RACISM, POLICY AND POLITICS

Karim Murji

D1612788

First published in Great Britain in 2017 by

Policy Press
University of Bristol
1-9 Old Park Hill
Bristol
BS2 8BB
UK
t: +44 (0)117 954 5940
pp-info@bristol.ac.uk
www.policypress.co.uk

North America office:
Policy Press
c/o The University of Chicago Press
1427 East 60th Street
Chicago, IL 60637, USA
t: +1 773 702 7700
f: +1 773-702-9756
sales@press.uchicago.edu
www.press.uchicago.edu

© Policy Press 2017

British Library Cataloguing in Publication Data
A catalogue record for this book is available from the British Library

Library of Congress Cataloging-in-Publication Data
A catalog record for this book has been requested

ISBN 978-1-4473-1958-0 paperback
ISBN 978-1-4473-1957-3 hardcover
ISBN 978-1-4473-1962-7 ePub
ISBN 978-1-4473-1961-0 Mobi
ISBN 978-1-4473-1959-7 epdf

Cover design by Andrew Corbett
Front cover image: kindly supplied by the Met Collection, New York
Printed and bound in Great Britain by Clays Ltd, St Ives plc
Policy Press uses environmentally responsible print partners

MIX
Paper from
responsible sources
FSC® C018072

For Rafi

For Rafi

Contents

Preface

This book is the culmination of my work over a number of years. One of the pleasures of marking that is the welcome opportunity to acknowledge some of the key people who I have worked with, learnt from and probably leant on at times: Gargi Bhattacharyya, Sara De Jong, Max Farrar, Vicki Harman, Michael Keith, Andrew King, Eugene McLaughlin, Andy Pilkington, Sarah Neal, Steve Pile, John Solomos, Sophie Watson and Kath Woodward.

A part of Chapter Two was presented at a seminar at the Centre Marc Bloch in Berlin; I am obliged to Sarah Masouz for the invitation and to participants for their comments. A version of Chapter Three was presented at a workshop on Racism and anti-racism in Nordic societies in Stockholm. I am grateful to Suvi Keskinen for inviting me and the participants for their feedback. Chapter Four was part of a conversation around the journal *Sociology* organised by Nasar Meer and Anoop Nayak, and I thank them for including me in that. Chapter Eight was first drafted for a Leverhulme Trust funded series on Framing Financial Crisis in Europe. I am indebted to Suman Gupta for including me in the seminars and to all the participants, especially Mike Hajimichael and Tao Papaioannou, who made it such a lively event to be part of.

I appreciate the helpful comments and support from the anonymous reviewers of the book proposal and the draft manuscript. I also want to record my thanks to Alison Shaw for raising the idea with me, and to Victoria Pittman and all the staff at Policy Press for helping me through to the end, even when it took a little longer than they expected.

INTRODUCTION

'The changing same'

Racism, policy and politics speaks to the contemporary and intersecting fields of race, racism and anti-racism in relation to policy, politics and policing. There already are many books on race, on policy (for example see Neale et al 2013, Turda and Quine 2018) and on the police, so what does this one add to all of those? I want to highlight two things that make this work distinctive. One is biographical: while various sections of this book are based on conventional social science research, they also draw on my own immersion in public policy. I say more about that at the end of this Introduction, but here I indicate that this can be seen most directly in the discussions in Chapters Six and Seven, though it had wider import in framing the general orientation of this book. This engagement and experience reinforced for me a sense of disquiet I had about the academy, in particular about the ways in which policy and politics are sometimes understood and represented in academic scholarship, as well as the nature of critical scholarship, and the circularity of some debates around race and racism. This is the basis of the second claim to distinctiveness I want to make. The chapters in this book review, engage, critique and maybe reconfigure academic and scholarly takes on impact, engagement as well as public sociology/criminology and any other way of framing a purposive critical encounter with policy and politics. The need for this perspective arises from the contemporary and recent issues discussed in this book, which illustrate various paths and trends that form an impasse around race and racism, and around policy, particularly in relation to the police, and the sense of familiarity and echoes of the past in all of that.

This book begins with a critical appraisal of sociological and social science debates about what race is, and closes with a final chapter that examines ways in which scholars frame riots. A key issue that recurs throughout the book is the sense that these things – not just riots, or debates about race but also many related matters – are always, seemingly, changing, yet at the same time, they feel as if they are unchanging. This paradox is what the term 'the changing same' speaks to, and I say a little more on this later. While racism and policing are public issues, they are also ones that have been the subject of sometimes intense academic scrutiny and commentary. The changing/unchanging puzzle is worrying, because it could be read as an indicator that a wide range of critical and engaged anti-racist scholarly research that aims to develop knowledge to analyse, reduce and even undermine racism, runs up against a political and policy environment in which its impact is limited; or perhaps that gains have been made and then lost, in a recurring cycle of progress and regress. Hence, the race-policy-politics nexus that this book is centred around is not another text on racism, sociology and the police; rather, its goal is to also draw into the frame an assessment of scholarly engagement itself.

As will become apparent, this focus is not done with the aim of assuming or reinforcing any dualistic view that positions academic social science 'outside' of the 'real' world; as I have already indicated, I am personally located within, and to an extent across, the frame. Through studies of others' and my own involvement in public policy around race, policing research and policy, I recognise that there are no straightforward ways beyond some of the difficulties that I will set out. Those entanglements are not a by-product of the academic-policy interface; they are inevitable and even constitutive features of that relationship in any arena where racism is a contested topic. The contents and arguments of this book are not a call for any withdrawal from that; nor does the book share the view that the proper role of social science is solely analytical (compare Hammersley 2014). Rather, in setting out and clarifying some of the problems, it aims to promote more and better forms of public, political and policy-engaged critical scholarship.

Outlining some events in recent times can help to set the need for this work and its themes in perspective. In early 2015, the US Department of Justice (DoJ) produced a report of investigation into the Ferguson Police Department. The report came out of protests, riots or disorders in 2014 that followed the fatal shooting of 18-year-old Michael Brown, an African-American man, by a white officer, Darren Wilson, in Ferguson. The protests spread far beyond the state of Missouri into other parts of the US and internationally. Michael Brown's death at the hand of a police officer was connected to other deaths of black men in encounters with the police, such as that of Eric Garner, a 43-year-old African-American man, in New York City. Garner's apparent last words, as he choked to death – "I can't breathe" – became a hashtag used across social media an estimated 300,000 times, which indicates the extent to which social media has become a space where public articulation of rights campaigns occur and are coordinated – itself a stark difference from previous decades. These and other deaths have sparked the campaign group Black Lives Matter,[1] which started in the US but has been evident in the UK also. In July 2014, I happened to be in the Westfield shopping centre in west London and saw about 50 young people lying on the floor 'playing dead', some of them holding placards with the words "I can't breathe". Later in 2015, the city of Baltimore witnessed further, sustained and extensive protests following the death of another African-American man, Freddie Gray, following his arrest by the police. The causes and analyses of these events are often on a par with, or at the very least reminiscent of, those that flowed from the civil rights protests in the 1960s, the riots/disorders/protests about policing in Britain in the 1980s, the events following the beating of Rodney King by the police in Los Angeles in 1991, and the riots and protests in France and Britain in the past decade. This connection between the recent past and the present, and from the US to Britain, is captured in an article title, 'From Tottenham to Baltimore' (Tyler and Lloyd 2015). The troubled histories of race and policing conflict across the ocean have been seen as 'the other special relationship' between the nations (Kelley and Tuck 2015); I say more on how some narratives of rioting link the past and the present, and 'here' and 'there', in Chapter Eight.

The DoJ report into the Ferguson police department called on it to improve its standards of law enforcement. On the subject of racial bias, the report is unsparing: 'Ferguson's approach to law enforcement both reflects and reinforces racial bias, including stereotyping. The harms of Ferguson's police and court practices are borne disproportionately by African Americans, and there is evidence that this is due in part to intentional discrimination on the basis of race' (DoJ 2015: 4). A 2016 DoJ investigation into policing in Baltimore is similarly stark, in reporting that the police department there uses 'enforcement strategies that produce severe and unjustified disparities in the rates of stops, searches and arrests of African Americans' (DoJ 2016: 1), in addition to making unconstitutional stops and relying on excessive force.[2] In 2017, another DoJ (2017) report, following the police shooting of Laquan McDonald in Chicago, found a similar picture of the police department there. These reports illustrate the Obama administration's strategy of using the DoJ to make the police more accountable. One equivalent with Britain is the way in which police accountability – a key concern for British campaign groups in the 1980s and 1990s – remains an unresolved topic, in spite of the many changes in governance of the police since those decades. This sense of 'unchangingness' around racism and policing informs movements such as Black Lives Matter that speak to, in Camp and Heatherton's (2016) terms, a 'planetary crisis of policing', rooted in systematic police brutality (Johnson et al 2015).

I also want, however, to do something further with this context. While there is a minor parallel in terms of internal and professional inquiries into aspects of policing (I will mention some of those in a moment), I want to draw attention to a bigger picture, formed by public inquiries in the UK, which are in nature quite different from the DoJ investigations in the US. The bias and stereotyping that the DoJ talks of in the Ferguson police department had been starkly revealed in the Stephen Lawrence inquiry in the UK in the late 1990s. The best known and remembered aspect of the Macpherson report (1999) was its finding of institutional racism to explain the police's poor investigation of the case, their treatment of Stephen Lawrence's family – including the suggestion that the police were 'spying' on anti-racist activists who were involved in the family support campaign – and the failure to bring a case against the main suspects for many years.

The case of Stephen Lawrence provides a continuity from the US to Britain in terms of a long, poor history of police race relations. But there are more key points to draw out. First, looking back almost two decades on from Macpherson, it is remarkable how institutional racism has 'risen' and 'fallen' in public discourse – from being widely implemented to its seeming dismissal some years later as too sweeping and complex a term. Yet it does not disappear and can be resuscitated, and not just by campaigners, episodically. So in mid-2015, the Commissioner of the Metropolitan Police accepted that the rate at which young black men are more likely to be stopped and searched than young white people provided 'some justification' for arguments about institutional racism in policing (Halliday 2015). Second, following ongoing and extensive investigations, nearly two decades after the murder of Stephen Lawrence, two men – two of the main suspects who had been named in the media in 1997 – were eventually convicted in January 2012. Throughout the Macpherson inquiry, claims were made that police inaction or incompetence was connected to corrupt dealings between officers involved in the investigation and members of the family of one of the suspects, David Norris, one of the two convicted in 2012. These apprehensions about both police undercover activities and possible corruption remained largely at the level of allegation during the inquiry and for some time afterwards. But they came to a head in 2015, when the Home Office announced an inquiry into undercover policing, while the Independent Police Complaints Commission (IPCC) said that it was investigating very senior officers, including a former Metropolitan Police Commissioner, over a complaint from Stephen Lawrence's father that full information about corruption was withheld from the Macpherson inquiry. Thus, even after a public

4

inquiry and years of media coverage, police investigation and academic research, the case of Stephen Lawrence remains 'unsettled' in several key ways; so too does institutional racism, and I look at that in Chapters Four, Five and Six.

Third, giving a public lecture in March 2015,[3] the Commissioner of the Metropolitan Police, Sir Bernard Hogan-Howe, did not focus on race as such. He did say that in a climate of economic austerity, the police service was at a crossroads, and it faced difficulties in squaring the squeeze on its resources with the demands made of it by the public and by politicians, a theme which became prominent in the 2017 UK General Election campaign. The events mentioned so far – events in the US; the continuing fallout from the Stephen Lawrence case; and issues such as stop and search, excessive force, public disorder, plus black young people as victims of gun and knife crime – position race at the centre of a public crisis in policing. Yet it is notable that in Hogan-Howe's speech race is epiphenomenal. Moreover, race is similarly marginal in the regular claims, particularly from police unions, that British policing is in a grave state, or crisis.

Whereas in the 1980s and 1990s, criticisms of the police were attributed to politically driven 'anti-police' agitators, in recent times the difficulties for the police are directly occasioned by governments, and where claims of a crisis have met with a robust response: for instance the crisis refrain was exposed by a Conservative Home Secretary speaking directly to the Police Federation, when she said at its 2015 conference:

> 'This weekend, the Federation warned that spending reductions mean that we'll be "forced to adopt a paramilitary style" of policing in Britain. Today, you've said that neighbourhood police officers are an "endangered species". I have to tell you that this kind of scaremongering does nobody any good – it doesn't serve you, it doesn't serve the officers you represent, and it doesn't serve the public. In 2002, you said David Blunkett [then Home Secretary] had "done more harm to the police in five minutes than others have taken years to do". In 2004, you said Labour were going to "destroy policing in this country for ever". And in 2007, you said the government had "betrayed the police". Now, I disagree with Labour policies – but even I don't think those things are true.
>
> 'You said police officers were "demoralised" in 2002, 2004, 2007 and 2012. You warned of police officers' "anger" in 2002, 2005 and 2008. And you warned that

the police – and the public – were being put in danger in 2001, 2004 and 2007. The truth is that crime fell in each of those years, it's fallen further since – and our country is safer than it has ever been.'[4]

Mrs May went on to become Prime Minister in 2016 and her certainty in this statement was a pressure point in the 2017 General Election. However, my point is that the recourse to a crisis discourse is another familiar and periodic trope that comes from critical scholars (for example Camp and Heatherton 2016) as well as the police themselves; in the latter, it is part of a much-used storyline about the 'thin blue line' (McLaughlin and Murji 1998). The sense of a crisis – or ongoing crises – has underlain regular pleas for change, even radical alterations in the structure of policing and their roles and functions. There are episodic calls for a Royal Commission into policing from varied sources, and this originates within and beyond the police. Yet those appeals rarely acknowledge that very extensive reviews, albeit falling short of a Royal Commission, have taken place in the past decade. For instance, Sir Ronnie Flanagan, a former Chief Inspector of Constabulary, produced an examination of police roles for the Home Office in 2008.[5] Although that happened under and during a period of Labour government, in opposition the Labour Party subsequently commissioned another analysis, under Lord Stevens, a former Commissioner of the Metropolitan Police, as a Labour-sponsored but independent review. It reported in 2013 and drew on extensive support from a number of academic criminologists. Their work is collected in *The future of policing* (Brown 2013). Underscoring the point about the past in the present, this title is itself a throwback, given Morgan and Newburn's (1997) book of the same title; some other books also use quite similar titles.

So inquiry after inquiry takes place or is called for. Race and racism feature in cases such as that of Stephen Lawrence and on topics such as undercover policing, recruitment, and employment practices (for examples, see Morris 2004, Home Office 2008, Race and Faith Inquiry Report 2010). Yet race and racism are otherwise on the margins of reform debates and proposals such as those from Flanagan and Stevens, and race itself has a more muted role in calls for a Royal Commission. It would be possible to go on with these types of example, but a couple of other recent stories help to draw things together about issues over time and the problem of what has – and has not – changed. First, in a 2015 report, *Dying for justice* (Athwal and Bourne 2015), the Institute of Race Relations reviewed 509 deaths in custody from 1991 to

2014 where there was some degree of suspicion about the role of the authorities involved. The span of time covered, as well as the main issue of deaths in custody – particularly involving black people – also reflects the ongoing unresolved problem of over-policing and the use of force that is so evident in the US cases and reports.

The second story I want to raise is of a different ilk, though it also reflects simultaneous and paradoxical continuities and discontinuities over a long timespan. In early 2015, Trevor Phillips, a former head of the Commission for Racial Equality (CRE) and the Equality and Human Rights Commission (EHRC, which replaced and absorbed the CRE into a pan-equalities body) made a documentary for Channel 4 Television called 'Things we won't say about race that are true'.[6] Its purpose was to assess some stereotypes about race, and to ask whether equality legislation and policy had been counterproductive. His message was certainly popular with one of the biggest-selling daily newspapers in the UK, the *Daily Mail*, which put the main headline on its front page as: 'At last: a man who dares to tell the truth about race', followed by a double-page spread on the findings in the programme. This, then, is an example of what had been called the 'anti anti-racist backlash', or more simply, the common refrain that political correctness has made race a taboo subject, which makes public sector workers, such as police officers and social workers, fearful of confronting ethnic minority communities and individuals for fear of being called racist.

Actually, Phillips' argument goes further and is indicative of one kind of 'post-race' thinking – the view that race is too generic a category to cover the diversity of groups and populations in Britain. So he went on to say that the use of ethnic designations such as 'BME' (Black and Minority Ethnic) in the UK is not useful, because it is too broad and obscures the significant differences between different segments of the BME population, not least religious differences, but also class and other social divisions. This is a view expressed since the 1980s at least, in the wake of the rise and decline of political blackness (see, for example, Modood 1994). At the same time, Phillips believes there is a 'deafening silence'[7] about ethnic segregation, and cultural norms, particularly among Muslims in parts of England (which itself goes back to Cantle [2001] and is resuscitated in the Casey [2016] report on integration). Hence, this trend indicates that race or perhaps ethno-race, dressed up as part of 'culture' does matter, but only as cultural separateness, not as a matter of institutional and systemic discrimination. The *Daily Mail*'s prominent attention to this focuses a lot on Phillips' stress that Britain is not a racist nation, even though claims about race as a taboo subject are hardly borne out by this programme itself. The highly critical response to it makes plain that racism is sometimes a public topic, although Song's (2014) analysis of some well covered cases does underscore how limited the scope of public discussion about racism is – or can be – in the mainstream media.

I have obviously brought these various reports and stories together for my own purposes, as they provide a quick route into the rationale and purpose of this book. The first and most obvious one is the ongoing and unresolved challenges around race and racism. The argument in this book is that this is troubling in academic discourse as well as in public policy and debate and, moreover, that the discussion of these is linked together, not in any causal sense but as some form of 'co-production'. I say that not only to get away from suggestions that academic work exists in an 'ivory tower', or that there is an implied 'real' world from which scholarship is somehow detached. Rather, in the course of the book, I chart the close connection between academic work on race and racism, the Macpherson inquiry and institutional racism, and my own policy and political roles in the interface between academia and race. Discussions of the relationship between academic social science and public policy are of long-standing and go to the heart of the ways in which the nature and role of social science is, or is not, conceived as a political/policy-oriented endeavour. These debates predate the rise of research 'impact', particularly in the context of the UK Research Excellence Framework, as well as the concerns with 'public sociology' (Burawoy 2005, 2014) and evidence and policy (Cairney 2016).

A second core theme is the extent to which the 'problem of race' is still largely formed through – perhaps dominated by – the question of policing for communities that are racialised, that is mainly people of African, Caribbean and Asian origins in the UK, and African-Americans in the US. That this should continue to be an issue is in some ways extraordinary. The riots of the 1980s led to the Scarman inquiry (1981); that, as well as the then unresolved murder of Stephen Lawrence and the Macpherson report's (1999) finding of institutional racism, each prompted waves of reform. These have led to considerable changes in the tone and leadership of the police, to the extent that the racist language and 'banter' once associated with the 'canteen culture' of the police (Holdaway 1996; Reiner 2010) had largely disappeared in research commissioned by the Home Office (Foster et al 2005), although that work did express concern about the extent of sexist language and attitudes. The establishment of Black Police Associations indicated the extent to which recruitment representation and, seemingly, the public face of the police had changed. The appointment of the first black Chief Constable in Kent in 2004, as well as the prominence of other ethnic minority senior officers in the ranks of the police also heralded a decisive shift. At the same time, critics and pressure groups, usually seen as 'anti-police', were welcomed in as independent advisers, with access to the highest ranks of the police, and on policy working groups on stop and search and gun crime, for instance. Independent oversight of the police was enhanced through the reorganisation of police authorities, including the establishment of a police authority in London. Subsequent reform led to the direct election of Police and Crime Commissioners in England and Wales. The investigation of complaints against the police was also changed and enhanced through the IPCC. Yet, with all of that, an inquiry into undercover policing, the persistent resort to a sense of crisis among some rank-and-file officers, and ongoing – and seemingly ever-present – proposals for further police reform speak to a rather dismal picture of continuity and familiarity, rather than change. The race dimension encapsulates that difficulty of what has – and has not – changed over more than three decades.

These two central pillars of this book – the questions of race and racism, and of policing and policy – are what the title *Racism, policy and politics* highlights. In many ways, the landscape around the politics of race and policing has altered dramatically – the extent and depth of research on race, policing and policy alone bears no comparison with the 1970s and 1980s; the same also applies to public and media discussions of racism. However, there is something very familiar, even unchanging, about the ways in which the same matters recur: complaints of unfair and discriminatory over-policing of black people, of racism and inequality in public policy, and the unresolved legacy of cases from the 1990s. These echoes provide the justification for the selection of the time frame of this book that the remainder of the contents fill out, although others may see different or longer parallels. These are all essentially public issues, in the sense of being played out in public debate, featured in the media, subject to sometimes intense scrutiny, and drawing in the policy role of academic knowledge production and engagement. The key role of the latter in explaining and analysing these things can be for the purpose of conceptual development that speaks to other researchers. Yet, even if viewed as merely applied social science, in most variants, whether in less or more critical ways, it has some import for policy change. Critical criminologists and scholars of race do at least gesture in the direction of ends that include better service delivery, in the form of fairer treatment, as well as less racial inequality.

The entanglements that this book considers are knotted for good reasons because of their location at the interfaces between academia, race and public policy. In a nutshell, we inhabit a landscape around race and policy that is utterly transformed from the 1970s and 1980s; yet, much of what I have raised in this Introduction looks very familiar to those who lived through and recall those times. Things seem to be 'always changing', while simultaneously and apparently 'un-changing'. Over two decades ago, Paul Gilroy adapted the term 'the changing same'; while he did that in the context of debates about identity, the term can still be employed in a different context. In interrogating whether cultural or diasporic identities were 'more or less' the same as before, Gilroy (1993) asked an important question about which side of the 'more' or 'less' matters (Fortier 2005). The 'changing same' captures this dynamic and dual sense that places it a step beyond continuity/ change and progress/regress. By conjoining 'change' with 'sameness', it aims to avoid linearity, while also suggesting that what is taken to be 'past' or precisely what is treated as 'continuity' and/or as 'change' is actively 'recovered' or re-made in the present. Stuart Hall captured this duality well, in commenting that, 'every new configuration contains masses of the old', as well as of 'the new as re-configuring elements of the past'.[8] In the same vein, while the changing same has usually been used to highlight 'sameness' over 'change', Chambers (2008) calls for more attention to what does change and how its meaning is shaped in each context. Or to put all of this another way, things repeat but that does not mean they are the same.[9]

Outline of the book

The centrepiece of this book is based on the case of Stephen Lawrence as seen through the Macpherson inquiry and the politics of race and policing flowing from that, the subsequent decade of policy and politics, especially the changing status of institutional racism, and the academy's role in that. To set that in context, Chapter One returns to debates on what race is. For some time, the dominant social constructionist approach in the social sciences has insisted that the only proper way to regard race is by refuting any connection with biology. Attention to the many ways in which race is socially constructed has been important; but, while a construction is not 'unreal', there is a common further step in which race is thereby deemed to be not valid, a fiction or 'bogus' (Better 2008). The rejection of race tends to treat race as something that would be 'real' if it were located in science and biology. I show how recent developments in the natural sciences and changing views on the relationship between the natural and social sciences problematise that view. Furthermore, it seems to me to be a weak place from which to confront racism when the starting point is treating race as not real. Yet in opposition to post-race views, as from Trevor Phillips for example, critical scholars can then be seen to draw on conventional categories of race to show that racialised inequality still matters.

While the ontology of race is not going to be resolved soon, I prefer to stress a focus not on race, but on racism – or more specifically on racialisation. The latter is a word subject to a wide variety of uses. In Chapter Two, entitled 'Racialisation', I outline a genealogy of the term, and some of the main ways in which it has been understood and deployed from its origins through to neo-Marxist and intersectional approaches, and beyond.

Chapter Three assesses a range of orientations to public engagement and critical race scholarship. I emphasise that there is no one correct way to be an engaged scholar, and each form contains some merit as well as various problems. The purpose of the discussion is not to build models or frameworks; rather, it aims to do several other things: first, to make the case for critical and engaged scholarship on race that is sensitive to the times and places it occurs in, as well as being aware of recurring debates about the relation of the academy to publics. Second, and unlike some other recent similar calls for engaged scholarship (Lewis and Embrick 2016), I argue that the academy itself needs to be situated; it cannot be treated as just a neutral or even a liberal place from which the practice of radical or critical scholarship occurs. This is quite different from Elias and Feagin (2016), whose critique of the 'white racial framing' of race and ethnicity studies is not accompanied with an understanding of the academy itself – and not just in the social sciences – as a site of racialised power-knowledge. Third, in introducing the topic of public sociology, Chapter Three sets the scene for the discussion that comes up in Chapters Four, Five and Six. Those three chapters move on to institutional racism, policy and politics.

In Chapter Four, 'Sociology and institutional racism', I chart the origins of the term 'institutional racism' in the 1960s in the Black Power movement, and its adoption and then rejection by policy makers and the academy, as well as its resuscitation by Macpherson. This history reflects my point about the 'rise' and 'fall' of institutional racism over at least four decades from the 1960s. Nonetheless, it is a term – and an idea – that refuses to go away, as events in 2014–16, mentioned earlier, show. I also link the public face of institutional racism – in relation to the police – with an 'internal' view of how it was utilised to critique the whiteness of sociology, itself something that has been revived to denounce universities and the social sciences through campaigns such as 'Rhodes must fall'.[9] Bringing this discussion in line with Chapter Two,

I submit that the idea of 'institutional racialisation' (Rattansi 2005) can be a more adequate and powerful means to capture the dynamics of race-making and re-making.

Chapter Five, 'The impacts of social science', examines Macpherson further, to analyse links between academic work and the politics of race and policing. I explore some of the significant academic evidence on institutional racism and on racial attacks presented to the Macpherson inquiry. While it is possible, particularly with institutional racism, to chart a connection between some of that and the conclusions of the inquiry (and in ways that speak to 'impact' well before the term was used as a means of evaluating academic performance), there is also a significant disconnection that, I think, provides a more nuanced idea of what impact is and how it occurs, as shown via the discussion of the internal politics of the Macpherson inquiry. An additional factor is that 'real time' events the police respond to indicates that they had, in some ways, already 'moved on' from institutional racism as early as 1999, even though that mostly precedes a decade of concerted policy implementation around racism.

The way in which institutional racism is 'killed off' – again – in 2009, at the tenth anniversary of Macpherson, is delineated in Chapter Six as a prelude to two particular examples – a legal case and an inquiry into race and policing – in the public arena. Chapter Six, 'The end(s) of institutional racism', looks at an employment tribunal case by a senior Asian police officer whose complaint of racial discrimination did not draw on, or refer to, institutional racism at all. I look at that alongside yet another investigation, the Race and Faith inquiry, where institutional racism could also have been expected to feature as a key issue but did so in a low-key and awkward way.

Although this period seemed to signal an end to institutional racism, I suggest that its multiple ends – in the dual sense that it has ended more than once, only to be reinvoked, as well as ends in the sense of diverse aims – is evident in the example of the BME recruitment target that is the subject of Chapter Seven. That also supposedly ended in 2009, yet the topic of race and representation continues to be seen currently, as this chapter shows. The BME target illustrates the policy and political manoeuvring around one of Macpherson's key recommendations: to increase the proportion of BME police officers. The acceptance, denial and termination of this 10-year policy target underscores the extent of 'game playing' with numbers/targets, but it also signals the ways in which the dynamics of race and racism are like a bubble that, when suppressed in one place, 'pops up' in another.

Finally, Chapter Eight returns squarely to the academic/scholarly role in relation to race and policing. In considering the 2011 riots, I present three ways in which those events were 'framed' or understood. By delineating the key features of each, I indicate their partialities and their consequences in terms of what academic framing does in shaping understandings of what matters in race and policing policy concerns. The 'messiness' of rioting is particularly useful for making this argument, though my overall suggestion is that it is a lesson that can apply more widely to scholarly research, and in writing on race and its connections to racism and policy matters.

This book is the culmination of an extended though not continuous period of engagement with and in policy and in policing, and most of that is about more than race. It draws on work in the past decade, though it seeks to make an argument that applies now. Some of the empirical material in this book draws on my own involvement in police, policy and political worlds. It is important to stress again that I do not want to imply that academic work takes place 'outside' politics, but there are quite differing levels and forms of engagement. In my own case, this is not unique but it is distinctive, and readers should be aware of this context. After researching some areas of law enforcement, such as drugs control, as well as writing on policing reform proposals in the 1990s, I observed some of the sessions of the Macpherson inquiry held in London in 1998. I subsequently interviewed a member of the inquiry panel and some others involved in and around the inquiry. After taking part in a panel on Macpherson at the Police Staff College, I was invited to observe some of the diversity training being carried out by the Metropolitan Police as one of its policy responses to Macpherson.

The main policy experience dates from 2004 when, following a public appointment process, I became an independent member of the Metropolitan Police Authority (MPA), the body that had been set up in 2000 to hold the Metropolitan Police Service (MPS) to account, as well as provide oversight and scrutiny. Members of the MPA were also responsible, in a quasi-judicial role, for dealing with complaints and the possible suspension of the most senior-ranking officers (these were called 'ACPO ranks', because they were members of the Association of Chief Police Officers), as well as 'forfeiture' cases where convicted police officers could have a portion of their pensions withdrawn under Home Office regulations. Even now, I feel that the combination of policy and adjudication in this role is not well understood and I point readers to Chapter Six, where I set out my own entanglements in a tribunal case and an MPA inquiry. It also brought me into proximity with the Stephen Lawrence case in ways that I could not have imagined as I sat in the public gallery observing the inquiry or the diversity training sessions. For instance, as the Deputy Chair of the MPA's Professional Standards Committee from 2004 to 2008, I was a co-signatory to agreed settlements, based on legal advice, between the MPS and complainants. While those are usually confidential, in one instance it turned out to involve Duwayne Brooks, and as the fact of a settlement was disclosed in the media at the time, I am not breaching that. Bringing this to light now is intended, even in its own limited way, to signal a world of policy 'realpolitik' that accounts of, say, public criminology (Loader and Sparks 2011) do not really engage. I have sometimes been asked by colleagues about why in this case or any others that settle before going to court, complainants do not pursue them. More rarely, people ask why the police settle, and this was a thorny matter for some MPA members who wanted to see complainants lose in public in order to discourage others. While I cannot speak for complainants, I do know why the MPA and MPS sought to settle in this and other cases. I do not think this makes me in some way 'complicit', but rather involved in a proper exercise of a public policy role that requires judgement beyond academic conceptions of engagement and knowledge transfer.

One of the other policy connections to Macpherson was that for some of this time I also sat as a member of one of the post-Stephen Lawrence 'trust and confidence' groups; the one I was on happened to be chaired by his mother, Mrs (later Baroness) Doreen Lawrence. This brought policy makers together to review progress and to an extent to 'chase' implementation of the Macpherson recommendations. During (as well as after) my term on the MPA, I had a number of other roles that I mention in order to be as clear as possible. These include consultancy roles as a Senior Selection Adviser for the National Policing Improvement Agency (NPIA) and for the MPA-led Race and Faith Inquiry. A smaller role includes taking part in 'crisis handling' training events led by the MPS that drew on the occasionally painful lessons of giving evidence to Macpherson (see also Chapter Six).

While I did not enter these positions with the aim of research, they are the involvement and context that inform some of the contents and most of the arguments about race, policy, policing and politics that I present here. These roles gave me privileged access to very senior figures in the MPS and beyond. I quote some of them by name in Chapters Four, Five and Six, and others without using their names, in Chapters Six and Seven. In all cases where they agreed to be interviewed or to speak with me, it was in full knowledge that my purpose was academic and that what they said could be cited; furthermore, the actual words have been available for review and amendment by the interviewees.

However, in the political climate around the BME target, discussed in Chapter Seven, a willingness to speak 'on the record' was harder to obtain, so that account does not name individuals.

So, in sum, *Racism, policy and politics* sets out a series of analyses and arguments that bring together the recent past and the present. It aims to locate academic scholarship as a player in, and not just an observer or analyst of, public and other debates around race and racism, and policing and policy. It argues for critical scholarship, better informed by an awareness of and need to reflect on the academy itself, as well as the political climate and context that research does, and sometimes does not, engage with and speak to.

Notes

[1] See: http://blacklivesmatter.com/

[2] Although Lester Spence argues that class matters as much as race in Baltimore. See: https://www.jacobinmag.com/2016/08/baltimore-police-department-of-justice-freddie-gray. Others argue for the continuing centrality of race. See: https://mobile.nytimes.com/2016/06/17/magazine/why-transcending-race-is-a-lie.html

[3] A report of this speech can be seen at: https://www.thersa.org/about-us/media/2015/commissioner-transform-british-policing-to-keep-the-public-safe

[4] Home Secretary's speech to the Police Federation Annual Conference (2015). See https://www.gov.uk/government/speeches/home-secretarys-police-federation-2015-speech

[5] Independent Review of Policing by Sir Ronnie Flanagan: http://webarchive.nationalarchives.gov.uk/20080910134927/police.homeoffice.gov.uk/publications/police-reform/review_of_policing_final_report/

[6] Channel 4 (2015) 'Things we won't say about race that are true', www.channel4.com/programmes/things-we-wont-say-about-race-that-are-true

[7] Phillips, T (2016) *Race and faith: The deafening silence*, Civitas report: http://www.civitas.org.uk/content/files/Race-and-Faith.pdf.

[8] In *The Stuart Hall Project*, directed by John Akomfrah, BFI films.

[9] This wording is a gloss from a line in Madeline Thien's 2015 novel, *Do not say we have nothing.*

[10] Rhodes Must Fall sprang from a protest at the University of Cape Town in 2015 and has evolved from opposition to statues of Cecil Rhodes at UCT and Oxford University into a wider movement against coloniality in higher education curricula.

ONE

Racial reality and unreality[1]

In his book *A theory of race*, the philosopher Joshua Glasgow observes that: 'When I first mention to civilian friends and students that many academics think race is nothing but an apparition, one common reaction is incredulity'; and that this 'departure from conventional wisdom ... might make academics appear to be unglued from the real world' (Glasgow 2009: 4). The academics that Glasgow is referring to are, in the main, social scientists, particularly those who insist on race as a social construction, a stance in contrast to the idea that race has any natural or biological basis. But it is an insistence that sets up odd ideas about the status and reality of race, and the relationship between society and nature. In a rush to dismiss biology, the natural and the real are sometimes conflated as if they mean the same thing, to be replaced by the social and constructed. Divisions between the social and the natural, or between culture and environment, or construction and essence are the core of a problem about the ontological status of race. To take one example, the opening to an introductory US textbook says that: 'the classifying of individuals by external physiological appearances is purely a societal product. Race, as used in social discourse in America, is a bogus term. There is no biological validity to the term "race"' (Better 2008: 3). This statement combines a fair opening statement with the view that race is false, because it is not founded in biology; hence the use of race in quote marks.

The long-standing, and sometimes circular, debates about what race 'really' is – and what it means – is pithily captured in Brett St Louis' (2005: 29–30) sharp observation that 'attempts at definitive racial understanding have arrived at the following conclusions: race does/does not exist and we should/should not use the concept'. As St Louis goes on to argue, the search for a conclusive understanding of what race is can obscure the more important issue of what race does, including what is done through race (Lentin 2015, 2017). Race in its many forms as racial identity, as self-classification, as observed and reflected, as phenotype, and as racial ancestry (Roth 2016) is summoned, debated, enacted, performed and measured in a great variety of ways in discourses that stretch across academic and non-academic divides. It is or can be both 'floating' as Stuart Hall (Jhally and Hall 1996) put it, as well as 'sticky' (Bobo 2014). Its contradictory and complex histories and present confront any easy certainties about it, whether those come from the social sciences or the natural sciences. This is far from a new observation; back in the 19th century, W.E.B. Du Bois suggested that: 'perhaps it is wrong to speak of [race] at all as a concept rather than as a group of contradictory forces, facts and tendencies' (in Moore et al 2003: 1). Thus, the reality or unreality of race, the relationship of nature to culture, and the role of scientific research need to be reassessed, not least due to developments in the latter.

Putting forward the argument that race is merely an idea or just a social construction might indeed make social scientists seem detached from reality, when viewed against a backdrop of national and global events of recent years. In 2014, 2015 and 2016 there were mass protests in response to the deaths of several black or African-American men in contact with the police in the US, a refugee/migrant crisis in Europe and the recurring depiction of Islam as other to 'western values'. Politically, the prominence of neo-fascist movements and parties also serves to show that race – even when it is 'ethnicised' as cultural difference – is only too real in political terms. In the domain of social policy also, race matters as a persistent and material factor in individual and group life chances.

A 2015 report on local ethnic inequalities over a 10-year period from 2001 to 2011 (Runnymede Trust 2015) found that educational inequality worsened for racial or ethnic minorities in nearly half of all districts in England and Wales; there were higher levels of unemployment for ethnic minorities than the White British for each of the Mixed group, the Black group and the Asian group. Health inequality is most severe for the Mixed group, which fared worse in terms of health than the White British group in the majority of local districts. Housing inequality for the Black group worsened in terms of the average level of absolute inequality in overcrowding across districts and the proportion of districts with a higher incidence of overcrowding compared with the White British group. The terms used in this report to describe broad ethnic/racial groups are derived from the categories used in the 2001 UK Census. Changes since then, particularly the rise of 'superdiversity' (Vertovec 2007) and EU migration in the past decade, make some of them seem dated.

Similar terms are used in a review of fairness in Britain by the Equality and Human Rights Commission (EHRC 2016), which over the more recent time period of 2010–15 evidences inequalities in health, employment and likelihood of living in poverty. The underlying and basic message is bleak: inequalities measured by race or ethnicity are stark and widening in some cases. Thus, in the criminal justice, social policy and political worlds the reality of race as a key marker of social inequality and mobilisations seems evident. Yet, it is a widely held academic and social scientific truism that there is no such thing as race; or rather, that it is a social construction but one that does have real effects, as Outlaw (1996) and Mills (1998), in different ways, conclude.

In light of the contradictory and genocidal history of race thinking and racial classification there are good reasons for social scientists and others to take issue with the idea of race and the use of racial categories, particularly when viewed in the context of the racial terror of slavery (Gilroy 1993) or the Holocaust (Mosse 1978, Stepan 1982, Bauman 1989). Race thinking, sometimes in the guise of science, has produced a multitude of racial schemas that subdivide human beings along definable and fixed physical and mental characteristics – Curnoe (2016) calls this undoubtedly 'the worst error in the history of science'. The uses, or rather misuses, of race signals its basis in historical and social relations of power, while scientific research has discredited any view that race can be found in unvarying rules of biology (Montagu 1942, Miles 1989, 1993). For much of the 20th century, and particularly after the Nazi Holocaust and the 1951 UNESCO statement on race, there has been a general scientific consensus that race is not a scientific category. Human genetic variation is greater within the 'same' racial group than between supposed racial groups and there is no scientifically reliable basis on which people can be grouped into races. Indeed, in 2000 the mapping of the Human Genome Project seemed to arrive at the same conclusion, in showing that the concept of race has no scientific or genetic basis. However, since then the science of race has not disappeared but grown in various ways that have seen the development of specific drugs for particular, seemingly 'racial' groups; and ideas about quasi race-like traces are apparent in the use of forensic DNA in the law courts and in tracing ancestry (Whitmarsh and Jones 2010). Race, in its scientific sense, has been reinvigorated by science, especially genetics (Bliss 2012), and bears out (even if the current context is quite different) what Barzun meant in stating that 'the idea [of race], although repeatedly killed, is nevertheless undying' (cited in St Louis 2015: 114).

Are these developments the 'rebiologisation' of race, albeit at a molecular rather than a phenotypical level? Critical social scientists who argue in these terms see any invocation of biology as modern-day developments of 19th-century racial typologies and their continuation in the eugenics movement, as the return of race science. For Hirschfield (1996), social constructionism is important, because it stands in opposition to essentialism, in which race is taken to be fixed in – or on

– bodies. In strong social constructionism, to conceive of race as having any connection to biology – whether in terms of blood and bones, or as patterns of genes, or propensity of particular medical conditions – smacks of biological essentialism. Yet although the anti-essentialist consensus in the social sciences has critiqued cultural essentialisms as well as biological reductionism, essentialism carries a range of meanings and can be a matter of degree rather than an absolute (Sayer 1997, Phillips 2010). Sayer argues that although the idea of essences as causal is both wrong and dangerous, a critical social science does require a kind of non-deterministic essentialism for explanatory purposes.

To approach this another way, Hacking (1999) understands social constructionism as a 'refutationist' approach that seeks to 'de-naturalise' views that assume that gender and race are founded in nature. In the case of race, there are two senses of the word in play – taking something out of nature, as well as throwing into doubt something that is taken for granted/a belief; this is akin to Glasgow's (2009) remark about disbelief. Race, in this view, is not in nature at all, and this means that it has no biological basis. Making that challenge is an explicitly political perspective, as its purpose is to contest and seek to overturn established ideas: it shows that 'something is bad and that we would be better off if it were radically changed, which becomes conceivable once we realize it is socially constructed and within our power to change' (Demeritt 2002: 769). In light of the legacy of scientific racism and the Nazi Holocaust, this has been an important argument to make. For Demeritt (2002), and following Hacking (1999), this can be distinguished from a less political (but not non-political) form of social constructionism in a more philosophical vein. This aims to advance an understanding of how reality is socially produced and without fixed ontological properties.

In opposition to constructionism, arguments that race needs to be 'reontologised' (Saldanha 2006) reflect a view that constructionist thinking has moved too far into treating race as socially produced through discourse and representation to an extent that its everyday, material, embodied and affective character has been neglected (Alcoff 1999, Monahan 2011, Garner and Fassin 2013, Pitcher 2014, Clarke 2015). Consequently, while construction as anti-essentialism has been very important in race studies, it is also contested – not least as social construction can produce its own essentialisms. While social scientists are critical of folk- and science-based versions of race, they are themselves accused of holding onto race in quasi-essentialist ways (Daynes and Lee 2008). Constructionists too often 'presume that the category of the social automatically escapes essentialism ... [while] the category of the natural is presupposed to be inevitably trapped within it' (Fuss 1989: 6).

Smaje (2000) makes the point well about reality and unreality and, by implication, essence and construction, in observing that the sociological analysis of racial ideologies has been:

> dominated by arguments against the 'reality' of the race concept. This stems from the sociological insight ... that social relations are ultimately arbitrary arrangements which are given the appearance of necessity by particular forms of legitimation. But the idea that race, or the social relations warranted by race, is not 'real' only have analytical force if it is also established that some kinds of social relations are non-arbitrary, or 'real'. Otherwise, one could establish that all social relations are 'real' in just the same measure they are 'unreal'; the notion of their reality would be entirely redundant. (Smaje 2000: 37)

A brief survey of recent debates illustrates the incompatible views of race that are present. Politically, essentialism can be the basis of movements around Blackness and black identity politics that draw on sociohistoric as well as cultural essentialisms (Gilroy 2000, Halady 2011, Sexton 2011) about a common African/black identity. Race and racial essences can be powerful for mobilising against racism, even while the basis of their presumed unity is questionable. In policy, social constructionist arguments are faced with the problem of what racial categories – if any – are useful for charting discrimination and inequality. For Krieger (2010), the advance of political and social justice has to be based on evidence of racial inequalities, which requires race categories. Moreover, when there are attempts to remove such categories, for instance through post-race or non-race 'eradicationist' views of race (Webster 1992, St Louis 2015), they are criticised by race scholars for adopting a colour-blind perspective that fails to grasp the extent and depth of racism and racial inequalities (for example, Bonilla-Silva with Ray 2015, Gallagher 2015). Administrative and social science measures using conventional race categories are used to demonstrate the scale of such inequalities also.[2] In addition, the opposition to proposals to investigate inequalities in their economic, social and cultural underpinnings – such as through traditional social-class-based arguments, or via intersectionality – can consist of calling for more emphasis on race, which is seen as being reduced by these developments.

The unreality of 'race': from political economy to social construction

Robert Miles and the many followers of his line of argument exemplify what Glasgow (2009) calls the 'rejectionist' approach to race. Miles sought to advance a political economy of race in reaction to the sociology of race relations as derived from the US and as it developed in the UK through the analyses of John Rex and Michael Banton. Rex's (1970) Weberian approach led him to make an argument for 'race-relations situations' occurring in conditions of structural conflict and discrimination. Banton (1967) offered a historical and comparative framework of race relations. These approaches have been widely debated and criticised, not least by Miles (1993; for a defence of his view, see Rex 1986; for an acknowledgment of the critique, see Banton 1991).

A key part of Miles' argument was that the 'race' part of race relations could not serve as an analytical category; indeed, it actually obscures the important task of analysing racism. Race, he argued, is fundamentally ideological; it is not founded on, or based in, science. It is the process of racialisation through which ideas about race are made. Miles' influential proposition was that some differences are coded as race because of relations of domination and subordination. Race is a historically and politically contingent construction that has changing meanings over time:

> The visibility of somatic characteristics is not inherent in the characteristics themselves, but arises from a process of signification by which meaning is attributed to certain of them. In other words, visibility is socially constructed in a wider set of structural constraints, within a set of relations of domination. (Miles 1993: 87)

In this way, Miles brought together a political economy of social structures with a social constructionist view of signification. For Miles, considerations of racial difference are linked to the distinction between the outer, observable differences between people – or phenotype – and the underlying genetic inheritance, or genotype. Ideas of race do correspond in some way to phenotypical differences among human populations (though see Roth 2015 for a wider range), although the relationship between them is open to variation and not clear-cut. There may be any number of phenotypical differences between groups, for example hair colour, facial features, body size. But, as these are not necessarily coded as 'racial' differences, it is clear that phenotype per se is not inevitably equated with race. They are, as Jenkins indicates, 'different orders of things ... phenotype is the material product of the interaction of genetic endowment (genotype) and environment, "race" is a cultural fiction' (Jenkins 1997: 78). In other words, race differences are not located in nature, and race is not the same as observable visible differences between peoples, since there are any number of clear differences; only some are usually seen to signify race. In recognising the critique of race relations, Banton (1991: 117) made the point in this way: 'People do not perceive racial differences. They perceive phenotypical differences of colour, hair form, underlying bone structures and so on. Phenotypical differences are a first order abstraction, race is a second order abstraction.'

Miles' critique of the sociology of race relations as it was conceived in the 1960s and 1970s argued that it took race for granted, whereas Miles argued it could not be used analytically. 'Race relations' was a term that appeared in everyday language, in Britain at least, and it was the phrase used in two landmark pieces of anti-discrimination legislation, the 1965 and 1976 Race Relations Acts (Layton-Henry 1984), and their updating in 2000 as the Race Relations (Amendment) Act. Yet by the time of the 50th anniversary of the 1965 Act, 'race relations' – as such – was not that evident in discussions of whether and to what extent social and economic inequalities for the main racialised groups had changed over time (EHRC 2015).

'Race relations' rarely appears as a phrase in social science to capture and explain 'relations between races', or as an expression employed in policy and legislation. In UK legislation and policy, this is also due to the thinking that informed the Equality Act 2010, which brought together the various strands of anti-discrimination legislation – race, gender, disability, age and so on – into a common framework, and the intersectional approaches to inequalities that informed it. In the European Union, the Racial Equality Directive of 2000 was also informed by an intersectional approach and a concern with 'mainstreaming' equality and anti-racism and, latterly, human rights (Bell 2008). It could be that 'race relations' sounds anachronistic and has been overtaken by more familiar terms such as 'multiculturalism' (or 'inter-culturalism' – Meer and Modood 2012), 'integration' and 'community cohesion' (Cantle 2001). Related and sometimes overlapping terms and words – 'incorporation', 'assimilation', 'citizenship', 'belonging' and 'superdiversity' (Vertovec 2007, Kyriakides 2008, Faist 2009) inform policy and academic debates in ways that trouble the boundaries of what is – and what is not – specifically race. Yet to add to the difficulties, it is also argued that, changes in terminology notwithstanding, the main thrust of public policy still looks like the assimilationist rationality of race relations policies of past decades, which treat 'minority' communities as social problems on whom there is an onus to integrate into the 'majority', 'indigenous' or 'national' culture from the era of New Labour to the Conservatives (Back et al 2002, Rattansi 2011, Bassel 2016).

Another aspect of Miles' critique of the sociology of race relations was due to its reliance on models developed in the US. In his view, this treated the black–white dichotomy as defining the subject of race, and so did not recognise the ways in which Jews, the Irish and Poles, among others, had been racialised in Europe (Kay and Miles 1992, Miles and Brown 2003). US studies showing how the Irish, Italians, Chinese and Slavs have been seen as 'darker' and 'lighter' (Warren and Twine 1997) over time are valuable, but often reflect a basic and underlying black–white colour scale. To an extent, so does the work on the ways in which whiteness has been constituted in the US (Jacobson 1998, Hughey 2015). The impact of US social science on race scholarship has been partial in understanding the diverse range of groups, contexts and issues in which race-like or racial processes, categorisations and 'xenologies' (Bhatt 2011) occur. This includes China (Dikötter 1992), Latin America (Wade 1997, Hanchard 1999, Loveman 2014), the Indian sub-continent (Bhatt 2010), Eastern Europe (Boatca 2007, Turda 2007) and various socialist/communist nations (Law 2010). This helps to explain Bourdieu and Wacquant's (1999) excoriating, though nonetheless questionable and much criticised,[3] view of the dominant and dismaying effect of the US sociology of race relations in framing race in the social sciences along black and white lines. They saw this as the lack of recognition in the US academy of diversity in racial formations and schemas. More significantly, the contemporary sociology of race – seen as largely formed through culturalist approaches emanating from the US and the UK – is, for Bhatt (2004, 2016), seriously out of step with the global geopolitical and international and corporate contexts in which racial orders are shaped.

Miles' perspective combined Marxist political economy with social constructionism in ways that have not always sat comfortably together (Virdee 2010, Meer and Nayak 2015). The constructionist element led him to argue that race should always be written as 'race' – putting it in inverted commas – which 'problematised [it] ... as a sign of renunciation' (Miles 1993: 3). This became something of an orthodoxy in academic writing in Britain and can be seen in book titles across at least two decades, in Miles (1993) as well as *'Race' in Britain today*

(Skellington 1996), *Researching 'race' and ethnicity* (Gunaratnam 2003), *'Race', ethnicity and difference* (Ratcliffe 2004), and *Stuart Hall and 'race'* (Alexander 2009).

Whether referring to race in this way is still needed seems a matter that is more of an issue in Britain and other parts of Europe than in North America. The purpose of the scare/quote marks around race follows Miles' rejectionist argument for its negation as lacking any scientific or analytical basis (Nayak 2006), although Meer and Nayak (2015) see it as having a wider impact, even when the quote marks are not used. They note that sociologists:

> tend to portray the term under erasure by presenting it in inverted commas so as to indicate that we are referring to a socially constructed category, based upon a problematic idea, instead of something that is self-evidently real in the world ... [and] even those who do not repeat this practice agree with the thrust of the argument. (Meer and Nayak 2015: NP8)

Hence 'race' signifies a term that has been tainted by its roots in biology and disavowed and discredited in the 20th century. By placing it in quote marks, the writer intends to make clear that they are treating it as a social construct and to signal to readers that race should not be regarded as real in any scientific sense.

While a social construction does not make something 'not real' (Appiah and Gutman 1996, Glasgow 2009), it is the case that social science has sometimes become muddled by what it means to say that race is not real. The dismissal of any sense of race as founded in the natural sciences is key to arguments that insist that race is not real, but one produced through scientific racism and reproduced through social structures and everyday life. The case against science, or pseudo-science, is encapsulated in a wider critique of scientific method, particularly the observation and classification of regularities, which is fundamental to the schemas and hierarchies of racial typologies. As a means for ordering human populations, racial knowledge acquires its apparent authority from science; indeed, there is an intimate interrelationship between them, as Goldberg maintains: 'Race has been a basic categorical object, in some cases a founding focus of scientific analysis' (Goldberg 1997: 28). However, neither Goldberg nor Glasgow (2009), who shares the view that race should be freed from any biological associations, place race in quote marks. Yet, developments in science, such as the Human Genome Project and genomics, as well as longer-standing questions of the demarcation between nature and society, and human and non-human worlds (Haraway 1991, Latour 1993) have altered at the very least, or arguably transformed, the landscape and the context in which these issues are considered (Meloni 2017).

Rethinking race and science

Investigations carried on in the name of scientific research have produced a multitude of racial classifications, ranging from three to ten to thirty categories in which it has been claimed that human beings can be subdivided according to fixed characteristics (Stepan 1982, Blackburn 2000). While the content of such racial schemas has varied, the modes of classification have been more consistent usually with, as Whitmarsh and Jones (2010) indicate, a system that is based on hierarchy and fixity and placing whites at the top. Nevertheless, huge variations of the 'types' demarcated, and of the characteristics said to constitute race, signal the basis of such race thinking in European historical and social processes, rather than unvarying rules of biology (Omi and Winant 2015). Although the variability and inconsistency of the schemas can be regarded as self-evidently undermining the idea of race as an object of scientific knowledge, it is not their internal consistency that counts; rather, it is the capacity of racial classification 'to integrate divergent, sometimes contradictory contents ... [that] has been foundational to its extensive scientific and medical use' (Whitmarsh and Jones 2010: 4). Or, to state this another way, the relationship between what is regarded as fixed (in nature) and what is regarded as variable (in the social) is itself paradoxical, as Wade (2002) points out:

> Racial ideas do make reference to human biology, nature and phenotype but those ideas do not always straightforwardly invoke fixity or permanence. This means that what may appear to be a discourse of fixity may actually allow a measure of malleability and change, but it also means that a discourse of malleability can acquire meanings of permanence. (Wade 2002: 14)

To progress beyond the essentialist-constructionist divide, it is necessary to question: 'the constructionist assumption that nature and fixity go together (naturally) just as sociality and change go together (naturally). In other words, it might be time to ask whether essences can change and whether constructions can be normative' (Fuss 1989: 6).

Wade (2002, 2010) is among those race scholars who take on board Latour's (1993) important and influential critique – arguably insufficiently acknowledged within race and ethnicity studies – of the way in which modernity and the social sciences have drawn sharp distinctions between 'nature' and 'society'. As Meloni (2014) argues, sociology, in particular within the social sciences, has made it its sine qua non to assert social explanations and causes by driving out biology and nature. Despite this, natural and cultural realms have always interlocked and shaped one another in ways that involve, as Wade says, the naturalisation of culture and the culturalisation of nature. In regard to race, this indicates that 'the whole apparatus of race (racial categorizations, racial concepts, racisms) has commonly been as much about culture as about nature, that race has always been about shifting between these two domains' (Wade 2010: 45; see also Monahan 2011: Chapter 3). In the 1980s, Barker's (1981) analysis of the 'new racism' identified a strain of cultural racism based on difference and incompatibility, rather than biology or hierarchy. This influential argument (Centre for Contemporary Cultural Studies 1982, Smith 1994) was, however, read as suggesting culture as a new, rather than a revived, component of racism. As Hall (2000: 223) noted, 'biological racism and cultural differentialism constitute not two different systems but racism's two registers'.

In the late 20th century, biology was still heavily invoked in some conceptions of race that bore similarity to 19th-century conceptions (Malik 1996). Differences in sporting ability and achievements in intelligence tests became two of the most prominent arenas where arguments for race differences were aired. In the 1990s, there was, on the one hand, the well-known and controversial view around *The bell curve*, in which Herrnstein and Murray (1994) argued that disparities in intelligence scores between blacks and whites were due to a combination of environment and genetics. On the other hand, in relation to different sporting abilities or, rather, the superior achievements of some black athletes, Entine (2000) dismissed as 'political correctness' any denial of what he took to be self-evident: that black people are better equipped, physiologically and genetically, to excel at sport. However, each of these drew on elements of biology and environment, or nature and culture, thereby marking a departure from some 19th-century conceptions of race, making nature less deterministic by combining inheritance and environment.

At the same time, other 'anti anti-racist' perspectives were quite ready to draw on culture solely to identify a 'victim culture' among African-Americans (D'Souza 1995), or maintain that black inequality was due to 'liberal racists'; moreover, evidence of a degree of social and economic success for some ethnic or racial minorities led to claims that racism could not be a major cause of inequality (Sowell 2006). Nevertheless, some formulations drew on nature and culture in ways that returned race to a base level, rooted in a combination of physiology and genetics, with evolutionary psychology. J Philippe Rushton claimed to be able to identify numerous and consistent traits that distinguished what he saw as the three main racial groups. His view of a link between brain size and intelligence led him to put Asians above whites, with black at the bottom (Rushton 1995). More recently, Nicholas Wade (2014) has claimed the relative economic success of distinct racial groups as a product of genetic inheritance and cultural context. These instances indicate that a conventional division between nature/culture or between essence and construct has long been breached. The combination of nature and culture is not in itself novel (Goldberg 1993, Bhatt 2010) and their consequence does look like conventional racism, although sometimes the usual racial hierarchy is arrested, with blacks placed at the top for physical/athletic achievement, and Asians for intelligence.

Since then, the fields of commerce and governance have been at the forefront of delineating race, or something akin to race. Developments in health, law and genealogy – through the use of specific drugs for particular populations, the forensic uses of DNA and its role in ancestry tracing – signal some ways in which 'the relevance of race as a social, legal and medical category has been reinvigorated by science, especially genetics' (Whitmarsh and Jones 2010: 2). However, social scientists disagree about how this is to be interpreted (Bliss 2012, Lee 2015). Commerce around race-specific items has gone beyond the cultural consumption of designer and everyday goods that cultural studies scholars identified (Gilroy 2000, Pitcher 2014) and on to 'designer' drugs. BiDil (Kahn 2013) is still the best-known example as a combination of two existing medicines for treating heart failure, which has received support, following a clinical trial, from a range of black groups in the US. It became the first medical product to be approved in the US specifically for a particular racial or ethnic group, African-Americans. Despite criticisms about racial stereotyping, the trade in race-specific products has developed from particular vitamins to jogging shoes, as well as more everyday use in tracing genealogy and ancestry. Less than a decade after Craig Venter, one of the key mappers of the Human Genome Project announced, in 2000, that 'what we've shown is that the concept of race has no scientific basis' (cited in Bliss 2012: 2), Bliss maintains that race research has 're-emerged and proliferated to occupy scientific concerns to an extent unseen since early twentieth-century eugenics' (Bliss 2012: 2).

Social scientists have analysed and criticised these developments as: 'a troublesome recurrence' (Bobo 2015); a 'molecular reinscription' (Ossorio and Duster 2005); the 'rebiologisation' of race (Kahn 2013); race science (Whitmarsh and Jones 2010); 'racial ideology' (Williams 2016); or a further stage in scientific racism (Carter 2007). If race science in a genomic age oriented to a sub-molecular or nano-political (Gilroy 2000) level does mark a significant change, then whether it can be understood and explained within conventional social science rejections of racial science is arguable, as is the extent to which contemporary race science should be understood as marked by greater continuity with, or change from, the past. In either case, the 'reality' of race occurs in a different space to the blood-and-bones discourses established in the 19th century and the intelligence and evolution arguments in some 20th-century psychology.

While the ways in which scientists explain and justify their work on race can always be questioned – and remarkably, Meer (2014) provides a reminder that 19th-century racial categories like Caucasoid, Mongoloid and Negroid were still in use in the abstracts of medical reports up to 2003 – recent developments and analyses present contrasting insights into it. On the one hand, Bliss (2012) presents a view of scientists staking a claim for focusing on race through social justice arguments. It would be naive to accept this at face value – after all, even some racial scientists of the past claimed to be working in the public interest to improve the general status of populations. Nevertheless, this position does mark a departure from the stark exclusionary logic of eugenics and scientific racism (Barkan 1992), and the claim of fixed characteristics and innate hierarchies propounded in various racial typologies. Williams (2016) sees genomics and racial ideology as shaping each other, with the former informed by lay ideas of race. However, those who stress more continuity with the past have to take into account that the modalities of the production of racial difference have altered, deploying equality arguments and inclusion rather than exclusion (Epstein 2007, Bliss 2012). Hence, Bliss argues:

> It is time to rethink the character, aims, and implications of scientific knowledge. Formerly, scientists used biological inquiry into race to naturalize social difference in essential biological difference ... Biology was used to obscure social explanations for race. By contrast, contemporary inquiry into race begins with the concept of social disparities and

hierarchies and explores biological differences in order to correct those disparities. Instead of arguing that racial difference is impervious to social reform, scientists are expanding the definition of biology to include social actors, using their position to draw attention to inequalities; and applying scientific tools to create social change. (Bliss 2012: 15)

For Bliss, seeing racial science as racist and as a form of biological essentialism is to miss the nuances of contemporary genomic research. She uses the term 'antiracist racialism' to refer to an 'idea that there is no rank to races but that there are nevertheless discrete populations worth studying' (Bliss 2012: 15; although for some ways in which 'population' thinking stands in for conventional race, see St Louis 2005). Instead of the widely criticised post-race retreat from race, she suggests that an antiracist post-racialism, underlined by genomics, may become the framework for addressing racial disparities.

On the other hand, Outram and Ellison (2010) provide a different perspective on scientific practice. Their research indicates that scientists selectively engage with arguments about the use of racialised categories. Unlike Bliss's interviews with scientists, their perspective is based on a systematic citation-based literature search. They identified 335 papers that discussed the question of, and issues about, the use of racialised categories in biomedical research. Given the foundation of some of these categories in scientific racism and various racial typologies from the 19th century, it would be reasonable, as they state, to assume that 'geneticists and biomedical researchers would be only too pleased to abandon racialized categories' (Outram and Ellison 2010: 110). Their starting point is to ask why that is not the case, as well as whether the use of everyday racial categories in scientific research is a worry as it reproduces conventional ideas about race. In their thematic analysis, they found five main arguments against using racialised categories at all: that there is genetic variation within all racialised groups; that only a small amount of variation bunches within racialised groups; that there are no pure populations; that variations in phenotype do not necessarily mean underlying genotypic variations; and that the use of the terms and categories tends to reify and essentialise them. Outram and Ellison's work confirms a lack of agreement about the definition of any of the racialised categories used in biomedical research. It also highlights concerns about the ways in which the use of racial categories may erroneously infer genetic causality and lead to inappropriate and stigmatising services to particular groups.

In spite of their awareness of the extensive criticism of employing racialised categories, scientists are, Outram and Ellison (2010) suggest, involved in a process of 'selective engagement', which enables them to square the circle of acknowledging the problem, while maintaining the value of using the categories. This selective engagement permits the use of a wide range of racialised categories that remain largely unclear and unspecified, making them 'unexamined, common sense entities, sustained without critical examination by their frequent appearance in the genetic and biomedical literature' (Outram and Ellison 2010: 111). Furthermore, this lack of attention to the conceptual basis for using racialised categories produces a self-perpetuating and self-referential framework, in which the use of such categories makes it difficult to interpret disparities in health, for example, as anything other than genetically based. Consequently, the preoccupation with genetic causes narrows down the diagnostic and treatment options for racialised groups. Despite these problems, instead of an either/or approach that treats racialised categories as sociopolitical or biogenetic constructs, Outram and Ellison (2010) conclude by calling for a biosocial or bicultural approach that can cross over the natural and social sciences, and engage both the scientific and sociopolitical arenas (see also Malik 2008). From this perspective, they argue, racialised categories may be important for understanding and addressing the causes and consequences of disparities and injustices within racialised formations.

Beyond the dichotomies

Beyond either/or genetic or sociopolitical models and explanations of, for instance, health disparities, the emerging field of epigenetics – itself as development beyond genomics – provides another way of combining inheritance and environment (Meloni 2017). While the genome is inherited and does not change, except for mutations, the epigenome is the result of the genome interacting with the environment, thus showing how the social environment can become embodied as a biological and developmental pattern transgenerationally (Kuzawa and Sweet 2009). Using the example of black–white disparities in cardiovascular disease, Kuzawa and Sweet (2009) look at the link between that and the greater incidence of premature and low-birth-weight births among African-American mothers. The impact of that has consequences for developmental pathways that continue into adulthood and across generations, they maintain. Culturalist arguments could attribute that to maternal behaviour patterns, but they argue that the main predictors of low birth weights are factors such as racism, discrimination and stress, which are structural issues beyond individual control; this, therefore, calls for social and economic changes, as well as health and lifestyle ones. Consequently, changes in the terrain of science and of biology cross over into sociopolitical fields, such as health inequalities – though probably the overlap between them is much older, as Wade (2002) suggests.

Using race and racialised categories to chart inequalities and disparities – as in the Runnymede Trust (2015) and EHRC (2016) reports – again exposes the gap in treating race as 'race' in public policy, though it is more arguable in social and medical research. Like Outram and Ellison (2010), other social scientists take a pragmatic stance on racialised categories. This arises from the unexpected consequences of arguments for and against using race classifications for policy purposes, social and biomedical research and equality claims (Epstein 2007). Goldberg (1997) concluded that for all the racialised power-knowledge behind their construction and application in the US Census, the use of race categories was necessary as a baseline for the assessment of racial inequalities. Krieger (2010) criticised Proposition 54 in the State of California – an attempt to remove the use of race categories altogether – on the basis that it was based on a 'no data no problem' outlook, in which removing race counting would make racial disparities disappear from view, at least officially. Racial 'eliminativism' can be the logical end point of social constructionist arguments, but when tested in policy and in politics, there can be reasons to hold on to race and to oppose attempts to remove it.

The contention that race should – or could – be made to vanish by not using the word or the idea comes in both radical and conservative guises. A common thread between them is that 'race talk' is both misleading and damaging for people so racialised, because the appeal to racism breeds a victim culture (D'Souza 1995, Sowell 2006) or narrows identity politics into singular and exclusive forms (Gilroy 2000). This appeal to racial erasure crosses right-left political viewpoints (Lentin 2014, St Louis 2015), as when the late Bernard Crick called for the 'R-word' to be 'thrown away', because there 'is no such thing as race, only the destructive and false belief in the concept' (cited in Goulbourne 1998: viii). As Bonilla-Silva with Ray (2015), Gallagher (2015) and St Louis (2015) note, colour-blind or race-neutral views that underlie post-race positions share some of this outlook.

For others, the language of race is so corrupted by its antecedents and its folk uses that social scientists should adopt a different vocabulary in order to avoid the problem of contamination and misunderstanding (Glasgow 2009, Banton 2015). For Banton (2005, 2015), one answer to this is to use race as a category of expert knowledge rather than lay knowledge. However, race is arguably so steeped in the everyday that dividing it up between expert and non-expert knowledge and debate seems a forlorn hope. Thus, Blum's (2002) preference is for discussions to refer to racialised groups, rather than race, because the former designates a social kind without inherent characteristics, unlike the link to biology that the idea of race is said to contain. This, however, does not quite address the difficulty that Outram and Ellison (2010) pointed to: namely that racialised categories and terms are used selectively, and 'race-making' occurs through categories such as 'population' (St Louis 2005). As analyses and explanations produced in biomedicine utilise racial nomenclature and categories to account for observed variations in health and in illness this tends to reaffirm a biologically real basis for race. Thus it fails to address Banton's (1991) long-standing plea for a clear distinction between an *explanandum* (the thing to be explained) and *explanans* (the thing that does the explaining) – in this case meaning whether racial variation is what is being explained or doing the explaining.

The biosocial or biocultural approach that Outram and Ellison (2010) advocate calls for a changed understanding of the relationship between the natural sciences and the social sciences. Its implications for race theorising go well beyond the social constructionist argument for 'race' as a term of negation. Rapid developments in genomics and epigenetics, psychosocial and biocultural approaches, and materiality all trouble the division or dualism between biology and society that some social science perspectives on race have relied on (Meloni 2014). On one level, there is a need across the natural and social sciences for a different understanding of 'natural' and 'social' realities and their interrelationship. An argument that race is not real because it is not a scientific term nor founded in biology clearly concedes too much ground to the natural sciences as a basis for determining what is real. Social science understandings of biology can veer between blank dismissal and naive acceptance (Meloni 2014). In the former version, social science perspectives of the natural sciences can look like a kind of 'turf war in which social scientists claim to have superior racial optics and measures' (Bliss 2012: 204). In a similar vein, Monahan (2011) regards such social science understandings of biology as relying on positivist and essentialist views of science. Yet, the fixation with biology can overlook other ways that race matters, particularly in coloniality. As Hesse (2007) has demonstrated, race can be understood beyond and without corporeality as an assemblage that signifies 'Europeanness' and modernity. Relying on biology to make a critique of the idea of race is, for Hesse, insufficient, because it obscures the deeper roots of racialised modernity. Neither nature nor culture are enough in themselves or in combination as race, 'as ordering, as management, sedimentation, sifting, as correction and disciplining, as empowering some while causing others to buckle under that power has always relied on a plurality of processes' (Lentin 2015: 1403).

In this light, it is perhaps the 'real' rather than race that should be placed in quote marks as the key problematic term in the wide and numerous debates about the ontology of race. The assertion that 'race' must always be placed in quote marks includes a claim that they are needed so that other people know that 'we' are not treating race as real; this implies a 'they', who still believe the common-sense view that it must be biologically based. Imputing positions to an undifferentiated 'other' is an oddly orientalising move from critical or socially progressive social scientists. A corresponding view that failing to put race in quote marks means that it must be being treated as real fails to address what kind of social reality it may have, as well as implying that race could only be 'real' if it had some basis in nature. Furthermore, arguments for avoiding any hint of biology in race maintain that to do so smacks of essentialism, a view that barely acknowledges the essentialisms in social science itself, or various meanings of that (Sayer 1997, Phillips 2010). Indeed, whether in the guise of 'race' or anti-essentialism, social scientists seem as unwilling as anyone to give up on race, whether for progressive or other reasons (St Louis 2015). Daynes and Lee (2008) even attribute this 'desire for race' to a psychic fixation where, for all their critiques of essentialism, social scientists of all theoretical hues are unable to abandon race.

Glasgow (2009) partially clarifies the discussion of natural and social realities through his distinction between realism and anti-realism. (Mills 1998 provides another route into this.) While Glasgow personally takes the anti-realist view, following Appiah and Gutman (1996) and Zack (2002 – though see Monahan 2011 for a critique), for now the point is the distinction he makes between two forms of realism – biological realism and constructivism. The latter refers broadly to a position that something like race may be real because of its social construction through the 'sociohistorical relations that have been produced by widespread, significant and long-standing race based practices' (Glasgow 2009: 114), rather than having any biological foundation. As Glasgow indicates, this is a view that has wide purchase, particularly in the US, and among scholars such as Outlaw (1996) and Mitchell (2012). Glasgow rejects this, though, as, referring to Du Bois' view that race involves both a 'badge of colour' and a set of sociohistorical relations, he argues that because constructivists usually tie racial identifiers and race-making processes to physical differences, they continue to reference race as a visible physical feature. Glasgow's own anti-realist perspective acknowledges that constructs are real social kinds, but he maintains that race is not one of those things because, while race is not biologically real, constructivist arguments are unable to show that they can advance a notion of race that has no referent linked to biology (Glasgow 2009; for a critique, see Halady 2011).

Nonetheless, others take a stronger stance against racial eliminativism, in asserting the reality of race as distinct from racialised ideas and discourse. Halady (2011), for instance, seeks to make a case for the reality of race which combines biological and social construction. A different approach, in which race is also a real kind, comes from an attempt to 'reontologise' race. In contesting the predominant discursive and cultural approaches to race in the social sciences, Saldanha (2006) makes the case for an embodied materiality of race, based on the 'viscosity of bodies'. Other approaches, which draw on affective, embodied and materiality thinking, do not necessarily insist on the reality of race, though they do share Saldanha's view that materiality provides a means beyond treating nature/culture as a duality and might instead look to the ways in which ideas of nature and natural differences are invoked and put to work (Moore et al 2003).

In calling Blum's (2002) argument for referring to racialised groups rather than race 'substitutionism', Glasgow (2009) instead proposes what he calls 'reconstructionism'. This entails a conception that race (or, rather, race with an asterisk (race★), he suggests) can be used as long as it is free from any biological association, though this has not been taken up and is unlikely to be adopted widely in everyday use. In this regard, race in quote marks ('race') has been more successful in its reach in Britain – though much less in the US – among scholarly communities and, sometimes, in policy. However, demarcating race as race★ or 'race' takes us back full circle to the issue of the boundaries and crossover between biological and social realities, and the natural and social sciences.

Mitchell's (2012) argument for a view that retains the links between race and elements of genealogy and 'bloodlines' fails Glasgow's test (2009), because of its reference to biology and ancestral linkages. However, Mitchell's main purpose is to steer a course between the options of treating race as either real or unreal. Rather, drawing on psychoanalytical theories, he argues that race is both fantasy and reality (compare Daynes and Lee 2008, Clarke 2015), rather than natural or cultural. He treats race as a medium that we see through, rather than with. It is: 'an intervening substance ... something we see through ... a repertoire of cognitive and conceptual filters through which forms of human otherness are mediated' (Mitchell 2012: xii). This shares some common ground with Malik's (1996: 71) point that race is a not a single thing, but a medium through which the 'changing relationship between humanity, society and nature has been understood'.

The concept of racialisation, to be developed further in the next chapter, can be understood in similar terms, as a way of understanding the processes through which race-making and identification occur and vary. Like Omi and Winant (2015) it looks beyond the option of essence vs. illusion. The reality or unreality of race is an unhelpful duality, and it has dubiously based itself on a split between biology and society and nature and culture that cannot be sustained. Constructionism might better focus not on what race is in itself but, rather, what race does (St Louis 2005) and the ways in which race works to buttress racism (Lentin 2015, 2017). That would focus on the reproduction of racialised formations and inequalities, as well as how race is mobilised in racist and colonial imaginaries that position racialised groups as inferior, other or different. It would also examine the ways in which race and racism are articulated in specific and wider contexts – for instance, the war on terror and global and state racisms, debates around slavery and reparations, unequal development and exploitation, and the policy and politics of anti-discrimination measures.

Notes

[1] This is a revised and expanded version of a chapter that appeared as: K. Murji and J. Solomos (2015) 'Back to the future', in K. Murji and J. Solomos (eds) *Theories of Race and Ethnicity: Contemporary debates and perspectives*, Cambridge University Press. I thank the publisher and, especially, John Solomos for allowing me to re-use and re-work the material for this book.

[2] For example, see the case well made by Claire Alexander in her address to the British Sociological Association in 2016: https://vimeo.com/176452879

[3] For various critical responses to Bourdieu and Wacquant, see subsequent issues of *Theory, Culture and Society*.

TWO

Racialisation[1]

Scholars trying to make sense of the contemporary politics of race face a bewildering variety of perspectives, operating at macro and meso levels of explanation. That range and diversity reflects the unsettled status of race, as shown in the previous chapter, as well as the changing and dynamic nature of what count as 'race issues', what is specific to particular nations and regions of the world, and whether a time of 'post-race' has arrived. Consequently, debates about what constitutes the boundaries and content of race and ethnicity studies, and of racism, are both long-standing and contemporary (for example see Bulmer and Solomos, 1999a, 1999b, Murji and Solomos 2015). In the 21st century, Islamophobia or anti-Muslim racism has dominated public and media discussion; and the combination, or more accurately the recombination, of race and religion, alongside polarities around race and gender, such as the wearing of headscarves and in the European migration crisis, introduce new forces in the study of racial ideologies and processes. Their interconnection in policy and politics with issues of identity, belonging, citizenship and the boundaries of British/European/western values is prominent. All of this reflects the need for an analysis of the politics of race and racism that can go beyond seeing racism as either an undifferentiated, long-standing process beyond place and time, or as something superfluous and a relic of another age.

What is the nature and form of such a dynamic approach? While European theories of race and racism remain largely informed by classical and post-structuralist thinking, there is a notable and extraordinary range of perspectives emanating from the US. Critical race theory, once something relatively novel, has become quite familiar in the UK and beyond (Gillborn 2008, Cole 2009, Delgado and Stefancic 2012). It has brought to the fore the issues of white privilege and power, highlighting the role and power of whiteness and white social structures in the persistence and continuance of racism – what Martinot (2011) calls the 'machinery of whiteness'. But critical race theory has also split, or perhaps matured, into other and related strands of analysis, such as: the call for 'race critical' theorising (Essed and Goldberg 2002); or systemic racism theory, which is itself an extension and development of Feagin's (2006) white racial frame viewpoint, which posits a generalised meaning system, particularly among whites in the US, that enables them to systematically ignore racial disparities and inequalities, while relying on deeply embedded racial common sense knowledge. Meanwhile critical race feminism stresses the need for a gendered and intersectional perspective on race (Razack et al 2010; Wing 2015), while emerging arguments around 'afro-pessimism' (Sexton 2011) seek to bring together history, structure and culture with an emphasis on the violence perpetrated in the name of race. Other strands include the race optic (Kibria et al 2014), which draws on elements of Omi and Winant's (2015, originally 1986) racial formation theory; the latter is the subject of criticism from systemic racism theory (see Elias and Feagin 2016). These sit alongside prominent frames such as the focus on the role of racist ideologies as part of the racialised social system in the US (Bonilla-Silva 2001, 2006) and Goldberg's (2015) regional racisms analysis. There are also synthetic approaches that aim to combine some of the preceding strands (Emirbayer and Desmond 2015, Golash-Boza 2016).

Intervening in this diverse field, my argument is to restate the case for racialisation as the framework to make sense of race and racism in contemporary times. Gans (2017) has recently set out questions about the nature of the process underlying racialisation, its effects, and the relationship between racialisers and the racialised, and has called for more research. As this chapter goes on to explore, racialisation is not a single thing – there are diverse ways of understanding what racialisation is and how it occurs.

It is in many ways an older idea than many of the perspectives mentioned and the number of versions of it is both a strength and a weakness. Particularly when there is little or no account of precisely what racialisation means or how it is said to occur, other than in a quite loose sense that there are some racial meanings present and that it occurs or takes hold in some way because of the presence of those meanings, it is notably weak. My rebuke is aimed at the many ways in which the term is invoked and deployed without specifying the extent or appeal of racial ideas, and the mere presence of 'race like' terms; it requires an appreciation of their 'stickiness', to borrow a word from Bobo (2015). For Michael Banton, one of the first sociologists to use the term 'racialisation', there is a discernible lack of clarity about who and what is doing the racialising when the idea is utilised. Or, to put it in terms that Banton (1991) chooses, it can be difficult to discern whether racialisation is an *explanandum* – the thing to be explained – or an *explanans* – the thing that does the explaining.

Others also share Banton's concern from different theoretical perspectives. For example, Small (1994) comments that racialisation is used in a wide range of ways as 'a problematic, a process, a concept, a theory, a framework and a paradigm' (Small 1994: 33). This range is perhaps why there are some who are critical of using it at all. For instance, Carter (2000) argued that a lack of clarity about racialisation as a concept is why it is used so inconsistently. For Goldberg, the popularity of the concept of racialisation is part of the success of the 'cultural turn' in the social sciences, the usefulness of which he thinks has run its course. In his book *The racial state* he mentions, almost in passing, his feeling that racialisation has become a cliché, too easily invoked and used in discussion and academic papers, yet rarely used or assessed rigorously (Goldberg 2002). Where it is used to describe 'any race inflected social situation', it becomes for Goldberg too general and could apply in almost every context. Thus, it is one of the terms that he has taken to warning students against using in seminars, despite the rather shocked reaction it elicits from them. Goldberg (2005: 87) instead develops an argument for examining 'regionally prompted, parametered, and promoted racisms linked to their dominant state formations' to distinguish between types and levels of racism.

Despite these problems, its extensive usage underscores its appeal and value. The range of uses of racialisation almost defies capture (Murji and Solomos 2005) and it is applied and functions as both description and analysis. Its scope extends to a huge variety of issues, concerns and topics, such as immigration, the media, political discourses, crime and policing, housing and residential patterns, and poverty. Furthermore, the expansion of racialisation has been used to cover cultures, bodies, institutions, images, representations, technologies, landscape, the environment and art history. Racialisation is applied to whole institutions, such as the police, and educational or legal systems, or to entire nations and countries/continents, such as North America or Europe; indeed, even globalisation has been viewed as racialisation writ large. With regard to Islam and Islamophobia, Meer (2013) provides a nuanced approach to the racialisation of religion. Since 'mugging' in the 1970s (Hall et al 1978), other types of crime have been given a distinctive racial or ethnic spin in ways that indicate both continuity and change in racialisation processes (Webster 2007). It is now almost routine to hear about the racialisation of whiteness, of the Irish, Italians, Slavs, Chinese and many other ethno-national or ethno-racial groups (Warren and Twine 1997, Jacobson 1998, Bonnett 2000, Kushner 2005).

An indication of why it is worth returning to, developing and making the case for racialisation comes from asking whether the expansion of analytical terms and perspectives mentioned earlier has a reach beyond the US. This is not a problem that Golash-Boza (2016), for instance, considers. Similarly, arguments from afro-pessimism (Sexton 2011), which see slavery as foundational to contemporary racism, are framed in terms of the US only, while systemic racism theory (Elias and Feagin 2016) also seems to be systemic within national boundaries. In a related vein, Ray's (2017) wide-ranging critique of organisation studies and its lack of a race perspective also has a problem when it reaches the border of the US.

As a process, a concept and a framework there is a great deal of work done with and through racialisation. It can be deployed widely, as well with precision, to particular contexts (for examples, see Murji and Solomos 2005). The purpose of this chapter is to provide a genealogy of the idea and to examine its uses through the lens of neo-Marxist and post-Marxist analyses.

Racial formation and racialisation

While many variants treat racialisation as the process through which structural and ideological forces of race making and maintenance occurs, a related idea or framework – the concept of racial formation, as developed by Omi and Winant (2015, originally 1986) – shares common ground with that. It is useful to begin by looking at them together.

A connection between them is made in Barot and Bird's (2001: 617) observation that Omi and Winant 'use the concept of racial formation as a perspective that is not fundamentally different from the concept of racialisation as deployed in British literature in the 1980s'. An overlap between these influential ideas seems evident, as Omi and Winant maintain that race is an intractable and enduring feature of the US. (Critical race theory, the white racial frame, and systemic racism theory concur with this, but place more emphasis on the role of whiteness.) Racial meanings are pervasive and shape individual identities and collective action as well as social structures. Omi and Winant define racial formation as '*the sociohistorical process by which racial identities are created, lived out, transformed, and destroyed*' (Omi and Winant 2015: 109; italics in original). This view seeks to understand race as the subject of contestation in situated racial projects that make race meaningful, including struggles by people usually targeted by racism in mobilising against exclusion. This makes race both an 'unstable and "decentered"' complex of social meanings constantly being transformed by political struggle' (Omi and Winant 2015: 110), as well as an organising principle of social life. For Omi and Winant, racialisation refers to a specific ideological process, through which the shifting meanings of race are produced by the practices of various social groups. It signifies '*the extension of racial meaning to a previously racially unclassified relationship, social practice, or group.* Racialization occurs on large-scale and small-scale ways, macro- and micro-socially' (Omi and Winant 2015: 111; italics in original). Racialisation is a process through which racial meaning and identity are constructed, 'how the phenomic, the corporeal dimension of human bodies, acquires meaning in social life' (Omi and Winant 2015: 109). In other words, racialisation is just one part of racial formation and the racial projects it focuses on.

In both racialisation and racial formation there is a common emphasis on the process of race making, the influence of race thinking and the ways that racial meanings are variable and differentially applied. In something that looks similar to Miles' (1989, 1993) view, Winant (1994) states that racial formation theory suggests that: 'Although the concept of race appeals to biologically based human characteristics (so-called phenotypes) selection of these particular human features for purposes of racial signification is always and necessarily a social and historical process' (Winant 1994: 59). He notes three implications of this conception of racial formation: first, that racial meanings pervade social life; second, it helps us to grasp the expansion and intensification of racial phenomena in a globalising world; and third, it produces a new and revised conception of racial time and history.

In some of his earlier work, Goldberg also appeared to see a connection between racial formation and racialisation, when he writes:

> In using 'race' and the terms bearing racial significance, social subjects racialize the people and population groups whom they characterize and to whom they refer ... Conceived in this way, the concept that has assumed wide currency in characterizing the process by which human groups are constituted as races is racial formation (or, more awkwardly, racialization). Racial formation involves the structural composition and determination of groups into racialized form, the imparting of racial significance and connotation at given socio-structural sites to relationships previously lacking them. (Goldberg [1992] 1999: 375)

However, underneath the apparent affinities there are basic disagreements. Miles himself criticised Omi and Winant's conception of racialisation as underdeveloped and not used systematically. Miles (1993) and Miles and Torres (1999) argue that racial formation remains tied to the idea of using race as an analytical category, so it cannot be a critical theory of race, because it is rooted in a race relations paradigm that reifies the idea of race itself. They argue that 'the process of racialisation takes place and had its effects in the context of class and production relations and the idea of "race" may indeed not even be explicitly articulated in this process' (Miles and Torres 1999: 33). Miles' insistence that the purpose of racialisation is to take us beyond race is the means through which he combines his political economic perspective with social constructionism, as indicated in Chapter One. Thus, the concept of racialisation is intended as a critique of all concepts that treat race as anything other than ideological. Hence Omi and Winant's defence of the race concept is: 'a classic example of the way in which the academy in the US continues to racialize the world' (Miles and Torres 1999: 33). However, in a post-race or race-blind age, there are good reasons to hold on to and assert the centrality of race, as Lentin (2015) argues. Another argument about the baleful influence of the US comes from Bourdieu and Wacquant (1999), and there is a wider critique of Eurocentrism in race studies from Bhatt (2004, 2016).

The contrast between the US and the UK does show that the range of perspectives from the former, as mentioned at the outset, are not centrally engaged with the question of whether race is real or not, but rather – and more – with the structures and ideologies underlying racial exclusions and white dominance. As this chapter goes on to discuss, racialisation can also address the same structures and processes, and in ways that go beyond Miles' formulation and argumentation.

Tracing the origins of racialisation

In developing his own influential conception of racialisation, Miles[2] (1989, 1993) traces its origins to Fanon (1967) and its development within sociology to Banton (1977). This version has been widely accepted, although Barot and Bird (2001) supplemented this conventional history in their genealogy of the term, when they point out that the *Oxford English Dictionary* traces the first use to 1899: 'On the whole, racialization is used in the late-nineteenth and the first half of the twentieth century and then disappears to re-emerge within the sociology of "race" and ethnic relations' (Barot and Bird 2001: 603).

In its earlier incarnations in the fields of politics and anthropology, racialisation was used to mean the loss of racial qualities through increasing mixture. Even though the origins that Barot and Bird (2001) sketched remains underdeveloped in subsequent literature, the significant point is that the historical usage in the works of writers such as Arthur Keith and Arnold Toynbee (see Barot and Bird 2001) takes racialisation to mark or to mean not the presence, development or extension of race ideas, but rather the loss or lack of race – or a worry about the decline of racial stock through intermixture. This is important, because it cuts across any linear account where racialisation is, or would be, followed by deracialisation or even re-racialisation. Rather, these moments or phases can occur simultaneously and even in the 'wrong order'. This paradoxical and overlapping structure already makes racialisation a multiple and dynamic process.

Thinking of racialisation and deracialisation as conjoined and not necessarily opposing or contradictory processes opens a route to drawing into this discussion Du Bois' influential idea of the veil of race. Like the idea of double consciousness (Gilroy 1993), in *The souls of black folk* (Du Bois 1896) the veil captures a duality. While the veil means that black people are judged first and foremost by their skins rather than their souls, there is also a stage 'above the veil', where souls walk 'uncolored' and enjoy 'freedom for expansion and self-development' (Du Bois, cited in Posnock 1997: 326). These gestures towards an 'uncolored' humanity are not the same thing as a raceless or race-neutral future. To put it another way, the veil of race carries with it the tyranny of race as well as the possibility of its negation as the means by which black people are judged. So the importance of 'doublings' in Du Bois points the way to a condition where race does not disappear, but its meaning is changed. For Glasgow (2009), terms such as 'uncolored' and 'badge of color' do not escape the biologism that he sees as so problematic in race thinking, though Meloni (2014) maintains that it is possible to invoke biology without biologism in the social sciences. Winant captures the sense of the double aspect of the veil in his observation that Du Bois saw it as both confining and exclusionary, as it protected black people 'from at least some forms of white violence and domination' (Winant, 2004: 31). Thus one of the dialectical features of the veil is, Winant argues, that Du Bois searched for the 'means to transform the veil, [as] a way [to] preserve the differences it demarcated but not the status distinctions it reified' (Winant 2004: 26).

Du Bois can be linked to Fanon for the purposes of this discussion. In the section on national culture in *The wretched of the earth*, Fanon mentions the 'racialization of thought' (Fanon 1967: 171) as the process by which colonialism erased differences among and within Africans and blacks in terms of racial categories such as Negro. Racial thinking in turn affected native intellectuals, who adopted quasi-racial categories such as 'African culture', rather than proclaiming their own national culture. Fanon holds European colonialism responsible for this process or at least for beginning it, for 'colonialism did not dream of wasting its time in denying the existence of one national culture after another' (Fanon 1967: 171). Fanon's quite brief remarks on racialisation itself link it to European domination and to colonialism. He maintained that responding to European domination by affirming Negro-ism is a political dead-end, because the 'historical necessity in which men of African culture find themselves to racialize their claims and to speak more of African culture than of national culture will tend to lead them up a blind alley' (Fanon 1967: 172). Fanon instead advocated ways of looking beyond European models of thought and their influence – racialisation, racial thinking and racial categorisation are examples of this, which Fanon calls on anti-colonialists not to imitate. Anti-racism (or 'anti-racialisation' in this argument) rests not upon an assumed affinity between the national cultures of the colonised, but on the similar claims of colonised nations. Even though Essed and Goldberg (2002) feel that the notion of racialisation is now overused, they acknowledge Fanon's use of it, and especially his distinction between that and 'humanization' to 'suggest the ways in which racial conceptions and structural conditions order lives and delimit human possibilities' (Essed and Goldberg 2002: 6).

One of the wider legacies of Fanon's work is to draw attention to the relationship between the psychic and the social dimensions, and the ways in which subjugated identity positions can be internalised, even while they are unstable and being contested. While capturing racialisation in these terms is open to development, there are echoes of it in Miles. He suggests that his own conception of racialisation draws on it: 'by highlighting the process of categorisation as one of attributing meaning to somatic characteristics, [it] presumes a social psychological theory which explains the nature and dynamics of the process' (Miles 1989: 75). Racialisation in social-psychological and psychoanalytically influenced literatures on race (see Clarke 2015) sometimes can seem to use it as a synonym for racism and as the process through which differences are naturalised and legitimated. For Dalal (2002), for instance, the structure of the psyche and the structures of society reflect and reinforce each other, so that if one is colour-coded, both will be – though this suggests a rather deterministic link between individuals and social structure.

A different starting point for the uses of racialisation comes from Banton, who is credited with introducing the term into sociology in *The idea of race* (1977). In that book, he discussed the racialising of the west and the racialising of the world: 'There was a process, which can be called racialization, whereby a mode of categorisation was developed, applied tentatively in European historical writing and then, more confidently to the populations of the world' (Banton 1977: 18-19). Banton's view of racialisation highlights the process by which, from the beginning of the 19th century, others came to be seen and defined in terms of biological differences – so race came to be used to denote a physical category and not one that was to organise perceptions and ideas about differences. In *The international politics of race* (2002), Banton went on to state that he introduced racialisation in 1977 as a way of naming the modes of categorisation through which people and nations came to be called races. For Banton, if the language of race was present, then racialisation occurred; if it was absent, then there could not be any racialisation said to be happening. Banton's insistence that there has to be an explicit reference to – or resort to – race is a position that he has held consistently, throughout scholarly disputes with Miles in particular (see Miles 1993, Miles and Brown 2003). In 2005, Banton revisited the argument, by presenting an outline of the historical mode of racialisation, drawing on long-standing ideas about race as well as contemporary forms of racialisation through legislation and policy such as the Race Relations Acts in the UK (Banton 2005).

Banton's belief that social scientists can be responsible for the very racialisation that they claim to simply be describing finds an echo in Webster's argument about the racialisation of America: 'the systematic accentuation of certain physical attributes to allocate persons to races that are projected as real and thereby become the basis for analysing all social relations' (Webster 1992: 3). Webster maintains that social scientists and legislators generate a racial order by their use of racial classifications in demography and official documents, in ways that give race a 'life of its own'. He says: 'It is social scientists who classify persons racially, announce that race is a social reality, admit that race cannot be defined satisfactorily and claim to be dealing with the enigma of race' (Webster 1992: 3). For Webster, deracialisation would entail the discarding of racial classifications, which, he argues, is what bedevils contemporary America, rather than race or racism. This kind of 'non race' outlook assumes that discarding racial categories and thinking in social science and in policy will itself do away with thinking of societies as structured in terms of race. This parallels the Proposition 54 debate mentioned in Chapter One, which Krieger (2010) criticised.

Neo-Marxism and its critics

In the past four decades, Miles (1982, 1989, 1993, Miles and Brown 2003) has done most to advance the concept of racialisation, though its usages may not have occurred in ways that Miles would be comfortable with. Like his view on 'race', Miles' (1993) approach to racialisation has been influential and widely taken up, but whether it achieved the intended break with race is questionable. In a 2011 interview, Miles reflected on it in these terms:

> The concept of racialization presumes that there is a product of the process of racialization. I resist talking about the concept of 'race' ... and I try consistently to talk about the idea of 'race'. (Ashe and McGeever 2011: 2018)

Miles' distinction between a concept and an idea enables him to accept that: 'there is an idea of "race" that is a historical reality'; for him, the concept of racialisation seeks to 'explain the origin, development and use of that idea' (in Ashe and McGeever 2011: 2018).

Initially, Miles' (1982) neo-Marxist analysis of race and class analysed how migrant labour, as sections or fragments of the working class, became racialised through state policies and actions. In particular, the state's attempts to manage the contradiction between the needs of capitalist economies to have free movement of labour, and the competing need to define and regulate movement through national boundaries and legal citizenship, make racism the medium or the modality through which class is lived. For Miles, racialisation indicated 'the existence of a social process in which human subjects articulate and reproduce the ideology of racism and engage in the practice of racial discrimination, but always in a context that they themselves have not determined' (Miles 1982: 177). Rejecting race as a basis of political organisation and progressive politics, Miles saw race politics as distillations of class politics; this is the point for which he has been most criticised (see, for example, Gilroy 1987, Solomos 2003), though it is a position he maintained (Miles 1993, Miles and Torres 1999, Miles and Brown 2003). Moreover, Miles and others have been criticised for laying too much stress on racism from and through the state, rather than seeing the state as potentially a bulwark at some times against racism in society, though others see no clear-cut division between them (Rattansi 2005).

Miles further developed the concept of racialisation in several works, initially treating it as a synonym for racial categorisation. He rejected 'race' and 'race relations' as analytical categories (for related arguments developed in France since the 1970s, see Guillaumin 1995), and instead uses racialisation to examine how ideas about 'race', as he puts it, are constructed, maintained and used as a basis for exclusionary practices. His main definition of it is: 'those instances where social relations between people have been structured by the signification of human biological characteristics in such a way as to define and construct differentiated social collectivities' (Miles 1989: 75).

A further point that Miles made is the basis for his disagreement with Banton, when he added that the 'characteristics signified vary historically and, although they have usually been visible somatic features, other non-visible (alleged and real) biological features have also been signified' (Miles 1989: 75). Thus, for Miles, racism is more than a black and white, phenotypical matter, as he shows, for instance, how Jews have been racialised through discourse and policy (Miles 1993, Kushner 2005).

This extension of the scope of racialisation makes it refer both to ideological practices through which 'race' is given significance, as well as cultural or political processes or situations where 'race' is invoked as an explanation or a means of understanding. The latter has been utlised widely in a broader conception of racialisation as expressing the ways in which social structures and ideologies become imbued with 'racial' meanings, so that social and political issues are conceived along racial lines. Among many issues that can be read in this way, Malik (1996) mentions class relations and poverty (especially in Victorian Britain), political discourse, and the idea of the third world and north–south relations.

Yet the broadening of the ways that the idea of racialisation is used has led Goldberg (2005) to reject it as an analytical term, as he sees it as vague and possibly vacuous. 'One cannot always tell, either explicitly or contextually, whether it is being invoked as a merely descriptive term or with deeper normative, critical thrust. Quite often it is put to work simply to suggest race-inflected social situations, those informed or marked by racial characterization' (Goldberg 2005: 88).

Hence, racialisation has itself been subject to 'conceptual inflation' on similar terms to Miles' observation about the concept of racism (which is the basis for his argument for a narrower use of racism as ideology, and not as an outcome or a practice). Miles has been accused of doing the same thing with racialisation, for instance by Carter (2000), who sees Miles formulation as asserting a connection between an actor's beliefs and the social structure. In other words, it entails a claim that changes in signification lead to the world becoming understood through a racial lens. From a 'realist' perspective, Carter saw this as conflationary, because it refers both to social relations and the structuring of ideas about social relations. For Carter, it is not 'racialization as a signifying practice itself that structures social relations but those who employ this practice' (Carter 2000: 89). Miles' formulation, Carter argues, is unclear about whether racialisation is an ideational or a structural phenomenon, or both (Carter 2000). In Carter's modified version, racialisation 'rests on race ideas, is posterior to them and is a description of their popularity within the cultural system. Its effects on social structures and social relations are a matter of the analysis of social interaction' (Carter 2000: 91).

Collins et al (2000) also maintain that the main shortcoming of Miles' use of racialisation is that it is treated as an ideological effect. Yet, they insist, racialisation is 'not simply an issue of representation, but of social practices through which political, economic and social relations are structured' (Collins et al 2000: 17), although Miles' neo-Marxist perspective did of course aim to stress social structure and practices, and not just ideas. For Collins et al (2000), racialisation is a tool to examine the dynamic between structural relations of marginalisation and the cultural representation of those relations. In these uses, racialisation requires an account of actions, cultural processes and their interaction with structures and ideologies.

Consequently, both the narrow and broader versions of Miles' conception have been critiqued by those who accept its main thrust but modify or develop some aspects of it, or reject it in part or altogether. The latter camp includes Banton, as well as Cohen (1994). In a series of exchanges between them, Banton (2002) criticised Miles' use and extension of racialisation, which Banton regarded as a claim that it occurred wherever its effects can be observed. In rejecting Miles' view, Banton also objected to claims made by analysts that race and racism are evident in statements even where there is no explicit use of either word. One of the best-known instances of this is in the (in)famous remarks made by Mrs Thatcher in 1978, when she addressed concerns about immigration, by saying that 'people are rather afraid of being swamped by those with a different culture'. This has been commonly assessed (Barker 1981, CCCS 1982, Smith 1994) as an instance of (coded) racial discourse, even though race as such is not mentioned, and instead 'different culture' and 'swamping' are used. Banton (2002) questions the imputation that the reader/analyst 'really' knows the thoughts of the speaker better than s/he does, although cultural analyses of racialised discourse are about their effects and context, rather than the intention of an individual speaker per se. Moreover, the reuse of words like 'swamping' by politicians in more recent times[3] does indicate that it is a touchstone term that carries more weight than Banton allows.

Cohen (1994) is also critical of the ways that racialisation came to be used to extend the categories of race and racism to a wider array of groups and phenomena. He maintains that anti-Catholicism, anti-Semitism and anti-Irish prejudice were the main forms of group discrimination in Britain prior to mass Commonwealth migration after the Second World War. Racism, Cohen argues, cannot be applied retrospectively in order to account for older forms of prejudice and discrimination. In the same vein, Cohen argued that anti-Muslim feeling draws on cultural and religious categories and not ideas about colour and descent. To make all or any these instances of racism requires a degree of 'theoretical inventiveness' that goes like this:

> of course the Irish, etc. are not a separate 'race' (but we all know that 'races' are artificial social constructs anyway), but as they are treated like a different race and alluded to in race-like ways, they are 'racialised' and can thus be considered the victims of 'racism'. In short we can have 'racism' without 'race'. (Cohen 1994: 194; on the racialisation of religion, see Brah 1996, Meer 2013; on the racialisation of the Irish, see Malik 1996, Garner, 2004)

Yet 'racism without racists' is precisely the frame that Bonilla-Silva (2006) reaches for to understand the contemporary US where racism is largely disavowed, and most people and public policy claim to be 'colour blind', even though manifest racial inequalities persist (see also Gallagher 2015).

In spite of these rejections of the racialisation framework developed by Miles, the more common response has been its adoption and even its extension. One valuable instance of this is Small's view of racialisation, which he takes to refer to 'social structures, social ideologies and attitudes [that] have historically become imbued with "racial" meaning [which are] contingent and contested and ... shaped by a multitude of other variables, economic, political, religious' (Small 1994: 36). This is akin to the broader view of racialisation sketched by Miles, but Small develops another argument from it. He sets out the racialisation problematic as a theoretical model or framework that allows the empirical data to be assessed against competing theories, 'for an understanding and explanation of the creation and variations in racialised barriers, boundaries and identities in various socio-historical contexts' (Small 1994: 33). This is more than a semantic issue, and he advocates 'changes in not just the language but also the framework and focus of the analysis, leading to a fundamentally different definition of "the problem" and to different types of policy and political proposals (Small 1994: 34).

Using racialisation as a problematic in this way potentially provides a more focused way to assess the range of theories and perspectives identified at the start of this chapter in terms of their adequacy and reach in explaining racialised inequalities and barriers. Like the CCCS (1982), Miles (1989) and others, Small sees racialisation as a means of redirecting the conventional gaze of race relations sociology away from the characteristics and actions of those defined racially, and instead as a means of focusing on the attitudes and motivations of more powerful social groups. In Small's (1994) own work on 'mixed race' identities (see also Bhattacharyya et al 2002), he defined 'racialised harmony' as non-antagonistic relations between blacks and whites, and 'racialised parity' as denoting equal access to privileges. Both of these are similar in tone to Reeves' (1983) idea of practical deracialisation. It is, however, unlikely that Reeves' use of 'anti-racialisation' as meaning the absence of race could fit with this, as Small's terminology indicates that groups racially defined in terms of blackness and whiteness would continue to be bases of collective self- and other-identification, though not antagonistically defined, which echoes the Du Boisian perspective outlined earlier.

Post-Marxist extensions of racialisation

Critiques of Marxism in the 1980s and 1990s, particularly of Miles' conception of racism by Gilroy (1987) among others (see Miles 1993 for his response), led to the development of analyses that placed more weight on black politics and struggle (CCCS 1982), on gender and intersectional analyses, and on culture and difference.

Anthias and Yuval-Davis (1992) made the case for placing gender relations centrally within race theory. Others arguing in the same vein include Davis (1981), hooks (1990), Guillaumin (1995), Brah (1996), Andersen and Hill Collins (1998) and Hill Collins (2000). This 'intersectional' approach has become the most common understanding of the links between ethnic, racial, gender and class phenomena (Hill Collins and Bilge 2016). Anthias and Yuval-Davis (1992) open the way to an even wider conception of racialisation through the notion of inferiorisation. They argue that Miles' approach excluded migrants and refugees, who are constructed as inferior in ethnic terms, though such inferiorisation may not include racial categories or nomenclature.

In their view, racism operates specifically through working on ethnic groupings and it is:

> a discourse and practice of inferiorizing ethnic groups. Racism need not rely on a process of racialization. We believe that racism can also use the notion of the undesirability of groups ... this may lead to attempts to assimilate, exterminate or exclude. (Anthias and Yuval-Davis 1992: 12)

This enables them to broaden the scope to include anti-Muslim racism or Islamophobia, and to pluralise racism as racisms (see also Garner 2009). While this has clear possibilities of application to recent events such as the migrant crisis in Europe, for critics like Cohen (1994), the broadening of racialisation processes in the way that Anthias and Yuval-Davis propose makes the definition so wide that a number of otherwise diverse phenomena – including nationalism and xenophobia – collapse into one another, or are subsumed within race or racism.

The approach developed by Anthias and Yuval-Davis resuscitated the question of the relationship between what is specifically 'racial' or racist, and other instances of 'othering' and inferiorisation, which follows Edward Said's (1978) influential work on Orientalism. For Miles, racialisation – 'a process of categorisation, a representational process of defining an Other (usually, but not exclusively) somatically' (Miles 1989: 75) – is a dialectical process, in which the defining of others necessarily entails the definition of a sense of Self. (See also Collins et al 2000 for a view of racialisation as othering.)

Race and other axes of social differentiation do not exist apart from one another, but that is not the same as claiming that they are only defined in and through each other. The precise nature of the relationship between race and class – or gender, or nationalism – is open to empirical investigation, as are the links between racialisation and other related processes. For example, on class, see Alexander and Halpern (2000), and Martinot (2003); on young people, see Phoenix (2005); on gender and sex, see Brah (1996), Eisenstein (1996), Hill Collins and Bilge (2016); on migration, see Erel et al (2016). In similar terms, 'othering' has become, somewhat like racialisation, a generic term that can lack contextualisation as well as lacking an account of historicised and structural power relations that differentiate forms of othering.

A rather different take on racialisation starts from the analysis of political discourses around race. In *British Racial Discourse*, Reeves

(1983) treated racialisation as a process through which race is adopted in situations in which it was previously absent. He saw racialisation as occurring in any situation where race is used descriptively. Reeves introduces a temporal and historical dimension to this, in referring to 'historical racialization' as occurring when racial terms and ideas are increasingly used in situations where they were not used previously. He introduces the notion of 'sanitary coding' for situations where race is flagged in a coded form and Mrs Thatcher's 'swamping' remark would fit that, although Banton (2002) questions the reading of such 'coded' language.

Reeves' main distinction is between: *practical racialisation*, which refers to 'changes in the real world, in conscious or non-conscious social behaviour and physical and cultural characteristics'; and *ideological racialisation*, which is to do with 'changes in the symbolic world in the way human beings choose to account for what they perceive and how they act' (Reeves 1983: 174). Although the latter is Reeves' main concern, he does note that practice and ideology may correspond when a group seeks to justify its domination, or to implement policies that maintain group boundaries. Discourse is racialised when 'increasing use is made of some or all of the following: racial categorisations, racial explanations, racial evaluations, and racial prescriptions' (Reeves 1983: 174). In revisiting debates about race and immigration in post-war Britain, Rattansi (2005) finds this the most useful aspect in Reeves for the purpose of developing a multi-dimensional approach to racialisation.

The use of racial identity for anti-discriminatory struggles can be a form of political mobilisation to address racism and, indeed, organising through making race more visible can be necessary in societies where racial divisions operate without any willingness to do something about them (Winant, 2004). This kind of racialisation is an indication of a group's heightened awareness of, and a wish to reduce or remove, racial injustice and inequality. Reeves maintains that racialisation here 'involves the recognition of race as a means to non-racial moral ends' (Reeves 1983: 175), because a form of racial explanation is not used in an essentialist way. Rather, in these cases, race is invoked to highlight its superficiality. Reeves calls this 'anti-racialization'. This is comparable to the aims of social constructionist arguments on race, or 'race', as set out in Chapter One. However, in some African-American campaigns around race and black identity, it can readily become quite essentialist (Gilroy 2000).

While Reeves does not resolve how race-based struggles can achieve non-racial ends, his idea of ideological deracialisation does aim in that direction. This entails the attenuation, elimination or substitution of 'racial categories in discourse, the omission or de-emphasis of racial explanation, and the avoidance of racial evaluation or prescription (Reeves 1983: 177). Reeves makes a further distinction between systemic ideological deracialisation and self-conscious deracialisation, a dualism that parallels the one between ideology and individuals. Although this work advanced a developed account of racialisation and deracialisation processes in political discourse, it is not without its problems. It is applied to race relations in post-war Britain to argue that postcolonial black migrants experienced in practice their structural and social positions in racial terms, though ideologically there was an avoidance of discussing these as issues of race. Yet subsequent research revealed the extent to which governments were preoccupied with 'the race problem', meaning that migrants themselves were the problem (Solomos 1988). Subsequently, this entailed limiting immigration even while passing some anti-discrimination legislation in the 1960s (Layton-Henry 1984).

As well as the cultural turn in the social sciences and the impact of post-structuralism, feminist analyses underlie more nuanced analyses of racialisation. These aim to highlight the contingent, uneven and unexpected features of racialisation processes. Brah (1996) and Rattansi and Westwood (1994), for instance, explored the bases of differential racialisation as a mode of power that defines 'others' in racial and/or cultural terms. Brah (1996) highlighted the differences in the kinds of racism aimed at, and experienced by, blacks, South Asians and East Asians in the US, as intersecting modalities of power, and related these to social divisions such as gender, sexuality, class and religion. She treats differential racialisation as 'a concept for analysing processes of relational multi-locationality within and across formations of power marked by the articulation of one form of racism with another, and with other modes of differentiation' (Brah 1996: 196).

Mac an Ghaill (1999) also called for more complex accounts of racialisation. He shared the view that whiteness needed to be brought more into the frame, so that rather than taking black people to be the object of inquiry in race relations sociology, a different focus was needed, because:

> [an] issue that has tended to be underplayed in the literature
> on racialization is the collective subject position of whites,
> which operates in a hegemonic logic in which 'whiteness' is
> absent to the 'racial majority' who assume that racialisation
> is 'something to do with blacks'. (Mac an Ghaill 1999: 69)

This outlook chimes with a raft of work on whiteness (Jacobson 1998, Ware and Back 2000, Garner 2004, Nayak 2006).

Drawing on these accounts and a range of other resources Rattansi (2005) argued for the indispensability of racialisation as a multi-layered and multidimensional perspective that can cover both explicit statements and unstated assumptions. Race, nation, ethnicity, and cultural difference overlap and are articulated in specific ways. This means that 'racialization tell us that racism is never simply racism' (Rattansi 2005: 296) but exists within an imbrication that he calls the 'race–nation–ethnicity complex', and its articulations with gender, sexuality and class. This is a more intersectional outlook than that envisaged in Miles (1993) and most of the sources discussed in the neo-Marxist section of this chapter. The ways in which post-war migrants into Britain became synonymous with various social problems in housing, employment, policing and social services, presents an example of the racialisation of immigration through legislation and policy, media coverage and various forms of political mobilisation (Carter et al 1987, Solomos 1998, 2003). Through this analysis, Rattansi (2005: 290) makes a case for an extension of racialisation in one important respect, which he calls 'institutional racialization'. For him, this term explains – better than institutional racism – the 'articulations and complexity' of racisms that are both and differentially biological and cultural, gendered and classed, as well as providing a frame that is sensitive to the times and spaces of racialised discourses and policies.

Finally, there are several other extensions of racialisation which are striking. In each case, they point to the value of the idea, and its 'stretch' and development in newer ways. For Fassin (2011), racial discrimination must be understood in terms of embodied experience, as the body is the site of racial experience. Utilising a historical account of how bodies become racialised, and drawing on Fanon, Fassin understands this relationally as concerned equally with the invisibility of white bodies as the visibility of black bodies. Also referencing Fanon and ideas of relationality, Ann Phoenix (2005) seeks to understand racialisation as a form of differential positioning by race. The advantage of this approach for Phoenix is that the metaphor of position allows for a degree of flexibility rather than fixity in the ways that racial, ethnic, religious or national identities are negotiated and contested.

An intersectional analysis also informs Fassin's (2013) work on criminalisation and immigration control. In a related vein, Martinot's (2011) multi-layered approach to criminalisation in the US and its intersections with race and gender also draws on racialisation in a distinct way. Lastly, for Gržinić and Tatlić (2014), racialisation refers to contemporary imperial racisms that are part of the remaking of global capitalism, shifting from a politics of life to one that trades in death – or from biopolitics to necropolitics. Like Hesse's (2007) analysis of racialised modernity, these further developments widen the understanding of racialisation as an analytic that puts state power, 'crimmigration' (Stumpf 2006), coloniality/imperialism and whiteness at the centre of the frame.

In looking at some of the main uses of the idea of racialisation, this chapter has focused on what seem to be the most useful approaches. It does not exhaust all of the ways that racialisation can be – and has been – used, as indicated by Gans (2017), although a problem with the range covered by Gans is that the term can become conceptually nebulous. The approaches included here cannot simply be fused into any singularity and each of them is not without its problems. They do set out a number of lineages and contexts, through which the meaning of racialisation can be discerned, mapped onto or developed from in relation to legislation and policy, media and discourse, state and society, and the intersections of race with class and gender. They do not resolve the status of racialisation as a problematic, a framework, or as process, but this analysis can provide a yardstick by which the uses of the term might be assessed.

The unelaborated uses of racialisation have led to some rather frustrating catch-all uses of it. To echo Miles' criticism of the conceptual inflation of racism, racialisation is made to refer to a specific and narrow discourse of biologically distinctive races, a process of cultural differentiation, or as a code in which the idea or language of race may not be manifest at all. It is the overlaps and intersections between these and their uneven and differentiated articulation within and beyond 'race–ethnicity–nation' that provide more promising alternatives. Attention to its intersections, articulations and specificities can help to make racialisation more powerful analytic and less seamless and closed than it is sometimes made out to be. The larger the gap between the manifest and more hidden meanings of race, the more work is required on what makes something 'racial' and on the ways that is connected, by way of articulation or intersection, with ethnicity, culture, gender and so on.

Racialisation is not, therefore, a single analytic; it covers a number of different strands that are or can be interrelated, but also competing and point to different aspects and features of race making. The key issue is how to advance a notion that is analytically powerful as well as situationally complex to the multiple intersections of race in which racialisation is a multiple, ongoing and intersected process, and racial practices and racial meanings can encompass struggles over subjugated identity positions and racial categorisations.

Notes

[1] This is a revised and expanded version of a chapter that appeared as: K. Murji and J. Solomos (2005) 'Introduction: Racialization in theory and practice', in K. Murji and J. Solomos (eds) *Racialization: Studies in theory and practice*, Oxford University Press. I thank the publisher and, especially, John Solomos for allowing me to re-use and re-work the material for this book.

[2] For instance, it is the basis for the comparative and historic readings collected in Das Gupta et al (2007).

[3] See: '"Swamped" and "riddled": the toxic words that wreck public discourse', *The Guardian*, 27 October 2014 (https://www.theguardian.com/uk-news/2014/oct/27/swamped-and-riddled-toxic-phrases-wreck-politics-immigration-michael-fallon).

THREE

Race critical scholarship and public engagement[1]

The ways that academic scholars conceive of, analyse and debate race and racism are matters of theoretical deliberation within and across disciplinary boundaries, but such discussions, however abstract and rarefied, are rarely done just for the sake of speaking to other scholars. Their purposiveness may be far removed from aiming at policy relevance or even social action, but they commonly have a critical edge or intent directed at the demise, or at least the reduction, of racism in a world shaped by and divided on racial lines, where inequalities, life chances, social and international relations and everyday life are informed by race and racism.

For Golash-Boza, race scholarship cannot be an 'armchair exercise'; it should not be studied 'only for its intellectual interest ... [but for] the end of racial oppression' (Golash-Boza 2016: 139). In this light, race scholarship must always be a more than academic matter; however, what that entails practically is itself an issue of contention and, usually, an intra-scholarly debate about the relationship between the academy and politics. While race studies is far from the only arena where there is, or can be, a tension between 'academic' and 'applied' knowledge, or where academics seek to speak to and impact on publics and policy,[2] it is an acute place in the contemporary world to address such issues. Applying scholarly research and knowledge does not occur in a linear or direct manner, and Chapters Four to Six explore and develop that point further in looking at institutional racism and some of its consequences within sociology and in public policy around racism and policing.

The field of race and racism research does embody the difficulty of linking scholarly depth and precision with the pressing and evident need to tackle questions about racism, xenophobia, and racial inequality in the everyday social and political realities of contemporary societies. Just a few high-profile public events of recent years make the need and the difficulty evident: the ways in which forced migration and refugees have become central to European politics and counter-reaction to migrants has tested analyses of racism and migration (Lentin 2014). The furore about police brutality in the US against African-American men has challenged head on the limits of post-racial arguments, by making plain the realities of everyday racialised violence (Coates 2015, Goldberg 2015, Camp and Heatherton 2016). Both of these issues have united scholarly and political and policy domains via campaigns such as Open Borders[3] as well as the scrutiny of the role of states in policing borders and life and death politics, while simultaneous and overlapping processes in social media have made campaigns such as 'Black Lives Matter'[4] into a mainstream political question, such as during the 2016 US Presidential election and beyond.[5] For race scholars, all of these reflect new and resurgent racist mobilisations and resistance to them, and underscore the need for researchers in the field to remain attentive to new forces and processes, in light of historical contexts of race and racism, and the connections between them.

This chapter sets out to contextualise some forms of critical scholarly engagement with publics and with racism. In drawing on an overused term such as 'critical', the intention is to make plain that such engagement is not solely about the academy 'speaking to' the outside world. As Back (2007) reminds us, it also entails listening. Badgett (2016) also points out that it is what people hear as much as what is said that counts. Furthermore, any critical perspective on race and public engagement and involvement cannot escape the spotlight on the very institutional locus it emerges from – for most scholars, that is the contemporary university. While scholarship need not be confined to the academy, the university is an institutionalised setting that supports teaching and research in the social sciences and humanities. Both academics who are employed in them and the particular histories of disciplines such as sociology and philosophy (Goldberg 1993, Bhatt 2012, Bhambra 2014) are called into question in any attempt to examine racialised forms of knowledge and their partialities and exclusions, perhaps especially when disciplines and institutions present themselves as liberal seats of educational inquiry.

The nature and purpose of academic labour – particularly those that seek to be critical and engaged on matters such as racism and xenophobia – and the critique of the academy from critical, feminist and systemic race theories (Essed and Goldberg 2002, Feagin and Elias 2012) are therefore also of significance in interrogating the foundations of knowledge and its power relations (Young and Evans–Braziel 2006). The need for this perspective becomes apparent in contrast to a recent article by Lewis and Embrick (2016), where they make a case for race scholarship to engage public policy. They set out a number of ways in which engaged scholars can be more active in addressing racism in public policy, such as with the mainstream media through 'op ed' columns – which they call 'thought leadership' – through to community engagement and activism.

These are, of course, commendable aims and there is nothing intrinsically wrong with any of their suggestions; some of them do correspond with Burawoy's (2005, 2014) case for public sociology. It is, however, striking that the university is only situated in Lewis and Embrick's outlook by way of two instances of institutional spaces that support more creative engagement than traditional scholarly activity. In other words, there is no critical perspective on the academy as a site of racialised power-knowledge. This is surprising in a period where highly active campaigns to expose and challenge the racial foundations of universities, their staff and student make-up, and the content of the curriculum have been to the fore through Rhodes Must Fall, which started in South Africa and has spread to other parts of the world.[6]

Hence the outlook to be developed here maintains, or rather restates, that across a range of institutional and national settings, the academy is a participant and not just an observer in these issues; it is an intensely embodied and located place (Mirza 2009, Ahmed 2012, Essed 2013). This stance resuscitates some long-standing themes and debates about the connection of academic scholarship to political engagement and activity, and in particular the relationship between race, politics and anti-racism, where engaged and critical scholarship seeks to be both political and educational. Yet while the themes are not new per se (Goulbourne 1998 provides a reminder that well before 'impact' there were calls for social research on race to be useful for (and to) policy; see also Solomos 1999), the context is changing and different. Academic scholarship in the contemporary world of higher education exists in a climate marked by sweeping changes in universities and new challenges for the social sciences and humanities. Universities and disciplinary fields have been audited, regulated and reorganised in ways that mark considerable shifts in the nature, context and scope of scholarship (Bailey and Freedman 2011). Universities are becoming more diverse, not just in terms of fissures between research and teaching, but also the entry of new 'for profit' providers, while changing funding regimes make higher education an increasingly private – rather than public – good. All this takes place alongside the rise and intensification of audit, managerial and corporate cultures of higher education and a stress on measurable or demonstrable 'outputs'.[7] As even this quick sketch suggests, the processes are not unidirectional and are not just about contraction; expansion and diversification go alongside a narrowing focus, though underlying both is the baleful logic of consumerism and markets.

The field of ethnicity and racism studies, and race scholarship, is an instance of the contradictory processes occurring in higher education. The scope and variety of scholarship concerned either wholly or in part with racism and ethnic and racial studies has grown significantly in recent decades, as reflected in the numbers of publications and events. At the same time, the boundaries of what comes under ethnic and racial studies have also spread considerably, as indicated in the previous chapters. These developments underscore the spiralling of global racial inequalities and the widening fields of racialised thinking and action (Bhattacharyya et al 2002, Back and Solomos 2009, Murji and Solomos 2005, 2015). Yet at the same time it can legitimately be argued that race and racism remain marginal within the social sciences, while the clamour of 'post race' has occluded attention to racism, while race as a policy issue has disappeared from government agendas (Hund and Lentin 2014).[8]

The expansion of race and ethnicity studies alongside the constriction of scholarship through processes such as audit and regulation present a confusing picture about the contexts of academic work and the professional responsibilities of academics. Race and racism have become more pressing and urgent matters, and researchers seeking to be engaged with that in both scholarly and political ways feel that their status is being undermined. This forms the broad context in which concerns about the purposes of research, scholarship and knowledge production – and engagement – need to be framed. What outcome or impact does academic labour have? Who does it reach or who is it intended to reach? What are the challenges of addressing intensely political questions about race and racism in and beyond the academy for contemporary scholars? Such questions are, of course, not new, but the current conjuncture makes them a particular challenge for the academy and for scholars who want their work to contribute to social justice and the reduction of racialised inequalities. Although not all scholars see their role in these terms, it is the perspective or the framework for the intersections of policy, politics and racism that this book is concerned with.

A view that race and racism studies in higher education need to be better connected with racial inequalities in and beyond the university is apparent in Knowles' observation that:

> Race is over theorised and disconnected from social and political engagement. Elaborating difference provides complexity and depth, but it is over focused on identities and lacks political engagement. Yet, race politics is urgently

needed ... There is growing unease in academies at the disconnection between theoretical debate and political struggles addressing racism. (Knowles 2010: 27; see also Bhatt 2004, Hale 2008).

A decade or so before that, and in the immediate wake of the Macpherson report (1999), Solomos argued along similar lines, in noting that:

> One of the ironies of recent trends in the analysis of racism is that we have seen a move away from research on social action and on institutions and a fixation with theoretical abstraction and textual and cultural analysis. Whatever the merits of some of the recent theoretical debates, there have been few sustained attempts to link them to research on institutions and processes of social change. In this environment there has been, if anything, a retreat by researchers into abstracted theoretical debates and discourses. (Solomos 1999: para 4.7)

Knowles and Solomos are not alone in feeling a sense of dismay about the relationship between academic work on race and rather abstract theorising about ethnic and racial formations. There are numerous ways of closing that gap and seeking to make scholarship more engaged within and beyond the academy. Some prominent ones include – the notion of the public intellectual (Ritzer 2006), or of activist and committed scholarship (Hale 2008), as well as public sociology (Clawson et al 2007, Morton et al 2012). In this chapter I look at each of these; by not setting them as three separate strands, the aim is to treat them not as wholly distinct or compartmentalised approaches, but rather to regard them as tendencies or inclinations for scholars working on race and racism. An intellectual or a public intellectual could also be an activist; a public sociologist could also overlap with either or both. The term 'scholarship' is intentionally employed to mark a break from the overused notion of, and debates around, the academic-as-intellectual. It is also intended to signal that scholarship might be about more than research and its dissemination, and includes teaching as well as research, to reflect Burawoy's (2005) point that one of the main 'publics' for university-based sociologists is made up of students.

These orientations to critical and engaged scholarship are, in their different ways, attuned to concerns about the relevance of academic scholarship on race in analysing and addressing contemporary racial processes. While they do not cover all the ways that engagement can be done and thought about, they do provide a framework for exploring the issues of scholarly engagement in light of changes in higher education. Moreover, the purpose of such scholarship goes beyond, or aims to go beyond, scholarly communities and attempts to engage wider publics, in addressing the contemporary politics of race and racism. While some perspectives in social science warn against seeing it as having any direct political role (Hammersley 2013, 2014), engagement in race matters can rarely be apolitical, and the nature and meanings of political commitment go beyond a yes/no binary. Thus, as forms of *engagement* they assume that scholars or researchers want to contribute to political debate and campaigns and movements against racism.

In this context it is worth recalling that these are recurring issues and problems, particularly in the field of race studies. Writing in 1979, John Rex recognised that researchers were subject to being pulled in conflicting directions in regard to the politics of race research. One demand was that the only or main purpose of research should be at the service of policy. As Rex noted, this rather problematically assumed that there was a consensus about ends, and only the question of means to those ends were at issue. A second option was to retreat into academic theorising, in which public issues of race and racism are a secondary concern – this is what Solomos (1999) and Knowles (2010) express reservations about. Third, Rex saw that there was a route that emphasised activism and research to underpin and support that, but in his view that made research itself somewhat secondary to political ends.

Rex's Weberian perspective perhaps led him to overlook the combination of sociological fieldwork with political engagement advocated by Touraine (1981), particularly in relation to the events and protests of Paris in 1968. Instead of any of these, Rex made the case for 'a serious political sociology' (Rex 1979: 17), in which race research combined theory and politics, but set that within a structural view of race. As Solomos (1999) observes, Rex's summation captured the problems that researchers in the area of race and racism studies face, and Rex himself faced opprobrium for his analyses and his role in the academy (Bourne and Sivanandan 1980, CCCS 1982). Yet the recurrence of these issues in similar and varied forms speaks to the ongoing concerns of relating scholarship to engagement, and knowledge to politics.

The 'extra academy': from the margins to the centre?

A significant strand of thought in the area of racism and ethnicity studies has its roots not in the formal academy but in the social movements that emerge in opposition to colonialism and racism. In this there is a triple marginality:

- At one level, racism and the study of race is, broadly conceived, among the collection of political/intellectual endeavours that emerged in civil society and then fought to enter the academy. Nonetheless it could still be regarded as marginal, given the institutional whiteness of the academy in terms of its make-up, its precepts and its outlook (Puwar 2004, Mirza 2009, Ahmed 2012). The status of race studies and race scholars is at the same time both 'inside' and 'outside'; inside in the sense of the range of scholarly activity on racism, but outside to the extent that as a field of study it can still be regarded as marginal (or prone to being positioned at the margins) in terms of making critiques of the mainstream academy.
- Thus, at a second level, the study of race itself has sometimes been marginalised in the social sciences and humanities as an epiphenomenon to class, or subsumed under ethnicity, or collapsed within what, for some, are wider projects such as cosmopolitanism or social justice and human rights.
- A third aspect is the struggle and degree of marginality of racial 'minority' scholars, who can experience the double burden of being seen as 'responsible for race matters' in a department or within universities, and as troublemakers for raising issues about racism within the institutions they work in (Mirza 2009, Ahmed 2012).

It should be recalled, as well as frequently restated, that for all the apparent expansion of race scholarship, the study of race and racism has previously been marginalised in various social science disciplines, for the reasons suggested, and that the growth of 'race studies' has also led to concerns about the fragmentation of the subject and what the core theories and concerns of the field are (Murji and Solomos 2015, 2016).

The relationship of race to the academy needs to be put under scrutiny for both historical and contemporary reasons. Imagining race as a topic of study has animated various developments in the European academy, from biology and medicine, to anthropology and sociology (Kuklick 1991, Barkan 1992, Gilroy 2000, Epstein 2007, Whitmarsh and Jones 2010, Bhambra 2014) and this is the idea of race that social constructionism did much to contest (see Chapter One). Nevertheless, the need to give voice to the lived experiences and troubled histories of race and to analyse the continuing social impact of the idea of race in light of these knowledges has been tied, along with feminist analyses and theories (Hill Collins 2000), to a systematic critique of the exclusions and hierarchies of the traditional academy (Staples 1976, CCCS 1982, Young and Evans-Braziel 2006, Stanfield 2011, Morris 2015), and where the working environment can include the experience of daily racial 'microaggressions' (Pittman 2012).

All of these stress the need for deepening conceptions of what counts as knowledge, both in the sense of uncovering the global connections and inequalities that constitute such seemingly neutral terms as progress and reason, as well as re-inserting an awareness of the materiality that underpins the abstractions of learning. The struggle that Baxi (2007) charts and summarises with a quotation from Kwame Nkrumah, to 'reclaim the psychology of people, erasing colonial mentality from it' (Baxi 2007: 100), draws from Fanon's (1967) idea of humanisation and struggles to assert a shared humanity. To understand the influences that underlie critical orientations to the field of race and ethnic studies, this is the battle that must be acknowledged – the ongoing struggle to reveal the violence on which the cultures of colonial privilege rest and the impact of such violence on the psyches and the bodies of those deemed less than human (Said 1978, Mignolo 2009). The 'changing same' contours and boundaries of 'sub-humanity' are evident in the routinised police violence and death of black people in Brazil (Alves 2014) and in the US (Camp and Heatherton 2016), that Coates (2015) movingly describes as a daily struggle to retain control over one's body, as well as in the 'border wars' of militarised controls and multiple irregular migrant deaths at the borders of Europe and beyond (Stumpf 2006, Bowling 2013).

Consequently, it is, or should be, unsurprising that some of the most influential ideas in the field of racism and ethnicity studies have arisen from outside the academy, such as the black consciousness movement inspired by Steve Biko (1986), the Black Power and political legacies of Malcolm X and Martin Luther King (Singh 2004), and the Afrocentrism of Marcus Garvey. Du Bois' research and ideas, such as the veil and double consciousness, have been excavated and imagined anew in academic settings that have at times forgotten him and his work (Gilroy 1993, Winant 1994, Morris 2015). Fanon's thoughts still shape understandings of the psychic costs of inhumanity for all parties (Fanon 1967), while postcolonial and black feminist analyses have criss-crossed institutional settings from the Combahee River Collective[9] and through writers as diverse as Audre Lorde (Lorde 1984), Angela Davis (Davis 1974) and Avtar Brah (Brah 1996).

Black Power and institutional racism have contributed to understandings of race and racism since the 1960s, and the latter term itself confronts the academy for its neglect of race as well as its impoverished understanding of racism, as discussed in Chapter Four. Singly or as a whole, these sources provide a rich heritage for teaching race 'differently' (Back 2007, Hund and Lentin 2014), although their 'other' or 'elsewhere' origins demand attention in their own right, and the relationship of 'parasitic' (Urry 2000) academic scholarship to that. In the UK, any teaching of the case of Stephen Lawrence must always be located in the context of the campaign by his family as something that came before and has continued well beyond a public inquiry (Cathcart 1999), and gave impetus to a decade of public policy on institutional racism, until the eventual and belated conviction of two people in 2012, nearly two decades after the murder. Recalling the 1970s Grunwick strike (McGowan 2008) by predominantly Asian women workers is a powerful reminder of intersectionality in action. Many more cases and examples could be added to these.

These observations underline Urry's (2000) comment about the 'parasitic' relationship between the discipline of sociology, in this case, and social movements:

> Most important developments in sociology have at least indirectly stemmed from social movements with 'emancipatory interests' that have fuelled a new or reconfigured social analysis. Examples of such mobilised groupings have at different historical moments included the working class, farmers, the professions, urban protest movements, student's movement, women's movement, immigrant groups, environmental NGOs, gay and lesbian movement, 'disabled' groups and so on. (Urry 2000: 210)

However, the ways in which such interests are taken up and developed in the social sciences and the academy are usually indirect rather than direct. It is the basis for an uneasy relationship between them that is too crudely dichotomised in terms of distinctions between theoretical reflection and practical action, or between ideas and policy, or knowledge and politics. Making such divisions too easily lets the academy off the hook, just as claims of a disengaged 'ivory tower' is also misleading. For Farrar (2013), sociology has tried, and in his view largely failed, to take account of and to provide an adequate framework for the social movements and issues that he has been involved in, although he does link this to the pressures of working in institutions of higher education that did sack friends of his for their association with student militancy in the 1960s, and which have since then become more corporate and risk-averse (Bailey and Freedman 2011). In another vein, Sandoval-García (2013) looks at collaborative work in a social movement and sets out the challenges as well as the possible gains, for scholars, of engaging and working with such groups in ways that might look more cooperative than parasitic.

The important point, as Urry further notes, is how: 'the "cognitive practices" of such movements have helped to constitute "public spaces for thinking new thoughts, activating new actors, generating new ideas" within societies (Eyerman and Jamison 1991: 161)' (Urry 2000: 210). One example of this is Eric Fassin's (Garner and Fassin 2013) reflection on how the wearing of the headscarf and the veil has shaped debates about race, culture and nation in France in the past decade. Social media campaigns and hashtags such as #Blacklivesmatter and #Rhodesmustfall have commanded mainstream media and political attention in ways that create space for combining a sense of historical perspective, research and scholarship, and activism in a digital age (Camp and Heatherton 2016).[10]

At its best, this is what the relationship between academic and extra-academic worlds can achieve: to widen the vision of what is possible and to draw together diverse constituencies to advance a progressive anti-discriminatory outlook. Essed's (2013) interviews with social justice scholars, for instance, shows the extent to which their pedagogic practices have been shaped and influenced by their links to, and rootedness in, social movements outside and beyond the academy. Such ends come under a variety of names and headings, such as critical social science, engaged and public sociology, activist research and scholarship, social justice scholarship, and others. This eclectic heritage has its own mixed consequences, including a tension between the wish to consolidate the credibility of an area of study – the analysis of racism and racialised exclusion – in the eyes of a wider professional social science community, alongside a desire to continue and extend the honourable tradition of contesting and re-imagining what can be considered as knowledge, and its range of sources and validities (Hill Collins 2000). As a result, work in this vein can span a range of registers – from professionalised discourses that echo more established disciplinary areas to the more interdisciplinary cut-and-mix style sometimes used in popular cultural studies.

With all of this there is the question of institutional responsibility, which comes with working in institutions that continue to practise forms of institutional racism and exclusion, in the sense of being both 'part of' the academy that perpetuates these things, as well as being located in a place and a positionality that provides and enables challenges to it. Taking account of positionality means that the academic voice is akin to that of a participant in a debate, not an all-knowing commentator or theoretical leadership of the movement; as bearers of a particular kind of contribution and not a hierarchical overview.

Public intellectuals and scholar-activists

A notable strand in the relationship between academics and 'publics', broadly conceived, is the role of intellectuals in communicating ideas, framing problems and questions, bringing some analytical clarity and perhaps advancing policy and other kinds of political solutions to contemporary political problems. Often though, the imaginary of the public intellectual tends to privilege the exceptional individual as one who through intellectual command or charisma straddles and maintains credence in different spheres – the academy and the wider public sphere.

This is a recurring theme in scholarship, suggesting that it is a category easily reached for as well as one that is well trodden. Readers can probably think of individuals they regard, or who are regarded, as exemplars of public intellectuals. Two prominent but differing examples are the interventions against globalisation of Pierre Bourdieu (on Bourdieu and politics, see Swartz 2003), and the relationship between sociology and government through the activities of Anthony Giddens.[11] While these suggest a particular form of engagement – the conventional political sphere – it is important to note that it can entail more than this, so there can be diverse forms and styles of political engagement. The life and work of Stuart Hall, for example, and his many contributions to crossing and linking the academic and activist spheres, speaks to the range of what is possible (see Alexander 2009, Back and Tate 2014).

While Hall's engagements are not just about race, in the field of racial and ethnic studies the involvements of Henry Louis Gates and Michael Dyson (Dyson 2003) on misogyny and violence in rap music, or Angela Davis on the devastating impact of the prison-industrial complex (Davis 2005) and the various interventions of Cornel West[12] provide examples of scholarly critique applied to public issues and concerns (see also Sudbury and Ozakawa-Rey 2009). The names of

Gates, Dyson, West and Davis have, among others, been marshalled into a category of the 'Black public intellectual'. Although this term could be of long standing and applied to Booker T Washington and Du Bois, Reed (2000) in an excoriating appraisal, depicted some of the people named here as latter-day colonial brokers, taking on in a self-appointed way, the role of 'interpreting the opaquely black heart of darkness for whites' (Reed 2000: 77), to 'explain the mysteries of Black America', and thereby have 'authenticity conferred by white opinion makers' (Reed 2000: 83-4). Some of the most heated assessments of the role of such figures occurs particularly in relation to their stance on the 2009–16 Obama presidency (see also Bonilla-Silva with Ray 2015); Dyson's (2015) criticisms of West provide an illustration of this.[13] The sometimes *ad hominem* arguments about the black public intellectual in the US show that these can become individual clashes. While the interpersonal battles certainly display the passions of race politics, they also provide an interesting instance of Baert's (2012) positioning theory of how intellectuals locate themselves in a sociopolitical field and, thereby, also how they position others.

There is a presentational problem with self-declared public intellectuals, not least who they claim to speak to and for. An anecdotal example of this occurred when a speaker at a session on race at an American Sociological Association conference stated that he had gone to the UN conference on racism in Durban in 2005 as an 'organic public intellectual'. As far as I could tell, this seemed to mean only that the speaker did not at the time have an academic post. Attaching an 'organic' status to being in a non-institutionalised location is just as much a problem as ruling that being in such a setting precludes people from it. Both claims – that being detached from the academy provides an 'organic' status, or that being in it is tantamount to being detached from such connections – are equally dubious. Following Gramsci (1971), any organic status has to be strived for and is, to borrow from Hall (1990), a matter of becoming – not a state of being.

A different angle is notable in Tariq Modood's many interventions and roles in public debates about race, religion and multiculturalism in Britain. Modood's biographical reflections do acknowledge a sense of his own positionality, and reveal the extent to which his stance on race and multiculturalism has been shaped by the 1989 Rushdie affair over *The satanic verses*[14] (as is the case for others of a Muslim background, see Jennings and Kemp-Welch 1997), as well as by policy work outside the academy. In an interview, Modood said:

> For me, public intellectual engagement is the gold standard. That's been my goal since I got into issues of equality and multiculturalism. I personally feel that if some academics only want to do very specialist academic work that is only of interest to fellow academics, that is fine. We need people like that. But, if everybody had to follow that track, I think that our public culture would be intellectually impoverished. Nevertheless, I have had to some extent argue with colleagues that what I am doing is legitimate. Some people feel that I sometimes simplify a complex theory into two or three sound bites, because that is what the media needs; that I risk being superficial or that I am not theorising enough and I am leaving arguments underdeveloped. There may be some trade-off between intellectual detail and public engagement but I feel that the kind of balance between theory and public engagement that I have been following now for 20 years or so, works for me and is legitimate. (Modood, in Martínez 2013: 735-6)

In almost all the instances mentioned, the figure of the public intellectual is often of an individual acting alone, commonly located at an elite university and often male. Of course there are public intellectuals who do not fit some or all of that description but as a conception of intellectual life I would argue that it can often look and feel like the 'great men' or 'men of letters' of history. In this light, interventions in the public realm are imagined as selfless individual displays of courage, free from any context of collective endeavour, perhaps in the spirit of the writer Emile Zola in the Dreyfus affair. Thus, as in Edward Said's (1994) conception, the intellectual is a figure who provides independent social criticism, against injustice and misuses of power, In fearlessly speaking out against accepted wisdom he (or more rarely, she) speaks 'truth to power' (Marable 1998). As well as being almost prophetic in its claim, this standpoint does little to address issues around the positionality of the speaker, or the need to be a listener and not just a speaker (Back 2007). In addition, if unqualified truth claims are themselves questionable – a notion of bearing witness or charting resistance is preferable – then so too is the unanchored, decontextualised and unreflexive way in which the academy itself is usually absent from relations of power and inequality. The ideal of a public intellectual is thus difficult to reconcile with the highly contested and often explicitly politicised practices of racial and ethnic studies, or even of the social sciences generally.

In considering black intellectuals, Dyson sums it up in these terms:

> The model of the charismatic black male leader has come in
> for deserved drubbing since it overlooks the contributions
> of women and children that often went unheralded in the
> civil rights movement and earlier black freedom struggles.
> Queer activists sparked the #BlackLivesMatter movement,
> underscoring the unacknowledged sacrifice of black folk
> who are confined to the closets and corners of black
> existence.[15]

There seems to be an assumption that there is a ready-made 'public'
simply awaiting the words of wisdom from scholars on Mount Olympus
who can pontificate on any topic. The oddly undifferentiated view of
'the public', rather than multiple publics, contained in that has been
taken to task by Burawoy (2005), among others. The view that reaching
or speaking to the public is evidenced by writing 'op ed' columns in
high-status newspapers and magazines to shape a climate of opinion
is a common instance. In the case of the prominent economist Paul
Krugman, a regular slot in the *New York Times* certainly provides an
outlet for his critical analysis of neoliberal capitalism, though its effect
or 'impact' is harder to pin down in any specific terms. In any case, as
Baert (2012) has argued, attention might more usefully be paid to the
effects of interventions rather than the dispositions and motivations
of individuals. The extent to which public intellectual figures are
reaching beyond particular constituencies and elites is questionable.
At the same time, the role and power of agenda-setting individuals,
groups and media must come into question at the very least in an
increasingly differentiated public and digital media space. The spread
of social media, and a multitude of internet spaces, dilutes the power
of the mainstream media, as well as of 'top down' opinion formation,
though they also assist the rise of an academic 'celebrity culture'.[16]

Thus, speaking, which includes writing in this case, is not the same
as being heard. In the case of black intellectuals, it may depend on the
receptiveness of white audiences to listen (Reed 2000). Intellectuals
from a range of disciplines and with different political positions have
expressed views on racism and racial injustices, but as Clair (2016)
points out:

> the representation of black subordination—no matter how
> carefully constructed—must also find a receptive audience.
> So much black intellectual energy has been expended

on convincing white audiences simply to care about the exploitation of the black poor and the alienation of the black middle classes. The receptivity of particular white audiences has fluctuated over time ... (Clair 2016)[17]

Reservations about the conception and role of public intellectuals are, of course, not new and go well beyond race studies. In part, the critique made draws on Foucault's (1977) observations on the political function of intellectuals. Foucault pointed to the changed circumstances in which the idea of the 'universal' intellectual as the bearer of a universal 'consciousness/conscience of everyone' became impossible to maintain. Instead, he stressed a new mode of connection between theory and practice, in specific sites where people are 'situated either by their professional conditions of work or their conditions of life (housing, the hospital, the asylum, the laboratory, the university, familial and sexual relations). Through this they have undoubtedly gained a much more concrete awareness of struggles' (Foucault 1977: 12). While his idea of the 'specific intellectual' is not without its problems, it is preferable to a notion of intellectual work as a distinct and specialised activity that brings knowledge and enlightenment to the masses or to the public.

The idea of specific intellectuals intersects or connects with an alternative perspective of how academic and public realms can or should be linked. Engaged and activist scholarship deliberately blurs the distinctions between intellectual and political work, combining both and seeking to bring the movement to the classroom and the insights of the classroom to the movement. Touraine's (1981) case for active 'sociological intervention' recommended that sociologists should not only be involved with social movements, but should also encourage them in their militancy. While that approach did not centre the academy itself, contemporary scholar-activist projects are on the same lines of praxis as Touraine, of putting 'theory into action'.[18] Others aim to dismantle 'the "ivory tower" syndrome as based on a false distinction between academia and wider society as sites for social struggle and knowledge production' (Chatterton et al 2010: 247; see also Isaacman, 2003 on African studies; and the essays collected in Sudbury and Ozakawa-Rey 2009).

While these are also familiar calls, they need not be any less important for that. Any assumption that the academy holds a monopoly over the production of knowledge is regarded as a key barrier to achieving a more inclusive and democratised process of shared learning. Whether as public intellectual, engaged researcher or scholar-activist, the wider argument that the perspective of race critical scholarship (Murji and

Bhattachayyrra 2014) offers is to centre the academy itself in the field of vision. That makes the academy a site of contestation in attempts to rethink how and for whom knowledge is made (Hill Collins 2000, Essed 2013). Campaigns against a curriculum dominated by white men were once dismissed as 'political correctness'; more recently, in relation to #Rhodesmustfall, they are de-legitimated as being against the spirit and ethos of a university as a space where 'free speech' and the free play of ideas is paramount. Curiously, the argument that universities are themselves sites of privilege and racist exclusion is one that is disallowed in this liberal space.

In a useful assessment of the pitfalls of attempting to engage activist groups in research, Chatterton et al (2010) suggest that the good intentions that motivate scholars with activist inclinations can be derailed by the imbalance in access to resources and the distinct, if not always contradictory, priorities and motivations of researchers and activists, as Sandoval-García (2013) also notes. They warn of the dangers of scholar activism becoming another professional 'output'. While the pressures on those working in the so-called 'neo-liberal university' (Bailey and Freedman 2011) increasingly demand that all activity can be measured and given value in the market, the move towards institutionalising activist research in such settings threatens to reconstruct the elitist barriers to learning that scholar-activism has sought to dismantle: 'scholar activism may undermine its own intentions by creating a cadre of professionalised, institutionalised activists whose potential is incorporated into the neo-liberal university' (Chatterton et al 2010: 266).

Addressing such challenges requires a flexible, pragmatic and emergent strategy rather than anything resolvable by fiat. Sometimes involvement in social movements may call for academic interventions in public debates that can usefully draw on the mythology of the professional scholar; in other times and places, the university and the bearing of a scholar may constrain political action and the possibility of other kinds of intellectual work. In either case though, institutional settings and identities cannot just be set aside; the persistent and unresolved racist exclusions of the academy shape politically engaged work in the cross-disciplinary areas of race and ethnic studies, giving a sense of urgency and political importance to ongoing debates about what should be included in conceptions of officially sanctioned knowledge. Inevitably, this also locates the academy itself as an interested and partial actor in a political arena that spans internal power struggles and a wider world (Young and Evans-Braziel 2006, Back 2007, Ahmed 2012, Morton et al 2012, Brown 2016). While some discussions of the need for a public scholarship appear to imagine the academy as a neutral space (eg Lewis and Embrick 2016), only recently corroded by the impure intrusion of the market, a critical approach to race studies is formed, in part, through a battle about the nature of the university, and its power-knowledge relation to 'others'. The invocation to scholars on race to become public needs to take account of the fact that race and racism are already public issues, even when scholars lay claim to social scientific detachment and the validation of professional codes of research practice and dissemination (Hammersley 2014). The tension between these is what Rex (1979) spoke to in weighing up the political and policy challenges of working on race; the politically committed approach he advocated was not the same thing as a politically driven, state-centred agenda.

This recalling of Rex (1979) serves as a reminder that even though the context of higher education has changed considerably since he wrote, there is no need to 'reinvent the wheel'. There already are instances of work crossing any distinction between public intellectuals or scholar-activists, and uniting academic work with a range of civic engagements. Indeed, such labels and categories are far less important than the issues and practices they have involved themselves in. To provide just one example, Stuart Hall for over four decades combined scholarly work with a wide variety of public engagements. Some of Hall's engagements with the politics of race, ethnicity, racism and multiculturalism are well established, such as his role as a prominent member of the Commission on the Future of Multi-ethnic Britain (Parekh 2000), sponsored by the Runnymede Trust, and his commentaries on the 1980s riots and on Stephen Lawrence (Hall 1982, 1999, Benyon and Solomos 1987). Others are less well known, such as Hall's role as an advisor to local inquiry into Policing in Hackney (Independent Committee of Inquiry 1989), an area of north east London marked by conflict between the police and black people; or his work on racial stereotyping for the legal team of Duwayne Brooks during the Macpherson (1999) inquiry. Alongside his analyses of Thatcherism in the 1980s (Hall 1989) and of neo-liberal politics generally, these demonstrate impressive testimony of scholarly analysis of critical conjunctures. They confound the distinction that Modood (in Martinez 2013) draws between 'reforming' (in which regard he named Bhikhu Parekh) and 'critical' (naming Hall) intellectuals, although Modood does say he has been inspired by both of them. Hall's work was both critical and practical; while there may be instances that are more of one type than the other, dividing them up in this way takes us backward into dichotomies such as practice/theory, or the idea of critical but 'armchair intellectualising'.

Public sociology in the neoliberal university

Another way into discussing critical public engagement takes its cue from Burawoy's (2005, 2014) famous manifesto for public sociology. This was articulated in response to a context where the academy is under attack by the assorted forces of marketisation. Burawoy called for a public sociology in a context of what he describes as 'privatization (diminishing public funds), corporatization (the turn to private donors), and marketization (appealing to the most vulgar instincts to boost student admissions and justify escalating fees)' (Burawoy 2005: 76) of universities. Burawoy's opposition to marketisation and neoliberalisation of higher education shares common ground with Sandel's (2012) critique of 'market societies' as ones in which everything is for sale.

There is much to commend in Burawoy's vision of sociology and of the social sciences that seeks to mobilise and activate, or even 'create' public audiences for intellectual work; as the examples of popular science and psychology show, this is possible. The appeal of Burawoy's approach is an emphasis on an 'outward'-facing academy, which asks itself for whom and to what end knowledge production is practised and intended. (Burawoy's schema acknowledges that there are other forms or types of sociology, which are as equally valid as public sociology.) Yet the impact of managerialist burdens on the professional autonomy of scholars[19] seems to be a more muted aspect of this debate than the populist call to connect with the public or publics. Moreover, while some of his proposals have potentially far-reaching scope, in other respects Burawoy's agenda is not far-reaching enough. So his call is not for a critique of the institutions of higher education, or even of a significant reconsideration of what the university is. Instead, this is a public sociology that seeks to defend the university 'against the encroachment of markets and states' (Burawoy 2005: 76), as if the university without these ongoing institutional pressures and carriers of privilege exists as an open space for democratic culture.

The celebrated as well as much criticised call to a public sociology initiated by Burawoy (*Sociology* 2007, *Critical Social Policy* 2008, Burawoy 2014) does not acknowledge the history and intellectual formation of US universities as in Lal's (2008) critique of it. This could be applied to a range of locations where universities have been at the service of the state and of the powerful, rather than a source of critical knowledges against racial and other forms of exclusion. Lal references some of the well-known criticisms of US-based area studies, not least their service to US imperial projects. However, her argument is more about the consequences of this provenance. For Lal, academic institutions have operated as a link in a chain that constructs attitudes to knowledge, usually around interest groups and institutions able to garner resources and influence. In this light, the marketisation of the academy, although a matter of concern, is more a continuation of the long-running interference by external forces on practices of learning and, through this, on public understandings of what learning can entail:

> The corporatization and marketization of American universities today continues this tradition of the academy in the service of state projects. Market needs, in harmony with state-led neoliberalism, facilitate the transformation of campuses in two primary ways. First, there is the commodification of the signs of the university by the market penetration and saturation of new public spheres. This 'logo' centrism brings the visibility and profitability of corporate logos into academic landscapes.... Secondly, there is the commodification (and reification) of particular forms of academic knowledge in the service of market demands. (Lal 2008: 173)

Burawoy describes a form of public scholarship that can include the professional recognition of public engagement, as well as the 'organic public sociologist' who is intertwined with local publics in a network of thick and active relations (Burawoy 2005: 72). In this optimistic outlook there is space for the re-imagination of academic professionalism for those linked to 'counter-publics', those explicitly politicised interest groups that develop knowledge in opposition to the mainstream. It is this ability to constitute and connect with counter-publics that is compromised by the market positon and sanctioned knowledge production of US universities, Lal argues. While there can be a space for a carefully thought-out display of expert and publicly respectable knowledge that is rooted in – and finds an echo in – the traditions of the academy, there is a problem of promoting the 'mass appeal of scientism and the public trust in "expert" knowledge ... both produced and maintained by the "professionalism" of academia, as well as by the state's legitimation of positivist social science through its sponsorship of and clientist relation with policy research' (Lal 2008: 178).

The ability to imagine otherwise, in the manner of counter-publics, may be harder to encompass within the various disciplinary mechanisms of the contemporary university. In differing ways, scholars acknowledge this difficulty, and struggle to overcome the limitations of the inevitably compromised and constrained institutional spaces occupied by scholars, critical and radical or not. For Farrar (2013), this means stepping away from the university into more effective interactions between learning and publics. For those, such as Mirza (2009), Ahmed (2012), Hill Collins (2013), Essed (2013) and Sandoval-García (2013), among others, the academy needs to be rendered accountable for the raced and gendered relations that it helps to create and sustain, if it is to be useful to social movements engaged in battles for social justice. Likewise, for Hesse (2007), Hund and Lentin (2014) and Bhambra (2014), it entails a recognition of the historical depth of colonial and racialised knowledge and relations embedded in academic institutions and disciplines – to the extent that these need to be fundamentally reformulated and reconceived (see also Connell 1997).

Public intellectuals, scholar-activists and public sociology each provide cues about the relationship of the university, and particularly for radical or critical scholars, to critical public engagement and social justice movements. Such publics and movements can exist within the university as well as beyond it, in the form of student and staff campaigns and solidarity movements beyond education, as Back (2015) shows in his review of sociology impact submissions. It is important not to regard them as separate domains, as that feeds into conceptions of the detached 'ivory tower', or of the role of scholars as being to speak 'to' the public. Instead, the view set out here seeks to implicate and acknowledge the university and scholarly activity as a contested space, itself tied into power-knowledge relations and hierarchies of race and its intersections. A wider, 'grounded' and de-masculinised conception of scholarly and intellectual activity than the figures of 'great men' would essentially invoke the positionality and complexity of, and for, individuals and groups working with – rather than on – publics.

While scholar-activists and, to an extent, public sociologists take a less hierarchical and elitist stance towards publics, they too must address internal difficulties, such as the danger that activism becomes a kind of badge; or in the case of public sociology, that it does not address the place and role of the university itself. While none of these provide a fixed position from which to advocate and practise critical work, and each signals some of the forms and achievements, including problems, of engaged scholarship, the key point is that it must always be a process of becoming rather than a state of being.

Notes

1   This is a revised and expanded version of an article that appeared as G. Bhattacharyya and K. Murji (2013) 'Race critical public scholarship', *Ethnic and Racial Studies* 36(9): 1359-73. I thank Routledge and, especially, Gargi Bhattacharyya for allowing me to re-use and re-work the material for this book.
2   Badgett (2016) provides a guide to some ways of being more effective in this regard.
3   For more information see: https://openborders.info/
4   See: http://blacklivesmatter.com/
5   For instance, this: *How sociology can support black lives matter.* www.asanet.org/news-events/footnotes/dec-2016/features/how-sociology-can-support-black-lives-matter
6   Rhodes Must Fall sprang from a protest at the University of Cape Town in 2015 and has spread from opposition to statues of Cecil Rhodes at UCT and Oxford Universities into a wider movement against coloniality in higher education curricula.
7   An insight into this can be seen at the blog site at: https://academicirregularities.wordpress.com/
8   See also the plenary lecture by Claire Alexander: https://vimeo.com/176452879
9   See: http://circuitous.org/scraps/combahee.html
10 See also this blogpost of a discussion at the American Sociological Association in 2016: https://policypress.wordpress.com/2016/08/23/i-dont-see-scholarship-and-activism-as-disctinct-plenary-at-the-asa-highlights-need-for-activism-resistance-among-scholars/
11 Giddens continues to discuss and reflect on his public work, such as in this interview: http://isa-global-dialogue.net/sociology-politics-and-power-an-interview-with-anthony-giddens/
12 For details see his website: http://www.cornelwest.com/
13 Dyson, ME, 'The ghost of Cornel West', *New Republic*, April 2015: https://newrepublic.com/article/121550/cornel-wests-rise-fall-our-most-exciting-black-scholar-ghost
14 On this aspect, see in particular: *On being a public intellectual, a Muslim and a multiculturalist.* http://renewal.org.uk/articles/on-being-a-public-intellectual-a-muslim-and-a-multiculturalist
15 Dyson, ME, 'The ghost of Cornel West', *New Republic*, April 2015:https://newrepublic.com/article/121550/cornel-wests-rise-fall-our-most-exciting-black-scholar-ghost
16 For instance, for an account of Slavoj Žižek as a superstar academic, see: https://www.thesociologicalreview.com/blog/slavoj-zizek-between-public-intellectual-and-academic-celebrity.html
17 Clair, M, 'Black intellectuals and white audiences', *Public Books*, May 2016: www.publicbooks.org/nonfiction/black-intellectuals-and-white-audiences
18 For instance, see the Transformative Studies Institute and its journal, *Social Justice*: http://transformativestudies.org/about-2/
19 See the Campaign for the Public University: http://publicuniversity.org.uk/

FOUR

Sociology and
institutional racism[1]

All the approaches to scholarly engagement discussed in Chapter Three looks towards a more outward-facing academy, although there are significant differences in what that should entail. Institutional racism, especially in the Macpherson inquiry (1999), provides a way into understanding public engagement by social scientists; it also sets the scene for assessing the impact of social science in policy and practice, and the academic–policy interface. These issues are developed in this chapter and the following two chapters.

The discussion cannot, however, be just about what scholars take to the public, in view of the discussion in Chapter Three, which argued that the university as well as the history of disciplines such as sociology are themselves implicated in, or maybe even foundational to, racial exclusion. Hence, racism and institutional racism can also be used to reflect on sociology itself. The interrelationship between them is what this chapter is about. It seeks to chart and explore several aspects of sociology – the link between US and British sociology, the different public stance adopted by their respective professional associations for sociologists, and the connections between sociology, social movements and the media. The origins and context of the term 'institutional racism' – which reached its fiftieth anniversary in 2017 – provides a way of reflecting on the development of race scholarship in Britain, and on the quite diverse public roles of the national sociological associations in the UK and the US, insofar as they reveal differing public and scholarly engagements with racism. Consequently, institutional racism provides a lens into the discipline of sociology itself, which it sheds light on or 'speaks back' to in ways that sociologists can find uncomfortable.

While there is a great deal written on sociology and on institutional racism, in this chapter I bring them together in different ways that reveal a set of connections that are less evident than they could be. On the one hand, the discipline, along with other social sciences, adopted and adapted the term, institutional racism, for social analysis and to critique systematic discrimination in society. On the other hand, it also fell out of favour in sociology and, rather like its public profile, the term has risen and then disappeared from social science,

79

only to rise and fall again in the years after the Scarman inquiry (1981) and, particularly, after the Macpherson inquiry (1999). Drawing on some sociological engagements with the latter inquiry, I propose that institutional racism has been useful as a vehicle for a kind of public sociology (Burawoy 2005, 2014), in which academic expertise contributed to the formulation of the term in the inquiry, though how that occurred is more of a 'wavy' line rather than a linear line of policy influence (see also Chapter Five).

The account in this chapter is also partly about an internal debate in sociology, as well as being about public and media discussion of racism after the publication of the Macpherson (1999) report. The kinds of public roles taken by scholars (which I consider here and in Chapters Five and Six) are not always recognised, for instance in accounts such as Loader and Sparks' (2011) version of public engagements by academic criminologists as either 'scientific experts, policy advisors, governmental players, social movement theorists, or lonely prophets'. In my view, none of these is that useful for understanding what went on within the Macpherson inquiry. The limit of Loader and Sparks' approach is not just in stating that such roles and categories overlap in practice.[2] Rather, it is to stress that it is analytically limited to adopt an 'academy led' viewpoint that does not take sufficient account of the environment and processes in which academic expertise or 'knowledge exchange' does have any impact. I provide a further instance of this in relation to another inquiry, into race and faith matters, in Chapter Six.

The idea of institutional racism, although aired in many places in and after Macpherson, is useful, because it sheds light on the problems, with versions of public engagement that do not take into account the academy itself (for example, see Loader and Sparks 2011, Lewis and Embrick 2016). Drawing on it in this context serves to highlight its use to critique the whiteness of the discipline of sociology itself, that are less prominent and largely absent in the discussions following Macpherson. In recent years, campaigns about racism in higher education, the representation and seniority of black and ethnic minority staff, the content of the curriculum, and the historic links between universities and slave owners, and racism have come to the fore. These campaigns, from South Africa to the US and Europe, have raised concerns about racism and white privilege in higher education. In these, racism is often understood as structural and historically rooted, as well as an aspect of unquestioned whiteness in the academy, which is treated as the unmarked norm to which racial minorities are expected to adapt and conform (Ahmed 2012). While this critique goes well beyond sociology itself, the purpose of going back to the origins and context of institutional racism in the 1960s is to revive some of the arguments that it was employed for – against white sociologies of race and for a black sociology.

Black Power and white sociology in the US and in Britain

A link between the two aspects of this chapter can be brought out through the opening paragraph of the entry for 'institutional racism' in *The Oxford Dictionary of Sociology*:

> In a remarkable episode in the history of ideas the concept of 'institutional racism' emerged in the context of radical political struggle and the Black Power movement in the United States in the 1960s and then traversed three decades, two continents and the social class structure to be adopted by a member of the British nobility. (Scott and Marshall 2005: 311-12)

This entry connects sociology and social movements, and indicates that the idea of institutional racism has travelled extensively since it originated in the latter. The 'member of the British nobility' referred to is Sir William Macpherson of Cluny, who chaired The Stephen Lawrence Inquiry. The inquiry received wide publicity, both while it was sitting and particularly after the publication of its report in 1999. (Cathcart, 1999 provides the most detailed coverage of the inquiry; commentaries on the media coverage include McLaughlin and Murji 1999, Neal 2003; later coverage of the media, the police and policy aspects includes Cottle 2004, Foster et al 2005, Holohan 2005, Runnymede Trust 2009, Hall et al 2009.)

Chapter 6 of the Macpherson report contains a discussion of the origins and meaning of institutional racism and points out that it is drawn from a 1967 book, *Black Power*, by Stokely Carmichael (later known as Kwame Ture) and Charles Hamilton, in which they introduced and first set out the main features of the term. That a radical book connected to the Black Panthers in the US should receive such significance in a UK public inquiry is itself noteworthy, as the Oxford dictionary entry suggests. While mainstream media coverage of that section of Macpherson commonly derided the term as a piece of sociological jargon – its association with sociology being what detractors used to damn both the idea itself, as well as sociology in general – it actually emerged from a 1960s civil rights political movement.

Black Power was an explicit critique of the white establishment in the US; it called for radical or militant black political activity to combat racism, which Carmichael and Hamilton argued was pervasive and systemic. They used the term 'institutional racism' to account for attitudes and practices that led to racist outcomes through unquestioned bureaucratic procedures, while they saw individual and institutional racism as analogous to the distinction between overt and covert racism. While individual racism is overt and could be seen and heard, institutional racism was a more subtle, covert process that could not be reduced to the acts of individuals. For them, white people clearly collectively benefited from that, even if individual whites did not wish to discriminate, so it went beyond whether people had good or ill intentions. In treating institutional racism as a form of internal colonialism in the US, they maintained that although blacks had the same citizenship status as whites, they stood in as colonial subjects in relation to white society. For Hesse (2000, 2014), this link to colonialism marks one of the most significant aspects of their approach. While neither of the authors of *Black Power* were sociologists,[3] the meaning and utility of institutional racism has been debated, in sporadic bursts but also sometimes in heated ways, in sociology, in the media and in public discourse ever since.

In the decade after the publication of *Black Power*, one of the key tasks in sociology for those who wanted to use the term was to develop an analysis of the key word 'institutional'. In the US in the 1970s, it was taken to mean that institutional racism usefully accounted for or explained racial inequalities that did not necessarily explicitly make reference to race or colour, but still resulted in systematic patterns of discrimination and disadvantage. In other words, racism was observable by its outcomes and patterns of inequality rather than the words and deeds of individuals. While there were some doubts about this view – which, like the original formulation in *Black Power* was considered to be overly dualistic, dividing blacks and whites into separate and opposed camps – its appeal was clear. Indeed, four decades on, similar arguments about racialised patterns of inequality are made as occurring through 'colour blind' racism (Gallagher 2015) and Bonilla-Silva's (2006) explanation of the persistence of 'racism without racists'.

In UK sociology, institutional racism came to be thought of as describing the process or mechanism that explained how racist outcomes were produced, even when individuals acted without obvious or discernible racist intent. It marked a shift from treating racism and racial disadvantage as a psychological or cultural trait of individuals and groups (such as 'the authoritarian personality'), or from anthropological models of a culture of poverty. Furthermore, the term helped to make the case for, or to reinforce, a conception of racism as a structural feature of society, rather than a psychological or cultural trait of individuals and groups. While seeing racism as a structural process, rather than a matter of individual prejudices, makes it difficult to detect, its manifestations are observable in patterns of systematic inequality produced by bureaucracies.

In both national contexts, sociologists adopted and developed the term as a way of accounting for racially biased outcomes and patterns and its underlying causes in institutional practices that embody assumptions and values that produce skewed outcomes. From its origins to these subsequent developments, some of the core ideas of institutional racism made it into the definition Macpherson proposed, although Rattansi (2007) sees that version as a jumble.

In this vein, the development of institutional racism within sociology was conceived as a radical or a critical concept, providing a lens or a tool to analyse racist exclusions. It also positioned sociology as a discipline and a practice committed to understanding and exposing racism. Its take-up within sociology and transplantation from the field of political activism is a clear demonstration of sociology acting 'parasitically' in Urry's (2000) terms. However, the idea of sociology as a discipline aligned with social movements and Zeitgeist moments is far from self-evident, and many sociologists and sociologies do not see the discipline in such terms. Neither is it merely a case of the academy being or becoming 'free riders' on the back of activist movements, for as Chapter Three argued, there is a complicated and uneven relationship between the academy, and social movements and publics in all their varieties. Nevertheless, such connections can – or do – generate new ideas, as Urry (2000) noted. Linking with them is an example of what Burawoy (2005: 260) sees as the 'passion for social justice … that drew so many of us to sociology'; a feeling that, recently, can also be seen in Hill Collins (2013), Farrar (2013) and Bauman (2014), among many others.[4] A gesture in the same direction also comes from decolonial approaches, which see social struggles as useful in challenging academic conceptual forms, perhaps to displace them for meanings based in 'political practices, alternative forms of justice, other ways of living' (Vázquez 2010: 41).

The context and consequences of Black Power as a social movement are significant for the public face of sociology. In the 1960s, the US witnessed a series of 'race riots' across the country, a burgeoning movement for civil rights and a prolonged debate about tackling the racial inequalities manifest in housing, employment, criminal justice and democratic representation (Singh 2004). To the degree that some sociologists supported the radical political and ideological shifts of that time (see Touraine 1981), it created a view of sociology as a discipline and a practice committed to egalitarianism and to challenging existing structures of power and authority. A picture of sociology's apparent radicalism then and since does needs to be tempered. As Burawoy (2005) points out, in 1968 two-thirds of American Sociological Association (ASA) members were against taking a view on the Vietnam War; he adds that in 2003, the same proportion favoured a resolution opposing the war in Iraq.

This mixed picture of sociology and its engagement with racism, institutional or otherwise, can be taken further in several ways that further connect the US and Britain. The first comes from a revisionist history of black anti-racist movements in the US, which starts from a critique of sociology's 'abbreviated periodization' (Singh 2004: 6) of the civil rights struggle as being from the 1950s. This, Singh (2004) argues, ignores the heterogeneity and depth of black struggles before that, particularly in accounts of the period that draw a sharp distinction between the conciliatory politics of Martin Luther King – and so neglect his radicalism – and the more revolutionary approach of groups such as the Black Panthers, to which Carmichael and Hamilton (1967) were connected. For current purposes, however, it is Singh's (2004) stress on the 'long civil rights' era from the 1930s that matters. Taking this longer view enables Singh to draw in various black intellectuals, particularly the neglect of the sociologist W.E.B. Du Bois in and by sociology (see also Morris 2015), as well as black social movements, which campaigned actively against imperialism and colonialism. Such writers and activists argued that blacks in the US experienced a form of internal colonialism, which would be repeated in Carmichael and Hamilton's (1967) characterisation of institutional racism. Singh shows that black intellectuals made a key link between racism and liberalism, and connected those to US globalism, making a powerful critique of nation-state institutional power across and over the globe. Thus, for Singh, Black Power in the 1960s marked a return to earlier radical and internationalist tendencies that connected equality and civil rights concerns with a critique of empire. While, politically, this internationalism was a precursor to the Black Power struggles of the 1960s, its importance in sociological terms was its criticism and rejection of the nation-state-centred vision of racial assimilation that was dominant in politics and policy.

While Singh (2004) does not use his historiography to label sociology as institutionally racist, the legacy of *Black Power* did lead other works of the time to draw on it to censure 'white sociology'. This is a second point of connection. In *The death of white sociology*, Ladner (1973) argued that a black sociology was needed as a counter to the mainstream, white liberal sociology that had, 'in the main, upheld the status quo' (Ladner, 1973: xx), although she left open whether there could be a black sociology founded on the rejection (rather than the acceptance) of traditional sociology. One contributor to Ladner's volume, Robert Staples, did castigate white racist sociology from the classical period through to the pro-segregationist arguments of early 20th-century US sociologists (Staples 1973). (Connell (1995) provides another critique of classical sociology and its links with empire.) Staples (1976) went on to develop a fuller account of a black sociology, in which the definition of racism as a form of dehumanisation and a system for the maintenance of white power draws from the *Black Power* view of institutional racism.

Furthermore, in one of the two case studies of institutional racism in the Ladner (1973) collection, Billingsley attacked social science research on the family for either ignoring black families or for producing distorted and pathological views of them when they were included, by using notions of the nihilism of ghetto culture and of matriarchal families to explain black disadvantage. (Anderson's (1999) ethnography of the 'code of the street' and Coates' (2015) biography provide more nuanced accounts.) For Billingsley (1973), such sociologies neglected the impact of institutional racism on blacks. Indeed, he went further and saw institutional racism as an endemic force within white social science that made it unable to correct its distortions and stereotypes of black families. It regarded unstable, low-income families as the cause of wider disadvantages that blacks experienced in society; it employed outdated methods based on statistical techniques; and it ignored stable black families as well as black scholars and experts. The works of John Stanfield (2011) have continued this critical tradition. Staples (1973, 1976) emphasised that the role of a sociologist was to be both a theorist and an activist; this is akin to the scholar-activist model identified in Chapter Three.

Turning from the US to Britain, there are interesting differences in the public face of sociology and this is the third point of connection. It would be incorrect to say that race and racism had been neglected by sociology in the period after the publication of *Black Power*, but it remained somewhat on the margins of academic sociology. The sociology of race and racialism was the theme of the 1969 British Sociological Association (BSA) conference. A book of essays from it, *Race and racialism*, was published a year later (Zubaida 1970) and for current purposes there are three notable features of that:

- First, the Introduction says that the aim of the conference was to integrate race into general sociological theory, which probably included a sense that more work on race in Britain was required, rather than on quasi-anthropological research in the former colonies. While the book's censure of race relations studies as largely atheoretical and ahistorical, unsystematic and as concerned with prejudicial attitudes rather than social structure is well founded, it is noticeable that this is not a criticism of sociology as such; rather it seems to be aimed at anthropology and psychology.
- Second, a reading of the book suggests that racism is mainly seen as a subject of internal debate in sociology, and with related disciplines. Although the Foreword to the book does indicate that racism is a pressing public issue, there is not much sense of how sociology could or would address that. Linked to that is the now striking and unexplained preference for 'racialism' rather than racism in the title, which perhaps marks the lack of a connection to *Black Power* or to institutional racism.
- Third, although Wolpe (1970) does employ an idea of structural racism as being akin to institutional racism – and as distinct from intentional racism – there is only one other chapter (Lockwood 1970) that mentions black power as a social movement at all, though Lockwood's main concern was whether race required a special theory or set of concepts, or whether it could be seen as a subset of class and stratification.

In retrospect, that 1969 BSA conference looked more like a statement of intent than any indication of the centrality of the study of race and racism within British sociology (Zubaida 1970). Although in the 1970s there was a noticeable development of research on race issues, through the founding of research centres at Bristol, Aston and then Warwick universities (Solomos 1999), British sociology lacked a distinct approach to such matters (indeed this was part of Miles' (1993) attack on race relations sociology). Sociology overlapped with social anthropology that focused mainly on the study of societies and communities in Africa and Asia and, with social psychology, which took as its object the measurement and explication of prejudice rather than racism.

This motley picture is evident even up to Rex and Mason's (1986) overview of the field. That volume contained chapters covering the disciplines of sociology, social anthropology and social psychology, as well as sociobiology, alongside macro-level approaches to race and ethnicity drawing on class analysis, the study of plural societies, and

Weberian and Marxist perspectives, as well as micro-level approaches such as rational choice theory and symbolic interactionism.

By the middle to late 1970s, sociology in Britain came to be attacked for the anthropological 'othering' of migrants into the UK as 'dark strangers'. This was a period when the Institute of Race Relations journal *Race and Class* became subtitled 'A journal for black and third world liberation', and it challenged the academy for its lack of critical analysis of racism (see, for example, Bourne and Sivanandan 1980). In a history of the BSA, Platt (2003) mentions an undated memo, in which the convenor of the BSA race group states that its main concern was to make a 'sociology that is geared to exposing and explaining white institutional racism' (cited in Platt, 2003: 57). She adds that the group sought to prevent John Rex from speaking. In the late 1970s, Rex became the second director of the Social Science Research Council (later the Economic and Social Research Council; ESRC) Unit on Race and Ethnic Relations. Highly critical views of his Weberian sociology as a governmental tool to manage race as an increasingly visible social problem appeared subsequently (Bourne and Sivanandan 1980, CCCS 1982). The field of race and racism studies was itself challenged and interrogated for the kind of knowledge it produced. A sense of the antagonisms of the time is apparent in the opening line of a chapter by Rex, where he states: 'The study of race relations, in common with other politically charged areas in the social sciences, seems beset with feuds and conflicts of a quite theological intensity' (Rex 1986: 64).

A key force behind that was the work of the Race and Politics group at the Birmingham University Centre for Contemporary Cultural Studies (CCCS) and the landmark 1982 publication *The empire strikes back*. In that book, Lawrence (1982) – in what is the most direct parallel with Ladner and Billingsley's work in the 1970s – analysed sociology's role in producing pathological accounts of black culture and families, as suffering from identity crisis and intergenerational conflict. He saw such analyses as easily incorporated into British state racism and policy, and explicitly attributes these failings to white sociology; that referred not only to white personnel, but also to the neglect of the historical conditions in which sociology developed (Lawrence 1982). In a review symposium of *The empire strikes back* three decades on, it is Lawrence's scrutiny of race relations sociology that stands the test of time for many. Meer (2014) describes Lawrence's two chapters 'as sharp as the day he penned them; and thirty years on, his complaint of "convergence between racist ideologies and the theories of 'race/

ethnic-relations sociology'" is no less searing (Lawrence 1982, 95)'
(Meer 2014: 1795).

A fourth point of connection is the different public roles of the
national sociological associations in each of these countries. Contrasts
between the American Sociological Association and the British
Sociological Association (the ASA and BSA respectively), the main
professional associations for sociologists in the US and the UK, reveal
quite diverse modes of engagement with publics beyond the academy.
Although the two associations are very different in size and operate in
different contexts and jurisdictions, it is noteworthy that the ASA has
been able to take a more public role on these things than the BSA;
indeed, the extent of that and the willingness of the ASA to get involved
in controversial public policy issues is striking. One example is the
ASA Council's statement that confirmed its view of the importance
of collecting and using data based on racial and ethnic categorisation
as necessary to address racial disparities. This was issued as a response
to the ASA's recommendation to voters in California to vote against
Proposition 54 that would have limited the ability of state agencies to
collect such data (Krieger 2010).

While the ASA has debated its role on campaigns such as Black
Lives Matter, a prominent role in race equality was its involvement in
cases concerning the University of Michigan's admissions policy. The
admissions policy went beyond exam scores in order to try to increase
the numbers of minority students enrolled at the university. In *Grutter
v. Bollinger* (2003), a white student protested that this policy denied
her entry into the Michigan law school. When the case reached the
US Supreme Court, the ASA – acting in concert with other learned
societies – prepared an amicus brief for the court. This drew on 'sound
sociological research that addresses the need for affirmative education
in legal education'.[5] The brief argued that race had a powerful impact
on life chances of black people in the US and so had to be taken into
account in admissions decisions. The Supreme Court did back the
university's admission policy in this case, although it also narrowed the
scope of affirmative action policies and the use of race-based admissions
in a related case and later cases.

While a more critical sociology may have stressed the historical and
structural legacy of institutional racism, this case is a demonstration of
the ASA's stated mission of advancing sociology and serving the public
good. This engagement in public policy advocacy is quite different from
its British counterpart. The BSA acts more as a learned society by way
of submitting evidence to bodies such as the British Academy or the
ESRC on matters such as research assessment, impact and teaching,

among other issues. Its status as a charity, and charity law within the UK, restricts wider engagement that could be deemed 'political'. Although the President of the BSA did speak out, by writing a letter to a national newspaper, about the underlying social and economic causes of the riots in 2011, Hammersley (2014) argues that it did not contain a particularly sociological viewpoint.

Scarman, Macpherson and the media

Institutional racism in Britain came into public view in the Macpherson inquiry, following many years after which it had apparently been laid to rest in and after the Scarman (1981) report. In Chapter Five, I look more at the content of social scientific evidence on institutional racism and how this helped to shape Macpherson's view. In this chapter, attention centres on some internal debates in sociology in the 1980s, following Scarman's rejection of the term institutional racism. The unresolved (or only partially resolved) dispute in sociology about the meaning and utility of the term shaped, to an extent, the formulations submitted by social scientists to Macpherson. Yet the media reaction to, and framing of, Macpherson largely bypassed that and took the discussion back to the state it was in two decades earlier.

Evidence submitted by sociologists, criminologists and other social scientists to Macpherson was usually done in an individual capacity, and not by professional associations. There were a couple of exceptions to that, one being the report prepared by Simon Holdaway in association with the Commission for Racial Equality. Another was a document prepared for Deighton Gudella solicitors – who were representing Duwayne Brooks, the friend of Stephen Lawrence who was with him on the night of the murder – by Stuart Hall and colleagues at the Open University. For Jane Deighton, Mr Brooks' solicitor, the rationale for seeking academic expertise was a feeling that:

> the Inquiry panel didn't have a grip on race. They couldn't see Duwayne [Brooks] as a victim, they only saw him as a witness. That was really troubling – they had a grip on some aspects and issues but they ignored the way Duwayne had been treated by the police. There wasn't a structure in place to explain this to the inquiry ... to explain why the police had acted in a racist way towards Duwayne – so we decided that one way to do this was to gather expert evidence.

This statement seems extraordinary in light of the way that race and racism were – and became – central in Macpherson. In turning to Hall for support, the solicitor was seeking a leading academic expert on race and, in light of Hall's profile, he was asked to draft a report. While the document he contributed to does not appear as a formal piece of evidence submitted to the inquiry, its contents seem to clearly inform the inquiry panel's thinking in one key respect particularly. The Open University document aims to unpick the process of racial stereotyping by the police. It argued that Stephen and Duwayne's race and gender meant that the police could only see them as dangerous young black men, perhaps as part of a gang, and not as victims. This stereotyping was a form of unconscious bias that informed the police's slow response (for a similar view see Holohan 2005). The Macpherson report reflects this view and it informs what it called 'unwitting' racism by the police. Hence, even without being acknowledged, social science can inform public policy and debates.

By the time the Macpherson inquiry sat in 1998, it had been over five years since the racist murder of Stephen Lawrence – years that had also been filled with a failed private prosecution and a famous *Daily Mail* headline 'MURDERERS', when in 1997 it named and printed photographs of the five white men who had long been the main suspects (Cottle 2004, McLaughlin 2005). Two of those five were eventually convicted of the murder in 2012.[6] Alongside allegations of police corruption and racism as reasons for the failure to prosecute the case, plus some concerns about Sir William Macpherson's own views and record on race matters (Catchcart 1999), the subject of racism was paramount in the inquiry. Thus, in the main, social scientists who responded to Macpherson's call for submissions concentrated on correcting the rejection of institutional racism in Scarman. During that inquiry into rioting in Brixton in 1981, it was put to Scarman that the over-policing of young black people was a major cause of the disorder and that, moreover, discrimination and disadvantage against blacks was due to institutional racism. He notably rejected the latter suggestion if it meant, he said, 'a society which knowingly, as a matter of policy, discriminates against black people' (Scarman 1981: para 2.22).

For Scarman, both an environment of inner-city deprivation as well as unemployment were associated with the feeling of injustice that police harassment exacerbated. That led him to acknowledge that 'racial disadvantage and its nasty associate, racial discrimination' did exist, and he accepted 'unwitting' discrimination as a factor, but not institutional racism, which he defined in intentionalist terms. This strongly framed the understanding of witting/unwitting racism in Macpherson's discussion. As Hesse (2004) indicates, Scarman is informed by an intentionalist view of racism and Macpherson by a consequentialist view of racism.

Scarman's stress on intentionality and his rejection of unseen institutional factors reopened the somewhat dormant debate on institutional racism, as well as sociology's contribution to anti-racist theory and policy. Sociologists observed that a lack of precision in the meaning of institutional racism had enabled Scarman to define it in his own way, and then to reject it as unfounded. Mason (1982) noted Scarman's 'simplistic rejection' of institutional racism, but he went on to acknowledge that the term suffered from:

> wide variation in uses ... imprecision in many of the formulations of the concept [and that] imprecise formulations, whose validity cannot be demonstrated, are a very poor basis indeed for the formation of policies or programmes of political action designed to combat racial disadvantage and oppression (Mason 1982: 44).

Similarly, Williams (1985) felt that its usage had become 'widespread and simplistic'; it had a 'catch all' character, as if it explained all situations where racial inequalities could be observed. Like Mason, she argued that the term was inadequate both as a guide to empirical research and as a means of policy formulation; she sought to interrogate the term to improve its 'political usefulness and [the] reform potential of anti-racist policies' (Williams 1985: 323). Others, like Miles (1989), argued against 'inflating' conceptions of racism, and called for more precise meanings. Although Hall (1982) stressed the need for nuanced readings of Scarman, the highly critical scholarly reaction to it is summed up in Barker and Beezer (1983), for whom the rejection of racism made Scarman's work as 'a liberal Report, but one within entirely racist parameters'.

In the 1980s, although the Metropolitan Police hierarchy accepted parts of the Scarman report, other sections of the force, and the Police Federation in particular, were said to have engaged in a 'backlash' to undermine even its limited policy proposals. Despite the clearly liberal, rather than structural, reform agenda in Scarman, Joe Sim argued that that was too much for the police, who viewed Scarman's recommendations as a threat to their power and autonomy. By mounting media and public campaigns drawing on the threat of the 'black mugger' and black street criminality (which Hall et al (1978) had analysed), Sim (1982) claimed that the police sought to undermine

Scarman and any changes in public order policing and structures of police accountability. What is noticeable about all of this is just how influential Scarman's framing of the term proved to be, as this is what social scientists sought to dismantle to produce a workable version in and for Macpherson.

Nonetheless, a Scarman-like formulation was still evident in 1999. In their evidence to Macpherson, the Metropolitan Police rejected institutional racism, by relying on grounds very similar to the ones used by Scarman. In their written submission and oral evidence to the inquiry, the police maintained that a finding of institutional racism would lead the public to regard all police officers as acting with racist intentions (see Macpherson 1999: chapter 6). Indeed, despite his personal acceptance of the argument for institutional racism, this is what worried Sir (later Lord) Ian Blair, the Commissioner of the Metropolitan Police from 2005–08:

> I know that the definition of institutional racism – of some form – has been around for some years before Macpherson reported. But, I think it was a profoundly difficult concept for the police service to understand, in particular for individual, relatively junior police officers to understand. It seemed to them to be literally an attack on their personal integrity, on whether they were racist or not. The definition that Macpherson gave is in my view a very good definition but I'm not sure that it was very helpful in the context of the Stephen Lawrence inquiry, it needed far more explanation, I think, than it was afforded. … It needed a very large health warning across it which said, this is about the organisation, it's not about individuals.

In the wake of Scarman in the 1980s and the critical reaction to it in sociology, the challenge for social scientists was to get beyond the individual/institutional dichotomy that was so strong in rejecting the idea of institutional racism and, moreover, which has proved to be a sticking point in police circles ever since (Foster et al 2005, Rowe 2007, Hall et al 2009, Souhami 2014). The nub of the individual/institutional problem is that it is taken to imply that everyone working in an organisation is being labelled as racist. Or, alternatively, that racism is just a matter of policies and processes, which can be seen as meaning that no prejudiced or racist individuals are required to produce institutionally racist outcomes, so even where there are well-intentioned individuals, institutional racism will occur nonetheless.

As Miles (1989) observed, in sociology this was taken to be a virtue of the term, because intentionality is regarded as secondary to the consequences of actions. If the cause and remedy are linked solely to institutions, individuals appear to be 'dupes' without agency. This re-hashing of the structure-agency dilemma (Wight 2003) is itself the problem. Essed (1991) pointed out that a dichotomous view of racism as either one thing or the other is dubious, because it places individuals outside of institutions, 'thereby severing rules, regulations and procedures from the people who make and enact them, as if it concerned qualitatively different racism rather than different positions and relations through which racism operates' (Essed 1991: 36). However, rather than giving up on institutional racism as a concept – used variably and often rhetorically – sociologists in the run-up to Macpherson, sought to refine and reconstruct it, so that it had greater clarity and explanatory power.

Macpherson – in contrast to Scarman – did accept the term institutional racism as a factor in policing, and the inquiry's definition of it became widely cited and commonly debated in policy arenas and in the media. Although Hesse (2000) sees both Scarman's and Macpherson's understanding of institutional racism as a superficial aberration in British society, or to western liberalism, it does bear repeating that a term from a radical black power movement had moved from the margins of political activism and sociological analysis into mainstream political discourse, three decades after its origin, and almost two decades after its rejection by Scarman. While sociology cannot take credit for coining the term, work in academic and policy fields probably contributed to its longevity and its currency, even as there was no settled meaning and use of institutional racism. Through empirical research, social scientists had developed more sophisticated conceptions of the workings of institutional racism, in housing and education, for example (see contributions in Braham et al 1992, Law et al 2004).

In 1999, the government welcomed Macpherson's report and accepted widespread recommendations to tackle institutional racism in the public services. Hence, in contrast to Hesse's (2004) view that Macpherson was institutionally specific to the police while Scarman was more generic on racism in society, it is astonishing how the policy consequences of the former spread far beyond the police. The government committed itself to tackling institutional racism across the board of public services. In terms of official policy from the 1980s to the end of the century, British governments had gone from completely denying racism as a facet of British society to official acceptance of it as a matter that exceeded the intentions of individual racists or groups, and required a policy response at institutional level, through race equality impact assessments. The scale and significance of this moment is missed by critics who suggest that the post-Macpherson Race Relations (Amendment) Act 2000 has achieved nothing in tackling racism.[7] That neglects not just the context of the 1980s, but also legislation and policy around institutional racism and race equality that would have been unimaginable only a few years before. Although the consequences of that have been mixed at best (the Runnymede Trust 2009 report provides an overview up to the tenth anniversary of Macpherson), changes in tone as well as of substance are served poorly in terms of history and policy by blanket rejections.

This account signals that sociology does contribute to public policy and debate, albeit not in any linear way and not without continuing difficulties within the discipline such as competing understandings of racism and institutional racism. Taking this into the media framing of Macpherson is, however, instructive for its indication of the difficulties of developing a public sociology. Policy debates involve more people than academic sociologists. In the crowded field that makes up public discourse – at least as far as can be gauged from media commentary – other views of the meaning of institutional racism reigned. While public sociology can be about more than the mainstream media, the media is inescapable in the story of institutional racism post-Macpherson.

In opinion pieces just after the publication of the report, some commentators were determined to stress the dichotomous view of individuals and institutions, to an extent that bears comparison to the backlash against Scarman (Sim 1982). In the *Daily Telegraph*, Janet Daley said that institutional racism was vague and dangerous; instead of confining racism to a minority – 'benighted and vicious members of society', as she put it – Macpherson disconnected racism from the intentions of individual people and it became a form of 'thought crime' (Daley 1999). In similar vein, McKinstry said that Macpherson's discussion of the concept sounded 'like a lecturer in sociology from the Sixties … indulg[ing] in a series of sweeping generalisations' (McKinstry 1999).

While it is easy to criticise these voices, the point is that sociology or social science can receive differential coverage in the media, rather than it being simply hostile or negative. While media interests and frames shape what gets included and how it gets covered (Fairhurst and Sarr 1996), the reception and treatment of two different sociological 'takes' on institutional racism illustrates this starkly. One piece of work on institutional racism that was given significant space in national newspapers was a report from a think tank, the Institute for the

Study of Civil Society (Dennis et al 2000). That rejected institutional racism entirely, which the report said was an incoherent and circular idea. In an almost line-by-line analysis of Macpherson, it argued that the public inquiry had been unable to demonstrate any instance or evidence of racism by the police. The response to Dennis et al (2000) was unsurprisingly to treat it as confirmation of the views about Macpherson that had been expressed as opinion in newspapers. For instance, in a *Sunday Times* column, Melanie Phillips (2000) saw it as clear evidence of 'the truth [that] the police are not racist'. If public sociology is simply about being in public and having a sociological voice heard, the wide publicity given to Dennis et al (2000) fits that. Critics might reject its sociological basis, though Dennis himself was portrayed as a sociologist in the media.

But why do other sociologists and other works not get covered? Sociology is sometimes derided as a form of 'slow journalism', suggesting that the findings of sociological research are banal, not especially novel and repeat what is already known. If that is even partially true, however, it also applies to Dennis et al, a report that came out in September 2000 (one and a half years after Macpherson), and in essence makes the same points as some newspaper commentators had in February 1999. Meanwhile, many other sociologists had responded much more quickly through a 'rapid response' special issue of *Sociological Research Online* (for example see Solomos 1999), which came out less than two months after Macpherson. As this received no mention of any significance in the media, the issue is not timeliness per se. While those contributions are highly varied, they do include thoughtful and balanced responses to Macpherson.

Hence the reporting of Dennis et al (2000) is more about how it confirms the viewpoints of some columnists in particular newspapers (for example Marrin 1999, Phillips 2000). The contrast in the treatment of these two sets of responses to Macpherson is a salutary reminder that social science analysis that seeks to provide a considered contribution to public and scholarly debate on institutional racism (as in the case of the special issue of *Sociological Research Online*) runs up against vested media interests.

A further example of this occurred with the report of the Commission on the Future of Multi-Ethnic Britain (Parekh et al, 2000), which did get a lot of media attention, though in a markedly different way. Overwhelmingly, coverage was dominated by one element of the report – the claim that it had said that 'British' was a racist term (Neal and McLaughlin 2007). The report of the Commission, which included prominent social scientists, including Stuart Hall, had set out a layered approach to and understanding of institutional racism, yet this was barely mentioned or considered in a media storm about one quite minor aspect of the report.

This discussion makes evident that, of course, there is no one version of public (or any other kind of) sociology. Social scientists presented a range of views that the Macpherson inquiry had to consider alongside all the other submissions they received on institutional racism. The different voices within sociology can be seen in Holdaway's (1999) post-inquiry reflection on his role in it. He concurred with the police's objection to the 'all officers are racists' understanding of institutional racism because, like the police, he also saw it as sociologists 'posit[ing] racialised inequalities at the societal and/or political levels and then, usually by implication, infer[ring] that all individuals are racists' (Holdaway 1999: para 2.5). Holdaway's objection to structural and Marxist sociologies of race is based on his preference for phenomenological sociology, which looks more to the everyday and routine actions of individuals in order to picture institutions as products of what people do. It is this processual quality that sociologists should pay attention to, in understanding police culture and institutional racism (Holdaway and O'Neill 2006). Notably, this approach, is many steps removed from the sketch presented by Better (2008), where individual and institutional forms of racism are laid out side by side, rather than interconnected.

Although Burawoy (2005) maintained that public sociology has no necessary normative stance, part of what is at stake is how effective and useful particular approaches are. This is evident in Burawoy's questions, 'Knowledge for whom and knowledge for what?' His charting of the multiple answers to these questions does not resolve – it obviously cannot – the question of what happens when differing forms of, or claims to, public sociology conflict. Are such differences to be adjudicated by other sociologists or by different publics, and on what basis? Burawoy (2005) stresses that public sociology is not just any sociology in public and it needs to be based on good sociology. The contested nature of sociological knowledge and differing views of what constitutes 'good' sociology mean that essentially scholarly disagreements are unlikely to appeal to media editors. Deep theoretical divergences within public and/or policy sociologies are not resolvable in public or in learned journals. As Ericson (2005) pointed out:

> There is a world of difference between communicating in the *British Journal of Sociology*, twelve-second news clip on television news, government policy report, and testimony

before a court of law or commission of inquiry. The sociologist's text escapes her as it moves into these new contexts that reconfigure how she thinks and acts (Ericson 2005: 369-70).

Burawoy (2005) also exhorts sociologists to take a more public role through writing 'op ed' columns in newspapers, as do Lewis and Embrick (2016) While the internet and digital media have made newspapers less significant, they can still play a role in shaping the nature and form of debates that will occur in other media. The opinions of media commentators on institutional racism seem to have been formed without any recourse to sociologists, as in the newspaper articles mentioned. Hence, sociology's uneven impact on the mainstream media, which can only provide a partial view of what sociologists do. Indeed, trying to fit into narrow media criteria of relevance can, Ericson suggests, produce outcomes that do 'not look like sociology at all, but rather journalism, government consultancy or expert witnessing' (Ericson 2005: 370).

In any case, the willingness of sociologists to speak and communicate to wider audiences has to be matched by an audience that is receptive, or at least open, to hearing such communication (Scott 2005). In this light, public sociology would be better thought of as 'publics' sociology – aiming to speak and appeal to multiple, differentiated publics at various times and in different places. As Burawoy (2005: 265) asks, 'why should anyone listen to us rather than the other messages streaming through the media?'; part of his answer to that is that sociology has an underdeveloped conception of publics and still has much to do in understanding how to engage them.[8]

This chapter has used the concept of institutional racism to pull together the ways in which it has been used to critique sociology itself, as well as its take-up in an influential public inquiry. In the latter, the sociological voice is evident and sometimes important, but in less than straightforward ways when there are multiple definers of the term and where a sociological perspective is just another voice, whatever privilege may be claimed for it. It may even be openly disparaged, as in some subsequent media commentary. I have outlined that attempts to take the discussion of institutional racism into public arenas may reveal some weaknesses in the organisation of sociological research on racism in the UK since the term was coined, echoing the view of Solomos (1999). Furthermore, the more developed notion of institutional racialisation (Rattansi 2005) is analytically more useful, though that does not mean it can be translated into public forums any more easily (or probably much less easily) than institutional racism. At the same time, for most of the life of the term, sociology has not given equal emphasis to the critique of sociology itself as a white discipline, historically, in terms of its silences around race (Hund and Lentin 2014).

Notes

[1] This chapter is a revised and expanded version of an article published as: K. Murji (2007) 'Sociological engagements: Institutional racism and beyond', *Sociology*, 41(5), 843-55.

[2] In outlining a multi-level model McAra (2017) has recently provided a deeper sense of how academic work can engage with criminal justice.

[3] At the time it was published, Carmichael/Ture was one of the leaders of the Black Panthers, while Hamilton was based in Political Science at Columbia University, US.

[4] Although there is a view that Burawoy's vision is too narrow and a wider sense of engaged public sociology is required. See: Gillan, K 'Towards an ethic of public sociology', at: http://discoversociety.org/2015/01/03/towards-an-ethic-of-public-sociology

[5] From *Footnotes*, March 2003. This and other references to the ASA in this section are taken from its website: www.asanet.org

[6] Twenty years on from that, on 14 February 2017, the *Mail* reviewed its story on the case, including that headline – see: www.dailymail.co.uk/debate/article-4221790/Twenty-years-fight-Stephen-Lawrence-continues.html

[7] For example, see: https://www.theguardian.com/commentisfree/2015/jul/28/black-britons-failed-race-relations-cuts-racism

[8] Burawoy sees that public sociology in pursuit of popularity may be 'tempted to pander to and flatter its publics, and thereby compromis[e its] professional and critical commitments', or it may speak 'down to its publics, a sort of intellectual vanguardism' (Burawoy 2005: 277).

FIVE

The impacts of
social science[1]

The ways in which social science can enlighten public debate and
contribute to policy formulation have a wide scope. Public and
policy sociology, as discussed in Chapter Four, is one variant of
that, but public engagement by academics has a more varied span
than that. Engagement with non-academics is actively promoted by
research funding bodies such as the UK Research Councils through
a requirement to specify 'user engagement', 'knowledge transfer' and
to produce 'impact' summaries of research. This is more than a UK
issue, as higher education policy across large parts of the world has
deepened pressures for academics to engage with publics beyond the
academy, as can be seen in Badgett's (2016) 'how to' guide on being
more effective in communicating research. As engagement and impact
have become part of the audit culture of higher education, accounts of
these have tended to bifurcate into either a celebratory and uncritical
approach to public and policy engagement, or to decry the narrow and
instrumental ways in which impact has come to be defined, especially
by a neoliberal and market-based vision of higher education in the
21st century (Bailey and Freedman 2011, Sayer 2014).

   That engagement and impact have become critical in the framing
and pursuit of academic research is not in doubt, but what they mean
is unclear, not least in terms of defining and agreeing on the meaning
of these terms. The National Co-ordinating Centre for Public
Engagement (NCCPE), which exists to provide a space for developing
and disseminating good practice in this area, sees engagement or public
engagement as describing 'the myriad of ways in which the activity and
benefits of higher education and research can be shared with the public.
Engagement is by definition a two-way process, involving interaction
and listening, with the goal of generating mutual benefit'.[2] It adds that
that process is not something new; there are many and varied ways in
which academics engage with wider society.

   This is indeed so, although it raises a question about why impact
and engagement have become important now. While the demand
to be – or to become – 'more public' is itself a question or topic to
be analysed (Mahony and Clarke 2013), a concern with 'publicness'

has been notable across the social sciences and the humanities, such as in sociology (Burawoy 2005), anthropology (Erikksen 2006), criminology (*Theoretical Criminology* 2007, Loader and Sparks 2011) and social policy (*Critical Social Policy* 2008), as well as in geography,[3] history and theology, among others. There are differences between these disciplines in how the demands are interpreted, and how and whether they should be responded to. There are also divisions on what constitutes effective engagement, ranging from more 'scholar–activist' to 'public intellectual' conceptions (see Chapter Three). There are also significant variations in their orientation to government specifically, or to engaging civil society and social movements more widely. Among the worries about this rush to public engagement is Hammersley's (2014) view that the proper role of the social sciences is analytical and not political. There are also concerns that academic social science should not be evaluated in narrow terms of usefulness or the impact of research on policy making (aspects of this debate can also be seen in *British Journal of Sociology* 2004, *Critical Social Policy* 2008). While the context has changed, echoes of these views can be found in discussions about relating theory to policy (Smith 2007), as well as relating research to politics (Rex 1979, Solomos 1999).

One way of assessing the impact of academic research is to see what academics themselves say about it through the Research Excellence Framework (REF) in UK universities. In reviewing all the impact submissions made to the 2014 Sociology REF, Les Back reached this depressing conclusion:

> the 'impact agenda' has licensed an arrogant, self-crediting, boastful and narrow disciplinary version of sociology in public ... 'big research stars' are scripted ... as impact 'super heroes' advising cabinet ministers and giving evidence to parliamentary select committees. This version of public intervention is by definition narrowly concerned with evidencing its own claims. It is aligned with providing a kind of reformist 'empirical intelligence' that nudges at the edges of policy and political influence. 80% can be categorised in this way. (Back 2015)

While the dismal side of the impact agenda usually gets more attention, Back did see 'green shoots' in the other 20% of work he read, pointing out that such work showed 'radical ambition' and looked to:

a different kind of model of public engagement by challenging campus sexism through collaboration with Students Unions or creating archives of political activism. ... [or to] try and shift the public agenda through evidence and critical enquiry ... around race and segregation or casual forms of class stigma and hatred. (Back 2015)

The use of impact as an aim or as an output of research was often decried when it was raised as part of the assessment of research. Back's (2015) review and comments underline the way that sociologists have become adept at playing the impact game, but in a narrow, selective and credentialist manner. It is worth recalling that in terms of the REF, impact means 'an effect or change or benefit to the economy, society, culture, public policy or services, health, the environment or quality of life, beyond academia. It includes an effect on change or benefit to: the activity, attitude, awareness, behaviour, capacity, opportunity, performance, policy, practice, process or understanding of an audience, beneficiary, community, constituency, organisation or individual'.[4]

If beneficiaries cover all of the groups and categories identified in that statement, then that broad view of impact – although new as a measure of research – is not new at all. In recent decades, there has been a stress on using sound evidence to develop social policies, particularly by the UK Labour Party when it came into government in 1997 (though its emphasis on evidence-based policy stretches back before that, for instance in the work of the Commission on Social Justice 1994). Phrases from that time such as 'evidence-based policy' provided a strong spur to having a clear base from which to design and implement policies.[5] This became something of a cliché and a stick to beat governments with for their failures to act on the evidence and come up with workable policies, rather than seeking 'evidence' that supported policies they wanted to pursue anyway (Cairney 2016). Others also see the relationship of evidence to policy as much more complex than the phrase implies, and Keith (2008) and Hammersley (2013) provide two quite different arguments that nonetheless point in the same direction on this. Nonetheless, there is a general sense in which social science impacts on, and benefits, the economy, culture and society in many ways, some of which are measurable but some are not. Or, to put this point another way: there was – and perhaps always has been – impact before the impact agenda.

This chapter engages with 'impact before the impact agenda', by returning to the topic of institutional racism. It looks at some key academic contributions to the Macpherson inquiry, to indicate impact in the wider sense outlined previously. This extends the discussion started in Chapter Four and, to provide another angle, I add an examination of academic evidence to Macpherson on the policing of racist attacks. Through these two examples I argue that impact then (or now) does not take place in a straightforward or linear manner; it is, at best, 'a wavy line' as Hall (1982) suggested in a different context. So what 'real world' impact looks like, its shape and consequences is not something that can be gauged in a narrow time frame, or perhaps even a REF cycle. In pointing to situational and unpredictable factors, I propose that the link between academic impact and wider audiences is, or can be, indirect, episodic, contingent and even contradictory. This is not an argument against engagement or seeking impact. I do see social science as having uses and impact, but the ways in which that does and does not occur is about more than the quality of evidence or well-framed arguments. It is as much to do with politics and practicalities in the worlds of policy, as well as unpredictable individual factors. These are things that academic research finds it hard to keep 'in step' with or to account for.

The two issues that this chapters focuses on – the meaning of institutional racism, and the police response to racial violence – are in practice interlinked, but I set them out separately to make different points about instrumental and reflexive knowledge. For Burawoy (2005), the difference between the instrumental knowledge of professional and policy social science, against the reflexive knowledge of critical and public social science is plainest in the question about what knowledge is for. He differentiates them as forms of knowledge as a technical means, rather than knowledge for ultimate ends. While instrumental knowledge is concerned with puzzle or problem solving, reflexive knowledge is directed towards the fundamental direction of society and a willingness to question its values (Burawoy 2005). The utility of this distinction can be seen by considering the case made in a textbook by Stout et al (2008) that applied criminology should not merely be an adjunct to, or a policy science for, the smooth functioning of the criminal justice system and government. Rather, it should have a 'critical edge' that does not just aim to solve problems but also to raise them; and it should question the direction of policy. These statements encapsulate the instrumental/reflexive divide. My point is not about the validity of their aims, but to point out that they collapse instrumental and reflexive knowledge and purposes. The distinction between them may be fuzzy rather than firm, but it provides a useful starting point for pursuing the question of applying knowledge and its value for policy. In returning to Macpherson, I find it helpful to present social science as applied to social policy along both instrumental and reflexive/critical dimensions; while the former might be expected to be more useful, reflexive knowledge can also be powerful, as I now seek to show.

A 'simple, practical concept'? Instrumentalising institutional racism

The question of whether the police's shortcomings in the case of the murder of Stephen Lawrence were a chapter of accidents or something deeper is one of the key issues that the public inquiry confronted. To arrive at the latter, Dr Richard Stone, one of the three panellists advising Sir William Macpherson, told me that the inquiry needed 'something extra' and the term that did that for them was institutional racism. They received numerous submissions on it, and while many of those argued that the term could and should be applied to the police in this case, not all the evidence pointed in one direction. In particular, the Metropolitan Police argued that it was confusing, as they believed it would lead the public to think that all police officers acted with racist intent (see Chapter Four).

This view was, literally, shouted down in the inquiry by voices from the public gallery when, on 1 October 1998, Sir Paul Condon, the then Commissioner of the Metropolitan Police, appeared before the panel. He said to them that, 'if this inquiry labels my service as institutionally racist then the average officer, the average member of the public will assume the normal meaning of those words. They will assume a finding of conscious, wilful or deliberate action' (cited in Cathcart 1999: 358). Cathcart's account refers to 'noise from the public gallery', 'uproar' and appeals 'for calm' during Condon's evidence. From my own observations in the room, I heard shouted comments of 'resign' directed at Condon when he finished his prepared statement, and 'shame' following his remarks on institutional racism. Denis O'Connor, then an Assistant Commissioner, and who sat next to Condon that day, told me that:

> when I went to the Inquiry that day, the Inquiry were not in the mood to think about the way forward, they wanted to establish guilt and where blame lay and that seemed to be the primary focus ... We were not going to go that Inquiry and say that we didn't have some real thoughts and deliberations about finding a way forward, which was part of the acknowledgement of what had gone wrong ... It just so happened that the Inquiry at that point didn't want to

hear about how to do things better, that wasn't their prime
mission that day.

The need to be prepared for such bruising encounters is part of what
went into subsequent Metropolitan Police Service training on the
strategic management of critical incidents (see Griffiths 2009). Despite
the obvious negative reaction of the audience and the tone of the panel,
John Grieve – at the time a senior officer in the Metropolitan Police –
says the finding of institutional racism came as a 'shock' (Bowling with
Grieve 2009: 47). It was an 'intelligence failure' by the police, who had
not seen it coming. This was, and has remained, the most controversial
aspect of Macpherson, although since those events and the report, a
persistent and dominant problem has continued to be distinguishing
institutional and individual racism (as seen in Chapter Four).

To follow this tortuous path, I turn to the published report and the
evidence submitted to the inquiry. In the former it is evident that the
contributions of social scientists were valued, as the report cites two
notes on the meaning of institutional racism submitted by Dr Robin
Oakley, where he aimed to 'clarify the meaning of the term as a simple,
practical concept'.[6] It is important to recognise the consciously policy-
oriented instrumental thrust of his approach. He focused specifically
on avoiding and resolving the confusion between institutional and
individual forms of racism. Oakley's evidence emphasises that it is
manifested in routine practices, where the effect or outcome may be
discriminatory even if it is unintended. Or it is evident in informal
cultural practices, for example taken-for-granted assumptions and
stereotypes about minority groups. Oakley's perspective on institutional
racism combined individual, cultural and structural factors as interacting
processes. This construction sought to get beyond the point at which
Scarman (1981) stopped – that is, whether institutional racism was
a witting or an unwitting form of racism. In bringing individuals,
cultures and structures into one framework, it was an instrumental/
policy-oriented contribution, because it tried to resolve a conundrum
and produce a conception useable in policy and practice.

Other social scientists also stressed that a social or institutional
dimension exists beyond individual intention and action, and sought to
fuse and transcend cultural and structural aspects of racism. For instance,
Bowling sees it as distinct from both individual and cultural racism, and
more than the effect of their combination.[7] Such formulations offered
an approach to police racism that was way beyond the well-worn 'rotten
apples' one. It also went beyond the search for individual racists in, or
those seeking to join, the organisation. While these criticisms were

well established long before Macpherson, it is the framing offered by academics that the inquiry panel seems to have found especially useful (see Macpherson 1999: chapter 6).

Extensive subsequent academic commentary and research on institutional racism has followed in the wake of Macpherson. In an approach broadly equivalent to Oakley's, Pilkington (2003) points out that institutional racism is usually employed in three ways or levels: the occupational culture of policing; discriminatory practices (which may be direct or indirect); and patterns of racial disadvantage. For Pilkington, this wide range lacks precision, which mirrors some of Carter's (2000) reservations about the term. So, while the academic advice to Macpherson suggested a resolution, it is not one that escapes the problem of explaining and accounting for institutional racism.

Why, then, did the Macpherson inquiry find the term useful? When I asked Dr Stone about this, his answer was not, as I might have expected, that it was because Scarman (1981) had been so opposed to the idea – as that is what Oakley's submission and other academic contributions tackled head on. Rather, Dr Stone said it was what the term appeared to explain:

> The answer is to my mind that we found no evidence of overt racism in the handling of the investigation but there was such a huge amount of incompetence or what we called a collective failure. And we found failure after failure, [so] we decided that we had to put together all those sections and failures to make them add up to something extra, beyond just each failure being excusable for a reason they apologised for, they'd made a mistake, they'd simply got lost, whatever it was. Each failure, each mistake could be explained away ... But if you add them all together, there had to be something more than just a series of incompetencies. We couldn't believe the whole Metropolitan Police Service was so incompetent .. we felt there was something extra there.

Institutional racism provided a key resource in understating failure and racism as more than individual culpability. This account reveals that, rather like Scarman, the Macpherson panel was not led by explicit racism in policy and procedure – this is what Dennis et al (2000) say Macpherson is unable to demonstrate. But, unlike Scarman, Macpherson saw that outcomes and processes could nonetheless still be discriminatory. While most research since then points to confusion in its application in practice and its formulation in Macpherson (Foster et al 2005, Rattansi 2007, Souhami 2014), that does not make academics responsible for the muddle. It does, however, indicate that even applied, instrumentally oriented approaches run into problems, and that the process of knowledge transfer through expert engagement with policy worlds is not simple or straightforward.

Following the publication of Macpherson, a colleague and I commented at the time (McLaughlin and Murji 1999) that a problem with the report was the viability of its definition of institutional racism. This is a matter of context and form. The contextual point is that the academic input is muddied by a combination of instrumental and reflexive purposes. The wish was to 'rebalance' a nearly 20-year-old debate, in which the concept of institutional racism had been powerfully rejected (Scarman 1981), hence so many contributions to Macpherson emphasised the need to establish it as a matter of record. Of course, the history matters, but however nuanced those contributions were, the inquiry's understanding entrenched divides about witting and unwitting racism. The adoption of a 'culturalist' approach, mediating the individual and the social, led Macpherson to use terms such as 'stereotyping', 'less favourable treatment', and so on – but these can be treated as individual or social processes.

Subsequent policy and practice have made limited headway in resolving how to account for culture as an intervening level or dimension, because it lacks precision in the ways in which culture operates contextually and situationally (see Phillips 2011). In a nutshell, this is the same difficulty that sociologies of so-called 'cop culture' encounter, in accounting for variation and heterogeneity (Holdaway and O'Neill 2006, Reiner 2010).

In trying to make plain the idea of institutional racism, the scholarly or academic briefs to Macpherson were probably also informed by an understanding that any workable definition had to persuade or 'carry' a recalcitrant police force into recognising the issue and taking measures to tackle it. This is the problem of form. The complexity of institutional racism is that it is about 'something extra' and more than individual prejudice or cultural norms. Fusing structure, culture and individual levels is a reasonable formal resolution, but how that is conveyed may be as, or even more, important than content. In this light, the submissions of non-academics may have been more persuasive for just such a reason, as in some of those, the 'institutional' nature of police racism is illustrated by particular examples of police racism against individuals, or by highlighting a lack of cultural awareness and sensitivity by the police. These 'narrative' rather than 'analytical' (Erikksen 2006) accounts are a way of making an abstract idea more concrete; they help to 'ground' a notion of institutional policies and processes that seem to persist without the need for any racist or prejudiced individuals. In other words, it is harder to be rhetorically persuasive in abstract rather than more concrete forms. It is harder still to advocate policy prescriptions.

In addition to the public written evidence, it emerged a decade later that, as well as the 'on the record' contributions of social scientists, there was also some activity behind the scenes. Thus, Bowling relates that he was invited to speak to Dr John Sentamu, another of the advisers to Macpherson. While Bowling says he 'can't really say how influential my intervention was', he also notes another occasion when he met Dr Sentamu, who said 'in his jovial way something like, "This man is responsible for institutional racism"' (Bowling with Grieve 2009: 49-50). This suggests that the influence of academic inputs can be far-reaching, although the process by which they were absorbed and fashioned into the final report is opaque. While academic inputs did have an influence, the nature of that is partial and goes beyond well-honed words and formulations, because the widely reproduced view of institutional racism emerged from some 'horse trading' between panel members in their private deliberations:

> I think the chapter on racism is the longest chapter in the report ... We spent more time on it certainly than anything else. I hadn't really quite realised it had come from the American civil rights movement ... how much it had been used or hadn't been used, all these academic advisers giving us advice on how you might word these things. Then you look at our definition; it was going to be one line, one sentence that was it. Then all of us felt that there were certain words that weren't in, which is why we had the second paragraph. Then we had to work out how you're going to typeset it so [that] the second paragraph doesn't get lost in the first paragraph ... that's why you've actually got two paragraphs looking as if they're one paragraph but in fact they're two ...[8]

The resulting definition was, Rattansi, says, 'an unsystematic jumble of different elements: impersonal processes, *conscious* attitudes and behaviour, and unwitting or *unintentional* prejudice' (Rattansi 2007: 134; emphasis in original). Whether the hitches came from within Macpherson or from the difficulty of the idea, turning it into 'a simple, practical' concept proved to be more complex than ideas about knowledge transfer. The agency-structure problem (Wight 2003) that is either inherent or at least deeply entangled in the idea remains resistant to definitional clarification. Importantly, it recognises that 'something more' than individual intention is involved. However, while it is covert, it can be seen through normal processes and biased outcomes of the workings of institutions. Because of this, policy measures aim to change working practices and to focus on people and processes, but unless there is a clear connection between those things – and which is not just 'culture' – the effect can be to mirror the individual/institutional dichotomy (Essed 1991, Phillips 2011). As it is 'unintended', this implies that even individuals with anti-racist motives can 'unwittingly' be racist, and this sense of people acting in unconscious ways to produce racist outcomes is the most problematic aspect of institutional racism. As senior and other ranks in the police have become more willing to express their opposition to racism, the view that an institution carries on discriminating in racist ways can become reduced to a matter of prejudiced individuals or of small groups and their cultural traits – or as a bureaucratic outcome that no one can control or change. Racist or racially skewed outcomes seemingly occur, despite good intentions, because of unwitting or unintentional processes.

The acceptance of institutional racism by Prime Minister Tony Blair upon the publication of Macpherson acknowledged that the report should be a watershed. It set the scene for subsequent legislation and policy, such as the Race Relations (Amendment) Act 2000. Such high-level support indicates the importance of the report and its role as a powerful driver or 'galvanizing force' (Tonry 2004: 77) for organisational initiatives within and beyond the police (see Runnymede Trust 2009 for a review). However, the application of institutional racism in practice, particularly with regard to the police, has been challenging. It has never 'settled' as a concept or a practical idea. While government policy after Macpherson certainly produced a great deal of organisational activity – not least the drive to put all Metropolitan Police officers through a two-day community and race relations (CRR) training programme, in which there was a significant focus on institutional racism – its impact has been questioned. Evaluations of CRR training (Institute of Employment Studies 2003, Rowe and Garland 2007) highlight the difficulty it had in convincing officers about the applicability of institutional racism to them individually or corporately. They reveal that a structural/institutional approach to racism – as opposed to an individualising one – is tricky to convey to sceptical officers. Indeed, at some times, a structural approach was missed out altogether.

Similarly, the main Home Office funded academic evaluation of police culture after Macpherson pointed to continuing misunderstandings in police ranks about the meaning of institutional racism, and a predominant understanding of it as branding all officers as racist (Foster et al 2005, Foster 2008). It did find that overt racism had declined, but as institutional racism was always about covert racism, it is much harder to gauge its level and scope. A benefit of such research, as well as my own observations of CRR training, is that they call into question Tonry's (2004: 76) view of institutional racism as unhelpful 'polar words' that are 'conversation-stoppers'. This is wide of the mark to the extent that officers are rarely unwilling to discuss it but rather do not accept what it implies about unintentional and unwitting racism. Overall, though, the attempt to proffer a plain and instrumentally oriented approach has been impactful at one level in shaping organisational activity, along with producing a certain amount (maybe a great deal) of confusion.

The gap between academic debates and the public or media framing of institutional racism is also evident, as in Chapter Four, in another example. When, in 2006, Sir Ian Blair, as Commissioner, said that there was institutional racism in the media, he was ridiculed for it, mainly by media commentators. The main reason for that was because he mentioned the reporting of the murder of two young girls in Soham, Cambridgeshire, as an example.[9] Sir Ian's comment that 'no one could understand' why it had received so much coverage was clearly insensitive. I was sitting about half a dozen seats around the table from him at a public meeting of the Metropolitan Police Authority and, at the time it was said, his words were not greeted with the shock suggested by a number of MPA politicians afterwards. In my view, that is because Sir Ian had actually been asked a question about the police resources devoted to two murders in London at the time. One was of a white, middle-class solicitor, the other of an Asian shopkeeper. The former got a great deal more media exposure and that was what he was reflecting on.[10] The furore over the infamous 'Soham' comments masked the fact that there were clear differences in how the police responded to the two murders, in part due to the high media and political profile of the former case. Critics who have long maintained that race crime – even when it is as serious as murder – does not receive the attention it should found that Sir Ian was actually agreeing with them. While he may not have seen this as institutional racism on the part of the police, he clearly did see that at work in the media coverage.

In light of Burawoy's (2005) distinction, the scholarly contributions to Macpherson are largely instrumental knowledge, because their purpose was to make the idea of institutional racism plain and applicable in practice. To the extent that, generally, they chose not to locate racism at the core of British society or even as a fundamental or systemic feature of policing, they are not reflexive in the sense identified earlier – although the radical origins of institutional racism mean that it could be pitched in that way. This is not a criticism of those who tried to make sense of the term for the inquiry. If it sounds as though it is, it suggests that Burawoy's conceptualisation valorises – either explicitly or implicitly – reflexive over instrumental knowledge.

A more significant matter for present purposes is that what follows from applied or instrumental knowledge is more complex than an instrumental/reflexive dichotomy, mainly because the instrumental strand has never 'stuck'. Public debate on institutional racism – at least in so far as media commentary can be regarded as an expression of that – reveals a repetitive and backward-looking strain. For instance, Blair's media critics after his 'Soham' remarks were mostly repeating the same objections to institutional racism as those directed at the Macpherson report, as outlined in Chapter Four. In a nutshell, these were that: it is merely jargon; only individuals can be racist; it is a form of thought crime; it expresses a form of political correctness; or it is simply wrong.

Instrumental and reflexive approaches to racial attacks

A second example from Macpherson is about the police response to racist violence. It is evident that Stephen Lawrence was racially abused and murdered by a group of racist men. The inquiry focused on the identity, motivations and actions of the five young white men commonly regarded as the key suspects. (Indeed, the Lawrence family brought an unsuccessful private prosecution against them, in the absence of police and prosecution action, see Cathcart 1999.) Apart from the appearance of Sir Paul Condon (discussed earlier), their day at the inquiry was one of the most crowded in the public gallery and in the level of media coverage. But the focus on the extremism of the alleged perpetrators individualises the issue of violent racism, rather than seeing it in context. Through the demonisation of a particular kind of residual white working-class masculinity (akin to the notion of 'white trash'), their attitudes were treated as exceptional and entirely uncharacteristic of 'mainstream' Britain, just as racism often has been seen (which Gilroy [1987] called the 'coat of paint' theory of racism, to suggest that it was superficial).

This also marks the treatment of the suspects and their mothers in the media, as McLaughlin (2005) shows. In so far as the approach of the inquiry also focused on those individuals, it provided a partial picture of the nature of violent racism, in which the 'othering' of a group of young men as the exemplars of racism obscures the wider manifestations of racism at a structural level. It also obscures the failures of the police to establish a case against the suspects, which is part of a wider picture of inaction in the face of numerous racial attacks, including murder[11] (Hesse et al 1992, Bowling 1998).[12] The limited perspective of the inquiry is certainly not attributable to the academic evidence it received. In looking at two examples of that evidence, I return to the usefulness of the instrumental/reflexive divide.

One, by Ben Bowling,[13] takes its cue from his book *Violent racism*, in which he discusses the well-documented history of racial violence in Britain and the failures of the police to deal with this due to their adoption of a reactive style that limits any preventative strategy. He advocated the employment of a victim-centred approach to racial incidents, in which whether an event is deemed 'racial' is based on the view of the victim or any proximate person, not that of the police. Bowling argued that in the absence of obvious racist intent, the police fail to see what it may look like to victims and the subjective definition is a way of addressing that – though some years on, Rattansi (2007) and Sian et al (2014) both criticise the subjectivity of this approach. Bowling stresses that victims experience racism as part of a process, while the police tend to treat them as disparate incidents.

Another statement of evidence was submitted by Barnor Hesse,[14] also drawing on research in east London (Hesse et al 1992). Hesse identifies two conspicuous problems in policing racism: first, a claim that there is a lack of evidence due to widespread underreporting of racial attacks; and second the police view that attacks are largely random. Hesse argues that there is no lack of evidence, but rather a deficiency in police willingness to treat racism as a serious social problem, a lack of organisational coherence to tackle it and a failure to appreciate the significance of racism as an issue in British society. On the second issue – the apparent randomness of incidents or attacks – he maintains that the lack of police organisational resources to combat racist crime is itself a problem. Hesse suggested that if the police treated race crime in the same way as, for example, organised crime, such an attitude would not persist. Close attention to the spatial location of racial incidents does reveal an underlying pattern of both entrenchment and dispersion, rather than the randomness that the police see.

Despite the differences in their presentation here, there is not a large gap between Bowling and Hesse. Both stress that racial attacks have to be understood in context rather than as a series of incidents. They make the same point that the key concern is the lack of priority given to racial attacks by the police and the criminal justice system, and this is what needs to be remedied. Both of them call for the police to take racist crime as seriously as they treat organised crime.

But, in spite of the overlaps, there is a significant difference of emphasis between them and in how the submissions can be treated. One sign of this is that Bowling provides a definition of institutional racism (and, as we have seen, that was the basis for further discussion between him and the inquiry), while Hesse makes no recommendations in his evidence. Bowling's approach is closer to instrumental knowledge, while Hesse's is more clearly reflexive – though this cannot be a firm distinction, given some similarities in their content. Hesse's contribution makes the recognition of racism its key theme, as it is occupied not just with the racism or motivation of the perpetrators of racial violence, but also with the organisational processes (this could be called institutional racism, though Hesse does not use the term) that shape the police non-response to racial attacks. Moreover, it locates racism as a structural feature of British history and society, and tries to identify the underlying roots of racial violence. Although it is not spelt out in these precise terms, the implication is that tackling racism is not just about the first and second aspect (racial motivation and organisational resources – which is what most contributions focus on), but also a wider and deeper engagement with the nature of a racially structured society. In this sense it is 'systemic' and directed to ultimate ends, though there is little on how that could be realised, apart from stressing that the police 'mentality' about race needs to be altered.

Bowling also gestures in this direction in calling for policing to be placed within a human rights perspective (see also Bowling et al 2005) that would provide a better service for victims of race attacks. However, it is primarily an instrumental approach directed towards policy development and probably had greater impact for that reason, as it chimed with the policy-oriented remit of a public inquiry; and beyond that, as Bowling recounts that he was approached by two Metropolitan Police officers asking him to spell out what he meant in his book by 'anti-racist policing'. He comments that: 'It was one of those terrifying moments in academic life when a practitioner signals their intention to act on your advice' (Bowling 1999: xvii-xviii).

The utility of the instrumental/reflexive distinction is perhaps evident in the fact that Macpherson did recommend the victim-centred definition, although Sian et al (2014: 133, n3) see that as making racism a matter of a clash of ethnicities that 'paradoxically, undermined the structural dimensions' of racism as it is considered in other parts of the Macpherson report. Whatever the panel made of Hesse's critique of the police mindset about the random nature of racial incidents, this view did not make it into the report. There is though an unexpected echo of that evidence in the concerted police action that did follow.

Even while the inquiry was sitting, the Metropolitan Police set up the Racial and Violent Crimes Task Force (RVCTF). Placed under the command of a senior and experienced detective, John Grieve, the force signalled its intent to take race crimes seriously and to pursue racist perpetrators as strenuously as it did organised crime, rather as Hesse had called for. A TV documentary from this time shows Grieve saying to his team that:

> You are the agents of change in this service. It's about us taking the lessons learnt from fighting terrorism and applying them to this problem. You've made London a hostile place for terrorists. You can make London a hostile place for racists.

In another meeting, he says, 'We'll change the culture because we'll lock people up for racism.'[15]

The thrust of this statement has attained iconic status in the senior ranks of the organisation as a call to 'let's nick some racists' (see Hall et al 2009 for accounts of it by Grieve himself). For instance, an experienced former officer, Bill Griffiths[16] said:

> in that phrase he [Grieve] absolutely nailed it ... What came out of that was not just [Operation] Athena, in terms of the Racial and Violent Crimes Task Force – which did go for some of the high-level, organised gangs. It led to Community Safety Units in every borough. That's another dividend of Stephen Lawrence – those units weren't there before.

Similarly, when I asked him about it, Sir Ian Blair also identified Grieve and the RVCTF as one of the key steps that had restored morale in the organisation after Macpherson:

> the third and cleverest things that Paul [Condon]... did was [to set up] the Racial and Violent Crimes Task Force and to operationalise anti-racism. By appointing John Grieve to that they pulled the finest detective the Met had at the time into this position and... a significant number of operational improvements, particularly in community support units and family liaison [resulted]. And John [Grieve] took all that

lot on board and went after the racists – not the internal racists, the external racists. So that was a very clever piece of manoeuvre because in policing terms if you can make, as John [Grieve] used to say it, catching racists as important as armed robbers, quite suddenly you've got somewhere that's really important to the organisation.

For how long that personal drive existed in the immediate aftermath of Macpherson is debatable, though the most positive views are that significant change had been embedded in the organisation (see Griffiths 2009, Hall et al 2009).

Nonetheless, in the immediate aftermath of Macpherson it is clear that Grieve's charisma and drive played a significant role in pushing race crime up the agenda of the Metropolitan Police. Indeed, it may be that his personal contribution was the single most significant factor, outweighing any input by academics or other evidence to Macpherson. Assistant Commissioner John Yates described it to me as a 'totemic appointment'. But when pressed about whether the priority that was evident in 1999 was still present,[17] he conceded that various factors meant that it probably was not. In his view, the commitment to tackling serious racist crime had not been diluted, but enhanced. However, in terms of other parts of the organisation dealing with lesser offences, he commented:

Is it the same on boroughs?[18] Probably not at the levels it was to be honest, but that is a matter for others. I don't think every borough has a Community Safety Unit, I don't think it's staffed in the same way [in terms of make-up of staff] …

This comment reflected the pressure on boroughs to deliver on centrally driven 'volume crime' targets, such as robbery. That meant that race/hate crime sat alongside many other priorities. Just as significantly, race crimes no longer had the high visibility they did in the wake of the RVCTF, under the leadership of John Grieve. At the same time, race issues had been reconfigured over the decade since Macpherson. For instance, Operation Trident (which investigates gun crime in black communities, or so-called 'black on black crime' – for a critique, see Murji 2002) became about ensuring sufficient confidence in the police for people to provide information to them. Or the widespread and later focus on knife crime in London was also approached as a matter requiring stronger social and familial networks and community partnerships. This has not been done by an independent act of will by the police; it is something that can be seen as a logical and intended outcome of the post-Macpherson stress on community involvement (see Stone 2009), and the role of independent advisers on race and community issues acting as 'critical friends' (Murji 2011).

A decade after Macpherson there was an obvious feeling among police officers that the agenda had moved on, in particular from race to faith issues in the wake of terrorist attacks in London in 2005 – this is covered more in the next chapter. Race was partially incorporated into a wider diversity strategy that Stephen Lawrence's mother expressed doubts about (see the Foreword in Hall et al 2009, as well as Chouhan and Sian 2010). The preference for diversity rather than race/racism seems to go hand in hand with the replacement of the vocabulary of race/racist crime by a hate crime discourse (Hall 2005, Iganski 2008).

Indeed, for all the emphasis on the RVCTF and the keynote 'let's nick some racists' message, this shift probably occurred much earlier than is recognised in research. In April 1999, only a couple of months after the publication of the Macpherson report, various nail bombs were targeted at gay and black communities in London. In September 1999, Grieve is cited as calling for a 'broad strategy on race ... [such that] work around race would give support to work around other forms of crime' (in Rock 2004: 473). As Rock (2004: 473) observes, 'It was in this fashion that racist crimes evolved within the policing sphere to become a sub-category of a larger and increasingly un-wieldy class of offence, hate crimes.'

There could be good reasons for connecting race with other bases of social identity and inequality. Yet there are reasons to query this development also. Encapsulating a wide variety of types of offences and social groups within a single word – 'hate' – is questionable, because it may not be an adequate way of capturing the motivation of perpetrators. To the extent that it individualises motivation, it misses the wider social context. Proponents of the term 'hate' argue that it is powerful because it harms the victim, the victim group and society (see Rock 2004). It invokes the sense that people are victimised, because of core elements of their personal and group identities such as ethnicity, gender, sexuality and so on. But, of course, all of these are relational terms, not fixed ones, and 'hate crime' can seem to rely on a view of power as something that is possessed largely or solely by white men. This overlooks the uneven dynamics of power across the main axes of social differentiation, not least social class. Meanwhile, the more practical or instrumental concerns with the police response to race/hate crimes is still dominated by the same premise that it was one, two or even three decades ago – such that increases in recorded incidents are treated as signs of increased confidence in policing.

Finally, returning to John Grieve enables me to bring together the two sides of this chapter and to cast a different light on the individual/ institutional problem. In a newspaper interview (*The Independent on Sunday*, 5 August 2001), he said: 'I'm a racist. I must be because Sir William Macpherson said that I am.' This disarming statement reveals Grieve's charismatic style and commitment. But, taken at face value, it is also ambiguous. Macpherson did not think that all police officers were racists – indeed, the inquiry was at pains to be seen not to be saying that, and it was what the academic evidence to the panel reinforced. The admission of racism by one individual, especially a high-profile one, is symbolically powerful, but it does not mean that it is accepted by other officers or by all in the same organisation. Nor does it follow that the actions and initiatives that result will be effective, as the example of CRR training indicates. Most problematically, the stress upon the 'I' is an individualising step that increases the distance from an institutional response/capacity. This is clearly not what Grieve intended – in the same interview he went on to say that he was for 'change inside myself and in the behaviour of others'. But it does imply the extent to which the problem of institutional racism in Macpherson remains a – and perhaps *the* – key issue.

Policy, instrumentality and reflexivuty

In looking back at some of the main academic inputs to the Macpherson inquiry on two key aspects, I have, unsurprisingly, indicated that a public inquiry and public policy find it easier to deal with instrumental, policy-oriented academic constructions, rather than reflexive ones. However, the distinction between these types of knowledge is perhaps not as significant as implied by Burawoy (2005). Both approaches can have impact, in narrower and wider senses of that term, as it has come to be defined in relation to research in the UK. Institutional racism and an understanding of racial attacks can be employed in more or less instrumental and reflexive forms, and both of these operate in a critical register, whether in relation to other academic work or to police and policy understandings of these things. It is harder to apply reflexive approaches, because such knowledge claims can be too abstract or at a level of generality that makes the manner of its application or its usability unclear (compare Smith 2007 on applying theory to policy).[19] Consequently, what policy recommendations can flow from reflexive knowledge – such as a far-reaching critique of systemic racism in

Britain – is hard to specify, and this is at the root of one problem with institutional racism: is there a stage or a measure when an institution can be said to be not institutionally racist? Or, if it is fundamentally a social and structural issue, then no individual institution can ever be non-institutionally racist until the whole of society is.

While reflective critique may not aim to be useful in any narrow or instrumental fashion, the example of racial attacks does indicate some ways in which it impacts on policy. In spite of occurring in a crowded public space, the impact of academic social science on Macpherson was notable. To return to my criticism of Stout et al (2008), the discussion shows that Oakley's and Bowling's inputs to the inquiry aimed to both solve problems of definition, and to do so with a 'critical edge', seeking to reorient policy in particular ways.

Nevertheless, the usefulness of social science and of impact must be tempered by the additional insight into the Macpherson inquiry in this chapter. What appeared in the report is the work of many hands, and multiple perspectives. It is for these reasons, I argue, that impact and influence should be conceived of as a 'wavy' – and perhaps even a dotted – line. The passage of time makes that even more marked, as discussions of institutional racism in all the years after Macpherson repeated many of the same confusions. Up to the tenth anniversary of Macpherson, in 2009, individuals in the Metropolitan Police conscientiously tried to make the definition work (Griffiths 2009), yet the political drive behind it that was evident in 1999 had disappeared (I say more on this in the next chapter).

On racial attacks, police thinking was informed by instrumental and some reflexive knowledge. The sustained police action and resources targeted at that was at a high level, but identified very much with the drive of one key individual. The emphasis on charismatic leadership is another sign of how rooted the organisation is in individualistic, rather than institutional, thinking. An intense but short-lived focus on racial attacks was muted or lost in the turn to the wider category of hate crime. Thus, in spite of the efforts of Macpherson and various people who presented information and evidence on both institutional racism and on racial attacks, both issues were displaced or downgraded by events and political/contextual shifts that an inquiry and academics can find it hard to keep in step with.

Notes

1   This is a revised and expanded version of an article that was published as K. Murji (2010) 'Applied social science? Academic contributions to the Stephen Lawrence Inquiry and their consequences', *Journal of Social Policy*, 39(3), 343-57.

2   See: https://www.publicengagement.ac.uk/explore-it/what-public-engagement

3   For example, see: https://antipodefoundation.org/2014/10/20/doing-public-geography-making-scholarship-public/

4   See HEFCE at: www.hefce.ac.uk/rsrch/REFimpact/

5   Indeed, further back into the 1970s and in 1980, other precedents include the call for policies based on 'what works' pragmatically rather than ideologically.

6   NT1/49, National Archives. All subsequent NT numbers refer to documents in the UK National Archives.

7   NT1/167. However, it should be noted that evidence submitted by the Runnymede Trust, the Commission for Racial Equality, the Institute of Race Relations (IRR) and the 1990 Trust all made the same general point, though, arguably, their examples convey a personal and cultural approach. Rock (2004: chapter 9) says that several people lay claim to having suggested the term to the inquiry.

8   Tonry (2004: 76) describes Macpherson's wording as 'extraordinarily artless and almost incoherent'.

9   The two girls killed by Ian Huntley were Holly Wells and Jessica Chapman.

10 The people murdered were Tom ap Rhys Price and Balbir Matharu.

11 This was the thrust of the evidence submitted by the IRR, for example.

12 Thus, in the revised edition of his book after the publication of Macpherson, Bowling (1999: xvii) comments that the report 'lacks a coherent analysis of the problem of violent racism'.

13 NT1/167.

14 NT1/168.

15 Both quotes are taken from the TV documentary 'Race against crime', first broadcast on ITV, 25 October 1999.

16 At the time of speaking, Bill Griffiths was the Director of Leadership Development in the Metropolitan Police.

17 Assistant Commissioner John Yates was speaking to me in 2008.

18 London is divided into 32 administrative boroughs and each of these has a degree of local autonomy.

19 In this light, it is noteworthy that a blog post from Italy notes how the rejection of race as a category in the era since the Second World War has led to a denial of racism, also on the basis that it reifies an unscientific category – race. See: 'Anti-racism without race' at: http://africasacountry.com/2016/09/anti-racism-without-race-in-italy/

SIX

The end(s) of
institutional racism[1]

The double rise of institutional racism in Britain, once from the late 1960s and then in the late 1990s – is an extraordinary example of an idea moving from a radical or revolutionary movement into social science (Chapter Four), and then from the margins into the mainstream, becoming part of public policy initiatives that focused on institutions rather than on individuals and on structures as well as processes (Chapter Five). In spite of its prominence following the publication of the Macpherson report (1999), in the years after that, successive Labour governments are thought to have lost their early focus on racism, due to a number of events. One was the 2001 riots in towns and cities in northern England (Cantle 2001), which promulgated the idea that people of Muslim backgrounds were leading 'parallel lives', where they rarely mixed with white communities. Particularly under David Blunkett as Home Secretary this led to policies to develop community cohesion – a theme that persisted 15 years on in the name of 'integration' (Bassel 2016, Casey 2016). Another reason was the '9/11' terrorist attack on the US that heralded a long 'war on terror', overseas and 'at home', in which Islam has often been portrayed as an 'enemy within' the West, as well as a battleground of ideas about reason, progress, western and British values, and the limits of liberalism. An additional element was the rise of intersectional and diversity politics which, intentionally or otherwise, was seen as 'diluting' the politics of race equality, as Stephen Lawrence's mother implies (see the Foreword in Hall et al 2009).

At an organisational level, as I showed in Chapter Five, a shift away from race may have started earlier than any of these, as the response to attempted bombings by a far-right extremist in multiracial areas of London led the Metropolitan Police into targeting hate crimes. Thus, although a policy thrust behind institutional racism was nominally in place for many years, 'the end of institutional racism' began almost as soon as it was in its heyday in a period from 1999 to 2000.[2] Yet it is part of the paradox of the politics of institutional racism that, for all the difficulties in the term (see Chapters Four and Five), it persists into the current day. It 'ends' and it is revived or invoked again, often from the margins and by protest groups who use it to refer to events such as the 2011 riots, and deaths in custody and prisons, as well as police brutality in the US, and more widely to structural and ongoing racial inequalities.

For these reasons, I put the 'end' in quote marks, to signal some doubt about that – and also in a slightly ironic manner. I pluralise it as 'end(s)' in two key senses: first, it has had multiple ends rather than a single one; and second, the plural hints at, or brings out, the multiple aims or goals of institutional racism. The rise and fall of issues around race and recruitment, which I look at in Chapter Seven, also shows the same story: the apparent end of a process to recruit more black police officers and its subsequent recurrence.

In this chapter, the end(s) of institutional racism are considered via two cases that speak to the academic–policy interface, though in a different register to the ways it has come up in Chapters Four and Five. The two cases were ones that I was directly involved in, so I introduce a first-hand account as an academic 'inside' public policy. They are both instances where institutional racism could – and should – have been a key element, yet neither worked out that way. In exploring those cases and the reasons for that, I stress the significance of contextual factors – meaning the political environment in which they occurred.

In the Introduction, I provided an overview of my general role in public policy. This went beyond being either a 'participant' or an 'observer', or any combination of those. I add to that here only as needed for clarification. As will become apparent, this form of involvement is on a different plane to the public and policy sociology discussed in Chapters Four and Five, and in Burawoy (2005). Applied and policy sociology is usually accorded a secondary status, as when it is regarded as being concerned with addressing social problems or government agendas (Rex 1979, Burawoy 2005); or in criminology, as the 'administrative criminology' (Lea and Young 1984) of applied crime science. These views share some commonality with scepticism about social science designed to inform 'evidence based' policy (Hammersley 2013, Cairney 2016). While the roles I occupied could overlap with some of the terms and categories identified by Loader and Sparks (2011) – and could be framed in terms of impact, public engagement and knowledge transfer between higher education and public policy – my role was also more than all of those, as I aim to explain.

Engaging with policy and politics

There are several places from which to locate the nature of 'extra-academic' work. Pollitt (2006), for instance, distinguishes a number of kinds of advice for policy and political audiences, and looks at their consequences for engagement between academics and non-academics. Reports from the British Academy (2008, 2010) called for better engagement between research and policy makers, stressing the valuable role that the social sciences and humanities could play in that, and provided examples of their impact. In the main, these approaches focus on issues of research evidence and how that can be better taken up in policy making or in public debate. In other words, they are mainly about knowledge work and the blockages to realising the use of evidence.

However, academic perspectives on policy and politics that concentrate on knowledge production and dissemination (and in 'how to' guides such as Badgett 2016) can miss something about the nature of engagement required in the interrelationship of academic and policy worlds. There are problems of generality and specificity. In general, the range of academic expertise and knowledge is vast and connects to policy in myriad ways far beyond the social sciences. Expertise in health, medicine and technology, for example, cannot be subsumed in any catch-all accounts of academia and policy. The problem of specificity is that some accounts of research or advice acted upon or neglected may be so contextually dependent that to generalise from them is to do a disservice to meaningful discussion. The account here tends more towards the specific than the general, and I try to couch any wider lessons within appropriate boundaries and qualifiers.

To situate the cases to be discussed, I draw on two vectors – the relationship between knowledge and politics, and between being inside/ outside. In spite of the tenuousness of such dichotomies, I argue that in policy work they can matter in substantial ways. The inside/outside relationship refers to the location and depth of academic engagement. I can illustrate what I mean by pointing to some significant differences in how such academic engagements are conceived. A special issue of the journal *Public Money and Management* (2007) discusses interesting examples of the academic–policy interface, particularly the role of academics as consultants and advisers to public sector organisations. The contributions there all treat academic roles as research based, typified by acting as experts or consultants working on a specific area, perhaps commissioned by the government itself. Essentially, they are outsiders who come in or work alongside government for a limited period of time. In contrast, there are some, admittedly rarer instances, of academics engaged in policy worlds for extended periods of time, as employees not consultants, as advisers not necessarily researchers, and working on a range of policies rather than a single issue or topic. Two examples can be mentioned. One is Betsy Stanko, when she worked on policing and violence in the Number 10 Policy Unit,[3] which she explains as a personal career shift from academia into policy making (Stanko 2007). The other is Julian Le Grand, who saw his role in advising Prime Minister Tony Blair on public sector reform, especially in health and education, as a challenge of moving from academic detachment into a different space that does not fit the traditional academic/policy interface (Le Grand 2007). In each case, the time commitment also matters, in that Stanko and Le Grand went into their policy roles full-time, I believe. For each of them, their shift from one domain to another raises a question about being involved in a more 'hands on' way than shorter-term academic engagements.

Like my own role, these are different from the academic contributions to Macpherson that are, in essence, from 'the outside in'. They require becoming an 'insider', and what this can entail is discussed in the first case in this chapter. If this characterisation implies or reinforces a view that academics are 'detached' or operate at 'arm's length' from government and policy, I recognise the problem of dichotomies such as engaged/detached, along with ones like practice/theory and inside/ outside. Nonetheless, I try to show why these can matter. While being on the 'outside' is useful for critical voice (and there is evidence that such input can be significant – for an example in education policy, see Shattock 2008), there is also a hybrid category of being a 'critical friend' who can be inside or outside an organisation, although the lines between these things are often blurred (Murji 2011).

The relationship between knowledge, politics and policy is addressed in a wide range of fields, such as environmental policy making (Torgerson 1986), drugs policy (Stevens 2007) and criminology and science studies (Edwards and Sheptykci 2009). While those three sources use different terms, they do share a common approach to this relationship. Each sets out a three-part framework to understanding the links between knowledge and politics and, in each case, these authors then propose a 'third way' interacting model instead, as the way to understand how politics and policy connect with science. I agree that interaction brings out the dynamics between knowledge and politics, but I question the creation of 'third way' formulations, because they miss or underplay a couple of things. The first of these is that while there is no simple sense that the academy can (if it ever did) 'legislate' any longer, even the attendant claim about being 'interpreters' (Bauman 1987) is dubious when there are multiple interpreters, and the value of science or of academic knowledge cannot be taken as self-evident. The origins of the term 'institutional racism' (see Chapter Four), for example, mean that social science cannot claim some sort of dominion over it. Moreover, expert knowledge on race and racism comes from sites – universities – which are places where knowledge production about 'others' is legitimated through professional codes and practices that embody power relations (see Chapter Three). The relation of individual scholars to that is not simple but it is naive to claim to speak 'truth to power' when academics are themselves caught up in validating what the former is through the latter (Back and Solomos 1993).

Second, in these approaches to knowledge and politics, the form and content of academic engagements with policy and politics are not sufficiently distinguished. A stress on the interaction between knowledge and politics does suggest that more than the strength of evidence or the logic of ideas is required, as Cairney (2016) also argues. However, through the cases to be discussed in this chapter I argue that context is more significant than evidence or even rhetoric. To put it another way, the relationship between knowledge production and policies requires acts of translation. This is not the translation of academic expertise into a policy domain in a 'top down' way, nor is it just a two-way or interacting process. It may be quite one-way as political and policy priorities override the concerns of academic expertise. Thus, it is not enough to say that knowledge and politics interact; it is the form in which they do – and do not – combine in each context that matters.

Having stressed the importance of context, I briefly outline the setting that I think shaped the examples in this chapter: the tenth anniversary of the Macpherson report as it pertains to institutional racism. To mark the decade from Macpherson, the National Policing Improvement Agency (NPIA)[4] organised a major conference, on 24 February 2009 – this date sits approximately in the middle of the two cases to be discussed. Around 300 people attended the conference, which was addressed by three cabinet ministers, the Commissioner of the Metropolitan Police, and Stephen's mother, Mrs Lawrence. Yet the 'mood music' for it had been signalled prior to the event by Trevor Phillips, the head of the Equalities and Human Rights Commission (EHRC) – the establishment of which was itself seen as weakening attention to race equality and racism reduction (Chouhan and Sian 2010, Sian et al 2014). At the EHRC's own tenth anniversary event in January 2009, Phillips said that institutional racism had served its purpose in bringing about policy changes, was no longer needed or relevant, and that it was time to move on from it (Phillips 2009).[5] It had become 'a debate about linguistics' rather than evidence (in Home Affairs Committee 2009: 6). Another reason he gave for this – that it led to an assumption that all individuals become racists once they put on the police uniform – harks back beyond Macpherson to the debate as it was in the 1980s (see Neal 2003), which suggests that attempts by social scientists, or staff of the Commission for Racial Equality (CRE) and/or EHRC, to provide nuanced explanations of institutional racism had made little impact on the head of the UK equalities body.[6] While there was a very critical reaction to Phillips' speech, the most prominent critic in the media was Duwayne Brooks, the friend who was with Stephen on the night he was killed, rather than any social scientists.[7]

Phillips' speech appears to have been part of some 'political choreography' for the declarations that would become evident at the NPIA event. Jack Straw, who had set up the Macpherson inquiry as Home Secretary in 1997, said that the charge of institutional racism against the police was 'no longer' applicable and that 'by and large the police service has purged itself of the systemic racism Macpherson identified'. Sir Paul Stephenson, in what was his first major speech as Commissioner, concurred in stating that, 'I no longer believe the label to be either appropriate or useful'.[8]

While some internal and external voices, such as the National Black Police Association (NBPA), were critical of the Commissioner's view, the consensus between highly placed keynote speakers made it clear that a curtain was being drawn on the era of institutional racism. Significantly, Richard Stone, who had been an active proponent of the term, also read the 'political winds', when he said at the same event that he was comfortable with calling it 'systemic bias' rather than institutional racism; his only caveat being that the words 'by race' should be added.

From 'golden circle' to 'academic nuances'

The first case concerns an allegation of racial discrimination by a senior South Asian officer in the Metropolitan Police. The officer, Commander[9] Shabir Hussain, commenced legal proceedings after attempted mediation between him and the force had not been successful. Given his seniority in the organisation and the debates about institutional racism, not least due to the Macpherson report, this was a case that received national and some international media attention when it went before an employment tribunal[10] in 2008. The media coverage mainly occurred at the beginning, when the officer gave his side of the story. He stated that he believed that he had not been promoted because he had come up against a 'glass ceiling' in the organisation. In his view, 'promotion ... appears to operate by the earmarking of a "golden circle" of preferred candidates. ... I believe that I was excluded from the golden circle because my face did not fit, and that my face did not fit because I am not white'.[11]

His claim was evidenced in several ways. He was the only person to have been turned down for promotion on four occasions, in spite of the fact that he had been awarded the highest grades during the assessment centre activities that all candidates for seniority take part in, albeit at an earlier stage of his career. Furthermore, he documented that many other officers (who were named in his deposition) had been promoted beyond him, despite having lower grades at the same stage or being otherwise less qualified than him. All of those officers were white. He therefore concluded that the grounds for his non-promotion in the Metropolitan Police Service (MPS) must be due to racial discrimination.

My personal involvement in this case – including appearing at the employment tribunal – came about because I had been one of the panellists who interviewed Hussain on the last of the four occasions that he was not promoted.[12] At the time, senior appointments at Association of Chief Police Officers (ACPO) level were made by a panel of Metropolitan Police Authority (MPA) members, advised by the Chief Executive of the MPA and the Commissioner. The complaint was against both the MPA (as this was the body that had the final say on each of his promotion attempts), as well as Sir Ian Blair, as the Commissioner – Blair (2009) mentions the Hussain case quite briefly in his book. While only the Commissioner and the Chair of the MPA were individually named in the complaint of race discrimination, it also included each of the panellists at his interviews, including me.

Up to the time of that interview, I had had few professional dealings with Hussain and no private ones. My own view of the interview was that he had performed satisfactorily in most areas, but there were other candidates who, in terms of operational experience and performance, were better able to demonstrate the capacity to move to the next level of seniority in the organisation. I was aware that Hussain had been considered for promotion before, and heard from colleagues who had interviewed him before that his personal style in interviews, which some saw as being aloof, had been a drawback. I had not heard or seen any evidence of racial bias or preference against or towards him and, as far as I know, none of the panellists had, or would, be involved in that. Overt racial remarks or references would be very unusual in such an environment. The broader but unstated context that panel members were aware of was: that not even a handful of ethnic minority officers had made it into the ACPO ranks; that the rank and career progression of such officers throughout the organisation was a long-standing problem; and that the only two other senior ethnic minority officers had both had 'run-ins' with the Commissioner, over race and religious discrimination issues.[13]

Employment tribunal hearings take place in public, though the account I want to relate is more about aspects of the story 'off stage', and this draws on a privileged internal position to disclose aspects not in the public domain. A few qualifiers are therefore needed. Despite my role inside this case, my view is of course partial in the sense that I was not a party to the prior appointment panels or to the mediation. I am revealing some details from private meetings and discussions in ways that the other participants could not have expected; I try to address that difficulty by identifying directly only the two individuals already named and none of the other participants. The passage of time means that all of the people have long since moved on from the roles they occupied – both Hussain and Blair have retired – and the MPA has been replaced as the governing body for the police in London. Even though I look only at a part of the case here, there is an ethical responsibility involved in doing that.

The key element I want to bring out concerns matters of race and institutional racism. Before the tribunal proceedings began, I and some other panellists attended a briefing meeting with lawyers representing the MPA. Towards the end of this meeting, and because it had not already come up, I asked if we could expect to be asked something like 'do you believe that there is institutional racism in the Metropolitan Police?' One lawyer replied that we probably would be asked a question like that by Hussain's lawyer. My point in raising it was to think aloud about how the MPA might deal with it, but in a wide-ranging briefing on matters of strategy no such discussion took place. I was surprised that what I thought would be a key issue and a problem for the MPA (and the MPS, which was represented separately) was not aired. Afterwards, I discussed with some colleagues my view and a possible response, which was to find a way to articulate simultaneously the opinion that: institutional racism is a complex and problematic term; but it did name or identify a form of racism that is not reducible to individual intentions, and indeed may occur and persist despite the good intentions of individuals and the MPS's anti-discrimination policies. In other words, while I could not point to manifest racism in the Hussain case, the meaning of institutional racism made it inescapable in some way.

In a case alleging racial discrimination occurring in a period when the MPS was still officially implementing policies to address racism and institutional racism, it is remarkable that the latter never came into the tribunal. A major challenge that the MPS had grappled with for years before the tribunal became 'the elephant in the room' – everyone aware of it but no one raising it. The lawyer for Hussain did not ask me or any of the other panellists about it, and concentrated on a key point in legislation: that his client had been subject to 'less favourable treatment' under the Race Relations Act, by comparing the treatment and progression of Hussain with various white colleagues. If the claimant and his lawyer did not raise it, the lawyers for the MPA and the MPS presumably saw no reason for them to do so, though the Commissioner had suffered from antagonistic media coverage for his liberal views on race. Indeed, he had been caught up in a public furore, after talking about institutional racism in the media less than two years before, as mentioned in Chapter Four (see also Blair 2009).

It seems incredible that institutional racism could be entirely absent in this case. While my own position sought to reconcile a tension or a conflict between my insider/outsider, or policy and academic, roles, my position as a panellist and a member of the body being complained about led me one way, but my academic perspective led me in another direction. Despite an attempt to merge them, my point is that the roles are not easily divisible when one is neither wholly in one camp nor another. Being on the 'inside', even partially, entailed compromises that cannot be resolved by turning to some kind of interstitial space between the inside/outside, or a third category between knowledge and politics. Ethical dilemmas are a familiar aspect of social research, especially in qualitative methods. A crucial difference that I am pointing to here is that, unlike situations such as fieldwork or consultancy or seconded roles, where the researcher sooner or later withdraws from the scene, the scenario I have described does not offer the same opportunities for detachment or withdrawal (compare Le Grand 2007).

This case raised three other dilemmas about race and racism:

* First, in a private conservation, one of the other panellists told me that while the interview was fair 'in the room' (that is, in our appraisal of the candidates during it), we could do little or nothing about the inequalities that came before that. This is a classic liberal distinction between formal/procedural equality that does not (or cannot) take account of the substantive inequality of which racial differentiation

is one key aspect, without – in the liberal view – causing detriment to the procedure or to other candidates. Yet critical views see this as precisely the superficiality of liberalism, where such decontextualised thinking neglects the social or structural dimension that the concept of institutional racism aims to highlight.

- Second, in the briefing meeting previously referred to, one of the lawyers commented that Hussain had no track record of supporting other ethnic minorities, either as a senior officer or through the internal staff organisations that represent black, Asian and Muslim police officers and staff. In the lawyer's words, Hussain had 'played the white man's game'. I took this to mean that the lawyer saw Hussain as having tried, and failed, to de-racinate himself, so by now presenting himself as a victim of race discrimination his case was deemed questionable or even invalid. While I cannot offer a view on Hussain's previous actions or his commitment to race equality, it is at the very least an uncomfortable space to be 'inside' a case buttressed by questioning the right of an ethnic minority man to claim racial discrimination. Although the overriding instrumental or practical goal was not to lose the case – because the publicity would be highly damaging to the police and to the MPA – a critical perspective is not just to assert that it must be 'racism what dunnit' (Cohen 1992) but, rather, to understand how and to what extent race or racism (maybe working with or against other bases of social discrimination) could be an important factor.

- Third, part of the grounds of resistance for the MPA was that the final panel of five members (that is, the one that I sat on) contained two people of South Asian descent and that one of the other panellists was partly of Indian descent. (The latter and two other panellists would normally be seen as white; four out of five were men.) In the briefing meeting, this was seen as a strong point; one of the lawyers said it would be 'hard to imagine a more diverse panel'. Similarly, in its judgement the employment tribunal – which dismissed all of Hussain's claims – commented that the panel 'was diverse in terms of colour and ethnicity'. These viewpoints were never called into question by anyone, yet what do they rest upon? It was treated as largely self-evident that people of Asian descent would not be racist or biased against another Asian. The only question mark about 'reverse racism' was raised by the MPA's own lawyer in the briefing meeting, when he asked me if it was possible that I had judged Hussain more harshly because I had higher expectations of fellow Asians, or because I might think that he had to be better than an equivalent white colleague in order to survive in the organisation.

I saw this as a question based on anticipating what I might be asked by Hussain's lawyer. A critical outlook would accept that racism is not simply what 'whites' do to 'others'; that members of the 'same' ethnic group may be alike and not alike in many ways; and that unconscious or subconscious factors may be at work in unintended negative discrimination (see Essed 1991). Perhaps, paradoxically, this could be a form of institutional racism as defined by Macpherson in the sense of unwitting or thoughtless prejudice or racism.

This account deals only with a few points of this case; my purpose in doing so has been to address some dilemmas about being an insider and an outsider in addressing racism. It would be possible to delve into academic accounts of ethics, codes of practice on social research or wider theory, in which comparable difficulties and dilemmas are raised. The point here though is that being 'inside' entails complicities and contradictions beyond academic detachment. Taking part in public policy requires participation in politics in ways where a purely academic position can have limited purchase (compare Keith 2008). Faced with a binary yes/no choice, there is not just limited scope, but actually no scope to enunciate open-ended answers based on a critical/reflexive orientation about the nature and extent of racism.

That, for instance, is what happened when, in the briefing meeting, I indicated what my response to the opening question from the MPA lawyer would be. He asked whether I and other panellists believed there was a 'golden circle' in the MPS, from which Hussain had been excluded. My response was that I thought not, but was concerned about a perception that such a circle did exist; it was met with a flat statement that a tribunal was not the place for 'academic nuances'.

While the reflexive and critical qualities of academic knowledge are certainly invaluable in providing analyses of ethical choices and value judgements, my involvement in this case study shows that instrumentality closes down almost any space for reflexivity. As a member of a public body and a direct participant in one of the instances of alleged discrimination, I became part of an 'inside' closing ranks.

A 'sterile debate'?

While institutional racism failed even to get a mention in the tribunal case as previously discussed, the second example is quite different, but its outcome is perhaps no less surprising. I sketch this to develop my point about the relationship between knowledge, policy and politics via my role in relation to an MPA-led inquiry into Race and Faith issues.

The background that led to the setting up of that inquiry was that in 2008 a number of race issues came to a head in the MPS. These included an allegation of racism against the Commissioner by the most senior Black and Minority Ethnic (BME) officer in the force, an ongoing battle with another senior BME officer, and tension between the senior management of the MPS and the representative organisation for BME officers, the Metropolitan Police Black Police Association (MetBPA). Frustrated by a lack of progress on race matters, and amid claims that racism in the force towards officers and staff already in the MPS was not being addressed by the management of the MPS, or only as 'lip service' (see Cashmore 2002), the MetBPA said it would no longer support MPS efforts targeted at recruiting more BME officers. (This was a target that the MPS was supposed to achieve by 2009, and which is the subject of the next chapter.) The establishment of the inquiry occurred in a changeover period in London government and the MPA. Ken Livingstone, who had been the Mayor of London for eight years until 2008, was replaced by the Conservative politician Boris Johnson, who would go on to become the Mayor for the next eight years. One of the first actions of Mayor Johnson was effectively to dismiss Sir Ian Blair as Commissioner, on the grounds that he did not have confidence in him. Curiously for a Commissioner widely regarded as progressive on a range of equalities issues, including racism, Sir Ian had become embroiled in conflicts with senior minority officers and with the MetBPA (see Blair 2009).

The Race and Faith Inquiry, chaired by MPA member Cindy Butts, with three independent advisers/members, was established to provide a means for the MPS and MetBPA to address and resolve issues raised by the latter. The inquiry held a number of public hearings in 2008–09 and heard from all the parties to the dispute. In the summer of 2009, I agreed to be an adviser to the inquiry, after the panel decided it needed a fresh approach because it had not been satisfied with the report drawn up by MPA staff. While there are several elements to all of that, my concern here is only with the issue of institutional racism in this inquiry. Having heard from many sources – including academics, policy makers, senior police officers and the BPA – the panel had not arrived at a view on what it wanted to say about racism. If this is surprising in the wake of a decade-long policy drive to address the Macpherson (1999) recommendations, it is also unsurprising for the same reason, due to the position emerging around institutional racism, as charted earlier. So a key concern for the inquiry was how to handle that in this climate of opinion. In spite of the rush to declare the end of institutional racism – to put it in the past, as something that had been dealt with or that the police had done more than anyone else to address (Loftus 2008, Hall et al 2009, Shiner 2010) – the events that led to the Race and Faith inquiry showed the extent to which race, racism and institutional racism could still play a powerful role.

In the evidence sessions held by the inquiry, it heard arguments both for and against the value of institutional racism as a term. On the one side, groups such as the MetBPA and their counterparts the National BPA, alongside some members of the MPS's Race Advisory Group all maintained that racism had not disappeared in the years since Macpherson, and more action was needed.[14] On the other side, Trevor Phillips from the EHRC, the new Commissioner of the MPS and the new Chair of the MPA expressed varying degrees of doubt about institutional racism as a term. My main advice to the panel members was to avoid a soundbite, either for or against, as that would be seen as a clear victory for one side and would discredit the inquiry for the 'losing' side. Just as importantly, after nearly a decade of public and policy arguments, the panel would be unwise to merely restate the Macpherson view, or to completely reject it. Rather, in the political milieu of the time, the inquiry was an opportunity for the panel to provide a new impetus to tackling racism, while also acknowledging that other matters – especially faith and gender – also needed to be part of the equation. (Rattansi 2007 similarly advocated the need for gender and class to be included alongside race in the later New Labour years.)

This is the first time I have written about this inquiry and, as an example of policy sociology, I set out here in full[15] my advice in the form of the text on racism that I drafted for the panel to discuss:

Racism – institutional or otherwise

Our inquiry inevitably has to deal with the question of institutional racism because this is a term that has been prominent since the Macpherson inquiry. It has been the subject of a great deal of discussion and research. We do not intend to go through all of that. There is already a detailed literature review that examines policy and academic works on the term after Macpherson.

We raised the question of the meaning and existence of institutional racism with our witnesses and can distinguish two broad strands in the current discussion. On one side, the MetBPA, some BME officers and Mrs Doreen Lawrence maintain that institutional racism is still evident in the policies and procedures of the MPS, that it has not been properly dealt with and that bodies such as the MPA have to some extent colluded with senior managers in the MPS in the victimisation of senior and junior officers and staff. On the other hand, people such as the Commissioner, the head of the EHRC and the Lord Chancellor uphold that the term has served its purpose, is no longer applicable to the MPS and that it is time to move on.

Both sides agree with the views of the Stephen Lawrence Inquiry that institutional racism was a factor in the poor police response to Stephen's family and in the investigation of his murder and [has] been a powerful galvanising force for action in the MPS and beyond. The difference between them boils down to whether the term is still relevant or not. This has become a polarised debate.

Although Dr Richard Stone told us that he was happy to accept 'systemic bias' as an alternative, as long it took account of the 'r word', racism, his recent report makes a distinction between 'institutionalised' and 'institutional' racism, where the former refers to the situation in apartheid South Africa or Nazi Germany and does not exist in Britain, but the latter – meaning the discretionary and discriminatory exercise of power – does. Others, such as Sir Paul Stephenson believe that debate over definitions is sterile and that "actions not definitions" are required.

It is worth recalling Macpherson's approach to the term, which saw it as:

> The collective failure of an organisation to provide an appropriate and professional service to people because of their colour, culture or ethnic origin. It can be seen or detected in processes, attitudes and behaviour which amount to discrimination through unwitting prejudice, ignorance, thoughtlessness, and racist stereotyping which disadvantage minority ethnic people. (Macpherson, 1999, para 6.34)

The impact of Macpherson and the Race Relations Amendment Act has been important in driving policy changes in the police service, as many of our interviewees including the current and previous Commissioner agreed. However there is a good deal of evidence that institutional racism is both poorly understood and resented. The impact of training programmes in this area has been mixed at best. Research for the MPS and the Home Office found that the term was poorly understood or resented by many non-BME officers. This is also supported by other academic research.

One response to the debate and the evidence is to say it is time to move on – although move on to what is not always made clear by the people who take this position. The other is to say that we need better and more forceful leadership to drive out institutional racism.

We agree that it is time to move and that leadership and action against racism – and other forms of discrimination – is needed. That does not mean we are simply placing ourselves in a half-way house between two poles. Our considered view is that both sides are wrong. One makes claims that are too general and alarmist, while the other is too complacent and defensive. A new approach is needed.

To map out that approach we need to delve a little into the debate about the meaning and applicability of institutional racism. Originally, the term was used to identify pervasive and systemic racism. It meant something more than individual and group prejudice and discrimination ('rotten apples' in terms of police culture).

The confusions around the term arose from its lack of clarity about what distinguished – and what connected – individual and institutional forms of racism. Implicitly the former seemed to mean the same thing as overt racism while the latter seemed to refer to covert racism. Both and all of these seem to be included in Macpherson's idea of institutional racism as occurring through 'unwitting prejudice, ignorance, thoughtlessness, and racist stereotyping'.

Dr Stone admitted to us that the use of 'unwitting' has caused him problems with audiences who have failed to understand why it seems to overlook or exclude 'witting' racism. So whether racism is intended is a difficulty, and the research evidence is that many officers resented the accusation that they were acting with racist intent in their day to day work.

At the same time, 'processes, attitudes and behaviour' could mean and cover both intended forms of racism and intended or unintended outcomes. The perplexity about intentions and whether these are evident in policies or not is what underlay Lord Scarman's rejection of the term institutional racism if that meant that the police discriminated 'knowingly as a matter of policy'. To the extent that the terms as set out by Macpherson have confused rather than clarified issues we do believe that it is time to move on.

Our starting point is that we do not believe that racism has disappeared from the UK. It may have altered and be more subtle than it once was but nonetheless it still exists.

Where racism is evident and intended we expect the leadership of the MPS to condemn it unequivocally. While the Inquiry was sitting, we heard press reports about an 'apartheid culture' in one London police station. Commissioner Sir Paul Stephenson made it clear that was unacceptable but called it 'bigotry' and 'pockets of stupidity' within the Met. At an NPIA conference on 24 February 2009 marking the 10th anniversary of the publication of the Macpherson report, an open row took place between the Commissioner and the MetBPA about his choice of words.

We heard from Professor Simon Holdaway that in his research where he asked BME officers for examples of institutional racism they usually mentioned examples of personal bias or mis-treatment; and that when he asked for recent examples, they sometimes brought out things that happened quite a long time ago. Both findings are important, the first because it highlights the difficulty of evidencing institutional racism, the second because it makes clear the importance of institutional memory in the police service which cannot be brushed under the carpet by maintaining that was a long time ago, or to a list of achievements in the last decade.

Leadership from the Management Board and at all levels of management in the MPS is also needed in ensuring that all the policies and procedures of the MPS are rigorously 'equality checked' through impact assessments. We have heard how this has become a superficial 'tick box' exercise. Reports by the MPS to MPA committees sometimes demonstrate that, but more important than individually challenging officers is to inculcate a diversity culture where it is no longer seen as an 'add on' to the real issues in a report. That could mean that equalities implications are 'mainstreamed' but for reasons we set out [in the new vision] we do not believe that the MPS is yet at that level of maturity. So equalities implications will need to be spelt out in a separate section but the leadership of Management Board and the DCFD [Diversity and Citizen Focus Directorate] acting as an 'internal inspectorate' will have to oversee that – and own it when or if they are challenged on it by the MPA and other bodies.

No one could direct us to specific rules and procedures in the MPS that are systematically biased against BME officers and staff, though we heard a lot about informal cultures and networks – and some specific calls for greater openness in how decisions about temporary promotions and mentoring schemes work.

The examination of outcomes also requires a new culture of openness. We know that the MetBPA and the NBPA have drawn attention to the fact in the past three years only one BME officer has been appointed to ACPO rank by the MPA. We heard that in the past two years no BME officer has made it through PNAC [Police National Assessment Centre]. We also have data about the lack of progression of BME officers in Chief Inspector, Superintendent and Chief Superintendent ranks in the MPS.

These are patterns of statistical inequality that we think are important. The MPS should monitor, report and act upon them. Whether racism or institutional racism accounts for all racially biased outcomes or effects is not an easy question to answer, but we place the onus on the organisation to inspect all its policies and procedures every time there is a pattern that cannot be explained. And because statistics can be used and mis-used in different ways we want that analysis to be supplemented by qualitative work that is used to complement the overall picture. So we want the MPS to look for and to act upon any and every instance and pattern of racial discrimination and exclusion – and not doing so would be an institutional failure by those in charge of the MPS.

As there are so few BME officers we are conscious that focusing on their success or failure makes them 'hyper visible'. A symptom of that is that each promotion or non-promotion is therefore treated as an example organisational success or failure as a whole. Until there are sufficient numbers of BME officers in all ranks of the MPS this unfortunately is a transitional issue to which there is no easy answer. However, the culture of diversity that we call for might lead to a more considered approach.

Adding to that culture, we recognise that across the diversity strands there are many forms of discrimination and disadvantage that cannot be encapsulated simply by adding the word 'institutional' into them to come up with 'institutional sexism', for example.

We asked witnesses about how they placed faith issues within that spectrum and some such as Dr Stone argued that Islamophobia is another form of racism and the Jewish Police Association spoke about anti-Semitism but without seeing it as equivalent to racism. We observed some stereotyping about Jewish communities when Kit Malthouse said that the Jewish people didn't see the police as a career because they aspired to become high-status professionals. Much the same used to be said about South Asian communities. But both Jewish and South Asian communities are internally diverse and should not be treated as homogenous in terms of their attitudes and aspirations. This Inquiry was set up to look at race and faith issues but as we have considered the evidence we have seen areas where the two areas join up and just as many ways in which they have to be regarded separately.

There is a need to cross-reference that with other strands of diversity in ways that combine the complexity of social inequalities without losing sight of the role of race in casting a spotlight on them in the first place. We welcome the widening equalities agenda around diversity, evident in the current Equalities Bill and the work of the EHRC. But our welcome comes with a caveat. Race has been and still is a 'totemic' issue for the police in London and elsewhere. That does not mean that the issue of race has stood still or that there are not many new communities and issues to respond to.

It will be up to the leadership of the MPS to demonstrate that an either/or approach will not do. What we mean by that is that suggestions that the police service is now un-recognisable from where it was twenty years ago are just as untenable that nothing has changed. In the same vein, using racism as an explanation for everything is no more helpful than the view that racism is not a factor. In a new culture, more nuanced positions and explanations will be required by all sides – and to be communicated transparently and in ways that do not seek to hide behind numbers, targets and boxes ticked.

As a matter of style, the panel decided they did not wish to draw on and cite witnesses as per my draft, and they rejected it. The more substantive issue is about the content and aims of the statement, and what they as members of an inquiry had to say about institutional racism. The draft aimed to manoeuvre between the irreconcilable positions of those who wanted to declare the end of institutional racism, and those representing black and minority officers in the police for whom it remained the core issue. Moreover, and in recognition that some complaints by of BME officers were at least as much about gender as about race, I sought to nudge the panel to consider an intersectional approach. The move towards a single equality body in the UK and the passage of what was to become the Equality Act 2010 also provided a spur to this.

None of this is something that the panel took up or developed; their deliberations continued without further input from me and in July 2010 the final report was published (Race and Faith Inquiry 2010). It contains a section headed 'Institutional racism' on pages 21–22, though only four or five of the twelve paragraphs deal with racism as such, one of which is just the Macpherson definition of the term. Of the four paragraphs on institutional racism, I want to cite two in full to indicate how it is raised only to be brushed aside rather abruptly:

3.3   Now, however, as a consequence of rhetorical inflation, the term is used too glibly as a blanket indictment and as such has become a barrier to reform. Paradoxically the concept of institutional racism has become a millstone around the neck of the MPS, obscuring our understanding of the nature of any continuing endemic racism in that or any other large organisation. There is also a risk, as Sir Paul Stephenson's quotation below highlights, that individual responsibility will be obscured within a quest for collective responsibility.

Defining a new vision

3.4   Rather than engage in sterile debate about the merits of the "institutionally racist" label the Panel commends an intelligent and balanced approach in which every case involving suspicions of racism should be investigated, firstly in terms of the broad conception of racism before progressing on to an attempt to discern the particular individual or structural (team, department, organisation etc) culpabilities. The truth is that any such example of racism is bound to have individual and collective elements, and recognition of this fact allows for a rational investigative, disciplinary and policy development strategy to be developed as a response.

Although this text concurred with my advice on not getting drawn into the minutiae, it is far from what I had mind. It is significant that institutional racism is called a 'sterile debate', a 'millstone' and a glib, obscure and blanket term. Yet their conclusion, paradoxically, illustrates why at least some engagement with the meaning and use of the term is unavoidable. In paragraph 3.4, the report both calls for identification of 'individual or structural' culpability and recognises that both 'individual and collective' elements are involved. The quotation referred to in paragraph 3.3 is where the Commissioner stated that:

> nobody acting in such a bigoted form in an organisation … should be allowed to hide behind some definition and some sense that this is an organisational problem and [say] my bigoted behaviour comes out of some wider sense of the organisation. I think we've got to find those people who do behave in an outrageous fashion and not give them the cover of some sort of comfortable broader phraseology. (in Race and Faith Inquiry 2010: 22)[16]

Here we have arrived at a virtually diametric reversal, where the Commissioner and the inquiry panel forget that rather than 'hide behind some definition', the usual complaint of police officers was that the definition was too sweeping and failed to differentiate between racist and non-racist individuals (Foster et al 2005, Loftus 2008). At the same time, officers disciplined for racist language or behaviour did claim that there was an organisational problem. By that they meant that senior officers were out of touch and unwilling to confront 'truths' about race, such as the view among some officers that black males are more involved in street crime. This bears restating in other words: officers are more likely to complain about institutional racism as a form of political correctness among senior officers that has the effect of restricting them in their work at ground level.

Moreover, the complaint of the MetBPA, for instance, is not about overt racism but consistent patterns of discipline and lack of promotion of BME officers and staff, a matter for which they held senior MPS managers – including the Commissioner – responsible. While that viewpoint tends to stress individual action, it does focus on the hierarchy of the organisation and so, to an extent, keeps the spotlight on the institution. How to make sense of the multiple forms and levels of individual and collective responsibility is a thorny theoretical debate (Wight 2003, Phillips 2011) – let alone a policy one. Just as the report provides no sense of how they could be addressed together and separately, the more intersectional approach I proposed to the inquiry was overlooked or discarded. Thus, any attempt to tackle race alongside gender and other bases of social inequalities – and to rework institutional racism into a new era – was missed at this point.

In my view, the panel's conclusions are to be understood within the political context they had to navigate; an attempt to steer around that and change the drift of the discussion was wholly unsuccessful. As an instance of policy sociology this looks like a fairly dismal outcome. Yet, there are other ways in which a form of policy impact does sneak through. This is apparent in the report's remarks on diversity, which state that it should become a routine, rather than exceptional, part of policing and organisational culture. This point came out of deliberations with, and wordings suggested to, the panel in my short role with them. While those comments remain aspirational and lacked a clear policy thrust, they were intended to signal a possible way forward on race and policing issues. They called for an awareness from senior politicians as well as police leaders that race and diversity should be regarded as the normal business of policing in a major cosmopolitan city, rather than as an 'added on' afterthought. This ambition can be thought of as (one of) the end(s) of institutional racism – to deepen the interrogation of a white male status quo treated as the norm from which all others are seen as different.

Both the employment tribunal case and the Race and Faith Inquiry signalled the end of institutional racism post-Macpherson, as became publicly evident in the political context of the tenth anniversary events. Yet they realise that in quite different ways, through omission and commission: in the former, there is a virtual silence about it; in the latter, it is raised only in order to largely dismiss it. In this chapter, I have set them as personal instances of being in the public domain, in order to suggest that the boundary between inside and outside is a shifting frontier. A recognition of the specific nature of that fluidity is required: sometimes they are separate, sometimes they overlap, and often they are matters of degree rather than absolutes. Yet, my argument is that it is not enough to show how the inside/outside are contingent constructs or to appeal to a third space or category, as those cannot deal with the kind of binary choice I illustrated in the employment tribunal. The example of the Race and Faith Inquiry also shows that 'third way' models that stress the interaction between knowledge and politics only take us so far and there is, again, a need to specify the relationship between those two things, with due attention to context.

However, 'interaction' may mean not some kind of meeting ground or combination of two things, but rather the dominance of one over the other in ways that call into question what makes for 'knowledge transfer'. While it is too easy to equate policy sociology with an instrumental rationality, and public sociology with a critical/reflexive outlook, instrumental logics dominated the nature of the defence at the employment tribunal, as well as the conclusions of the independent inquiry. In both of them a space for critical or reflexive thinking was squeezed out.

Notes

[1]   Part of the introduction to, and the first case study in this chapter appeared in K. Murji (2010) 'Race policy and politics: Two case studies from Britain', *Policy Studies*, 32(6), 585-98.

[2]   The view I present contrasts with Mayberry (2000), who saw the Macpherson inquiry as a 'pyrrhic victory', whose recommendations were undermined by a lack of political commitment from politicians and police leaders. Stone (2009) shares this view to an extent.

[3]   This is shorthand for the Prime Minister's policy unit, based at Number 10 Downing Street.

[4]   The NPIA was abolished in 2012 and its functions were transferred to new agencies, including the College of Policing.

[5]   Although in 2003 the then Home Secretary David Blunkett had stated that the term institutional racism has 'missed the point. See: https://www.theguardian.com/politics/2003/jan/14/immigrationpolicy.race. In an editorial The Guardian called his remarks 'unnecessary and damaging' - https://www.theguardian.com/politics/2003/jan/15/race.equality.

[6]   The other reasons Phillips gave was that there were other forms of discrimination based on age, gender, faith, disability, sexuality and not just race. This chimes with the remit of the EHRC, which replaced the previous 'single issue' equalities bodies in the UK. However, he does not make clear why that makes institutional racism invalid rather than sitting alongside, or in intersection with, multiple axes of discrimination. Interestingly, Phillips is prepared to draw on academic research that supports his argument, such as Ford (2008). Using the Social Attitudes Survey, Ford maintains that racial hostility is declining in the UK and this is principally

generational in nature, so that people born after the 1950s show a significant decline in prejudice.

[7] See 'A premature obituary', *The Guardian*, 21 January 2009: www.guardian.co.uk/commentisfree/2009/jan/21/stephen-lawrence-institutional-racism-race

[8] Quote as recorded in my own notes made at the event.

[9] Commander is a rank at about the third tier of seniority in the organisation. Mr Hussain retired from the Metropolitan Police in 2010.

[10] In the UK, an employment tribunal consists of three members, led by a judge.

[11] Stated in the plaintiff's deposition to the tribunal.

[12] There are several complexities here. British police officers are not formally employees but are Crown servants. They are entitled to take cases to employment tribunal proceedings only when alleging race or other forms of discrimination. Although the Commissioner of police is head of the organisation, a public body (the police authority) was formally the employer at this time, and one of its roles was to determine promotions into chief officer or 'ACPO' ranks. Police authorities were replaced by Police and Crime Commissioners by the UK coalition government of 2010–15; the same legislation enabled chief officers to directly appoint their senior management team.

[13] These have featured heavily in the media. One, Ali Dizaei, published a book on his experience inside the police service (Dizaei 2007) following a compensation payment to him by the Metropolitan Police. In 2010, he was convicted on charges of perverting the course of justice in a separate case, imprisoned and dismissed from the police service. In 2011, he was acquitted and a retrial ordered. In 2012 he was found guilty and dismissed from the MPS again. The other senior officer, Tarique Ghaffur, threatened to issue employment tribunal proceedings in 2008, alleging discrimination by the Commissioner. This was dropped and Mr Ghaffur received a pay-off, under which he retired from and left the police service.

[14] Their view can be seen in the report of the Home Affairs Committee (2009).

[15] The original version contained notes that I have excised here; all the references that were in the draft appear elsewhere in this and other chapters.

[16] This comment echoes Blunkett's 2003 understanding when he said that: 'It's not the structures created in the past, it's the processes to change structures in the future and it's individuals at all levels who do that. That's why I was so worried about people talking about institutional racism because it isn't institutions, it's patterns of work and processes that have grown up' (from: https://www.theguardian.com/politics/2003/jan/14/immigrationpolicy.race). Both Stephenson and Blunkett thereby hark back to and restate the individual/institutional dichotomisation that was used to criticise Macpherson in 1999 (see Chapters Four and Five).

SEVEN

Racialised numerics[1]

The politics of race, racism and policing has been a subject of controversy in some form in every post-war decade in Britain, making it a regular topic of public and policy discourse as well as social research from the 1960s. A principal theme across that span of time has been over-policing and the over-representation of black people through discriminatory policing. This has been a central element of debates about the nature of contemporary racism through the racialisation–criminalisation nexus (Gilroy 1987, Keith 1993). Sociology's contribution was to critique psychological and individualistic explanations based on prejudice and discrimination, in favour of cultural and structural models that identified a distinctive 'cop culture', through which the group solidarity of police officers combined with the everyday realities of police work to reproduce racist attitudes and practices (Holdaway 1996, Webster 2007, Reiner 2010).

Marxists and other critical sociologies took a more structural view of the police's role in 'managing the underclass' as part of their function within the state, which has been explored more recently in various cities in Europe, the US and beyond (Martinot 2003, Fassin 2013, Alves 2014, Camp and Heatherton 2016), where policing serves to keep young, usually male and often black, minorities and other marginalised groups in subjugated positions. In spite of sociological critique and many policy initiatives – such as more and different forms of police training, changes in the recruitment of officers, and employing more women and minority officers – the over-representation of black people, particularly males, in prisons, as subjects of policing and of criminal justice has been a dominant feature of race and criminal justice issues over many decades.

Sometimes, over-representation has been combined with attention to the under-representation of black (and Asian) people as employees in the police and in the criminal justice system, especially since the 1980s and the Scarman (1981) report. Nearly 20 years on from that, one recommendation from Macpherson (1999) to improve police relations with racial minorities was that all police forces should be mandated to increase the proportion of Black and Minority Ethnic (BME) officers serving in their ranks. In accepting this, the government set targets for all police forces in the UK to achieve a mandated number or proportion of BME officers in their ranks over a decade from 1999 to 2009. The national or overall target was 7% BME representation by 2009, while each local police force had individual targets. In London, the Metropolitan Police Service (MPS) target was 25%, a proportion based on and reflecting the BME population of the city. Police forces and senior officers, including the management of the MPS, pledged action to improve BME representation. About five years later, Sir William Macpherson (in the foreword to Whitfield (2004, xii) declared that he was 'optimistic for the future', while recognising that 'more must be done' to improve police race relations. This chapter explores some of the dynamics behind the BME target in the MPS and it demonstrates how the target was questioned or doubted from the outset and became negotiable while seemingly being fixed.

An important basis for increasing the proportion of BME groups in the police is due to pressure on public policy bodies to be more inclusive and representative. This is wider than race and includes gender representation and, commonly, it is based on the proportion in a local population or nationally. As a baseline, this form of measure is used in relation to employment, service delivery, consultation processes and the membership of various bodies and boards in local and national government, and other public bodies. It rests on a view that organisations will be better in various ways, if they are more 'equally' representative. The essence of this is captured in a 2015 speech by the then Home Secretary Theresa May, when she said that:

> if police forces do not truly represent the people they serve, if they are not made up of men and women of all backgrounds, if they do not properly reflect the communities where local officers police, then we cannot truly say the police are the public, and the public are the police. (Cited in Home Affairs Committee 2016: 4)[2]

However, what 'to reflect' means in practical terms is not simple. It is unlikely that government ever meant it in the sense of a reflecting like a mirror, where the proportion of particular groups has to perfectly match their presence in a defined population, although that is what black police associations, pressure groups and independent race advisers have called for and used as a baseline (Home Affairs Committee 2009, Murji 2011). There can be a culturalist and essentialist assumption that black and minority visibility will increase community confidence, or that their appearance will make for better relations with, and understanding of, communities. With increasing diversity (Vertovec 2007), the idea of racially or ethnically 'matching' officers to communities becomes more complex, though these assumptions do continue, as I show later.

In these ways, representation and proportionality can become part of 'a numbers game' (Brown et al 2006), where the quantity of staff becomes an end in itself, rather than the relationship of that to service delivery, and to the proportional and fair policing of minorities. The 'kill rate' of black police officers in the US suggests that being black in a uniform is no guarantee of procedural fairness (Tyler 2001), hence Bowling et al (2005) said that equal opportunities within the police had to be aligned with equality of service beyond that. Moreover, Afridi (2016) argues that equal or 'descriptive representation' of minorities does not necessarily lead to better policies and outcomes. Although Phillips (1995) makes an important argument for the 'presence' of under-represented groups, Afridi (2016) suggests that in the future better ways of assessing the quality of service to communities will demand more than just visible representation. Nonetheless, campaigns to address the visible exclusion of racial and ethnic minorities have pressed a range of institutions in national and local politics, through Operation Black Vote for example, for more and proportionate representation.

To achieve any representation in the police was a struggle from the 1960s (Whitfield 2004), and long predates the proportionality claim that Macpherson (1999) supported. The setting of a target for BME representation was intended to drive recruitment efforts to reach a set number in every police force across the country. A target is a goal or a directive set by central government that police forces were measured against annually, and it was overseen by the Home Office, which monitored progress. Hence, the BME target links practices of enumeration and categorisation. The politics around the target in London is part of a complicated context, marked by shifts and debates in race politics. These include the visibility of minorities and various race discrimination cases, and a worry among Black police staff that the MPS management was not committed to tackling racism thoroughly, such as evidenced in their backing away from institutional racism (as discussed in Chapters Five and Six).

The politics around the target are also complicated by the fact that although the target is set by central government and 'actioned' by local police forces, there is more to it than a central/local axis. Police forces in England and Wales are subject to local governance arrangements, namely police authorities up to 2012 and thereafter to local Police and Crime Commissioners, whose role it is to provide oversight and scrutiny of policing policies. In London, there was tension between a

Labour Mayor and a Labour-led Metropolitan Police Authority (MPA), something that has not been recognised in research on policing (see Murji 2011). The replacement of the MPA by the Mayor's Office for Policing and Crime (MOPAC) in 2012 gave the Mayor more direct control than the MPA had allowed. Hence there are several layers of governance and more than one line of accountability in play; these various levels can work both 'with' and 'against' one another. While numbers and targets are used to govern, the 'governed' (in this case the police as well as police authorities) respond to and 'push back' on such policies.

Attention to these issues from the public or the media is also a factor. Macpherson and the BME target was not just a matter of policy, but continued to be played out in public, albeit episodically. On 21 February 2009, the front-page headline of the second-largest selling daily newspaper in the UK, the *Daily Mail*, announced, 'Ten years after Macpherson, police race quotas are axed'. This was three days before the tenth anniversary of Macpherson and the National Policing Improvement Agency conference covered in Chapter Six.

Despite the claim in the *Daily Mail* headline, the issue of BME officer numbers and their proportion continues to crop up years later. In 2015, for instance, as Home Secretary Theresa May drew on diversity profiles – the percentage of BME officers against the percentage of the BME population – which showed no force had a black and minority ethnic representation reflecting its local population, to say that the proportion of black and Asian officers was 'simply not good enough', and the figures should be a 'wake-up call' to the police.[3] In 2016, the Home Affairs Committee (2016) stated that BME officer numbers in England and Wales had gone from 2% in 1999 to 5.5% in 2015 and no police force had a BME presence matching its local demographic. In its 2009 report the Committee had said it was 'disappointed' (Home Affairs Committee 2009: 7) with the lack of progress by the police. In 2016 the Committee called for more measures to speed up the diversity profile of the police, although the government rejected any idea of positive discrimination.[4]

Speaking in 2016 as the UK Prime Minister, Mrs May announced a race audit of public services, which would 'reveal difficult truths, but we should not be apologetic about shining a light on injustices as never before'.[5] While this audit is wider than employment in the police, these statements show that race equality can still be a public policy concern, and the numbers of BME officers in the police – and their proportionality to local populations – is still a political issue through which concerns about racism and policing occur.[6] In this regard, while institutional racism is not a term heard in these cases, it is an unsettled legacy of Macpherson, and of race in the UK more widely.

The political and public context of the BME target, as alluded to via the *Daily Mail* headline, is important for other reasons too. Race and recruitment have been part of an intense debate or argument, in particular from 2008[7] onwards, when the Metropolitan Police Black Police Association (MetBPA) announced its boycott of recruitment efforts. This contributed to the setting up of the Race and Faith Inquiry by the Mayor of London (see Chapter Six). At the time, positions were highly polarised, with senior managers being resentful of accusations that they had not done enough on race – including recruitment, progression and anti-discrimination policies – while black staff associations saw the force as still riddled with (institutional) racism, and any changes as mere 'window dressing' (Cashmore 2002). The sometimes hostile environment in which exchanges were conducted matters, because it frames the nature of the narrative in this chapter.

While media coverage of the BME target could be an advantage because it means more information is in the public domain, my view is that the opposite is nearer the mark in this case. A febrile, politicised context and an unwillingness to be accused of racism made senior managers defensive and guarded about what they said . Thus some of what I relate here is about discussions backstage or 'behind the scenes'; the manoeuvring around the target I describe usually occurred in private and is not 'official' in the sense of being recorded in documents or approved by the organisation. Even documents such as minutes or notes of meetings would not show that because, in the main, those relate the outcome of discussions, rather than process and background. The account I present in this chapter draws on privileged and insider access to people at the time this was occurring.[8] Public sources – reports, media stories – are cited where available, to indicate the issues at stake. However, to a significant extent, the key storyline relies on conversations that are not evident in public documents. Indeed, they cannot be, because they reflect private thinking and negotiations in meetings between officials and politicians.[9, 10]

Categorising and enumerating race

Public administration and governmentality provide two ways of bringing together enumeration and categorisation. They form part of an extensive literature about the use of key performance indicators, targets and, generally, on counting regimes as ways of directing, regulating and shaping the conduct of institutions and individuals

(Hood 2006, Miller and Rose 2008, Pidd 2012). Viewed as a distinct rationality of government (MacKinnon 2000), as well as being seen as a feature of managerialism or new public management, quantitative indicators and performance management are intended to improve public sector efficiency through business techniques (Pollitt and Bouckaert 2011). The BME target is an example of this, though it should be recognised that police forces faced a wide range of targets, particularly in the days of the so-called New Labour governments from 1997 to 2010.

Public administration, drawing from social and public policy studies, mainly concentrates on the processes of government and policy making, the role of key actors, and the relationship between politicians and civil servants (Bevir and Rhodes 2003, Hood 2006, 2007).[11] It examines the ways in which numbers and targets are implemented in fields such as health policy and their impact on the actions of practitioners and managers who see that targets are met – or 'finessed'. For instance, Bevan and Hood (2006) demonstrate how numbers/targets are the subject of 'game playing' by officials, and between local and central pillars of government and policy. So this perspective is concerned with the 'inner workings' of Whitehall, the civil service and public policy practitioners and managers. From an initial outlook that targets shaped organisational actions such that 'what gets measured is what gets done', it went on to highlight the limits of 'top down' government, which can be out of step with local realities and pressures.

In contrast, a Foucauldian-inspired genealogical approach to governmentality explores the emergence of numbers regimes as a means through which knowledge and expertise are mobilised to 'make up' and govern populations, particularly through instruments such as censuses and other statistical techniques of government (Hacking 1999, Miller and Rose 2008). While public administration tends to focus on government directives in the narrow sense, governmentality takes a wider view of how actions are shaped beyond public authorities.

In spite of notable differences in their style, there are some commonalities between the two approaches, in that both seek to historicise how particular rationales of government/governing have arisen, and how numbers/targets/performance indicators have become central to that. Some other overlaps are questions about how novel governing by numbers is, and the extent to which it is distinctively 'Anglo Saxon' or a particularly New Labour technocratic outlook (Kelman 2006, Pollitt and Bouckaert 2011). In relation to demands for public sector efficiency – a key underlying rationale for numbers regimes – both approaches recognise that this predated the Labour government in office from 1997 to 2010, as various efficiency reviews and managerialist initiatives since the 1980s show that this transcends a left-right political divide.

With regard to race, though, governmentality provides a more theorised account of its intersection with enumeration. It has examined the ways in which ethnicity and race are products of expert knowledge for 'knowing' population through quantification and classification techniques constructing racial and ethnic categories. Modern-day censuses and equalities policies are examples where enumeration and categorisation of race are conjoined but in which:

> the technical processes which materialise the world – in graphs, figures and other traces – necessarily perform an act of simplification. Expectations and beliefs are embodied in the framing of statistical enquiry, shaping what is counted.... They are embedded in systems of classification adopted, for example ethnicity rather than race, nationality, ancestry, caste or religion. (Rose 1991: 680)

Enumeration and categorisation go hand in hand and are irreducibly political because, like numbers, categories are not neutral descriptors but impart assumptions, frame knowing, fashion content and delimit the ways in which social relations are thought about. For Goldberg (1997), enumeration and categorisation 'naturalise' race as a primal category and as a quasi-technical object and identity. The power of legitimate naming is a mode of inscription, through which 'reality is made stable, mobile, comparable, and combinable. It is rendered in a form in which it can be debated and diagnosed' (Miller and Rose, 2008: 65-6).

Hence, race is routinely quantified in and for administrative purposes as an object to be 'managed'. While this is a compelling argument, there are some limits to it. Bureaucratic processes of course perform an act of simplification, though the analysis itself might underplay contestation around expertise, categorisation and counting. In particular, numbers and categories are both challenged and reinforced by social movements and pressure groups in ways that speak more to Omi and Winant's (2015) notion of racial projects. Racial categories are invested in by BME groups and black staff associations, for example, and changes to those may be resisted. Moreover, racial/ethnic categorisation can provide some political recognition by the state and serve to make the case for policy measures to address inequalities, as Goldberg (1997) and Krieger (2010) have argued. While racial categories and counting may be questionable in social policy as well as in research (see Outram and Ellison 2011), the absence of race – what is sometimes called 'non-racialism' or 'post-race arguments' – can be even less progressive.

Racialised numerics – through enumeration and categorisation – have played a strong role in UK policy and politics. Racial 'others' have often been labelled, through various ethno-national terms, as 'not British' (Small and Solomos 2006). In the post-war period, the main migrant communities into the UK – people of African-Caribbean and South Asian origins as well as their offspring – have gone through many and varied official terms and categories, such as coloured, West Indians, Asians, Black (with and without a capital B), ethnic minority, and Black and Minority Ethnic (BME).[12] Beneath that, there are a wide number of quasi-national identifications (Indian, Pakistani, Bangladeshi, Jamaican, and so on) and hyphenated terms, like Asian-British and Black-British.

The 2001 UK Census produced a categorisation system with terms that aimed to usefully capture ethnic diversity (Aspinall 2000) for policy purposes, although Vertovec's (2007) argument for superdiversity maintains that this has become too limited in light of EU migration. Across various 'white' and 'other' designations there are regular political 'numbers games', in areas such as migration (Erel et al 2016). But racialised numbers are also employed for anti-racist ends in highlighting the over-representation of black males in US prisons or in UK stop and search figures; or to make clear that the actual size of the minority population of the UK is much smaller than many people, and some media and racist discourses, make it appear. As such, numbers are both 'authoritatively' produced by governments and semi-independent bodies, as well as by pressure groups. Rather than being stable constructs, numbers are subject to multiple contestations, in which even 'independent' expert knowledge is called into question.[13]

Two further sources provide other ways of making sense of the politics of racialised numerics and the BME target. First, Omi and Winant's (2015) view of racial formation as an ongoing project, through which social movements for equality and justice engage the state in seeking recognition of group rights, helps in showing that such struggles can have diverse consequences. These include civil rights and equality legislation and group progress, as well as concerns about 'reverse racism' and 'white backlash'. In the present context, one instance of that is the argument by race equality campaigners for the primacy of 'old' (meaning post-war colonial migration) racial categories, rather than diluting race by using diversity (for an example, see the foreword to Hall et al 2009). Following Omi and Winant, I argue that these contestations of categories and designations are a type of racial project that is *'simultaneously an interpretation, representation or explanation of racial identities and meanings, and an effort to organize and distribute resources (economic, political, cultural), along particular racial lines'* (Omi and Winant 2015: 125; original italics).

Second, the unfixed character of targets can be seen in the topological approach to space and scales used by Allen and Cochrane (2007) in their work on regional government. They show how targets set by central government were amended locally in ways that indicate 'less government at-a-distance than part of a continual negotiation and renegotiation of political agendas' (Allen and Cochrane 2007: 15). They suggest that targets:

> offer a starting point for negotiation ... [they are] part of the way central government departments *reach out* through the circulation of priorities ... [they] are encountered as a form of negotiable authority where the manipulation of agendas and the translation of possibilities enters into the play of forces ...' (Allen and Cochrane 2010: 1080)

This stress on negotiable authority provides an insight into the fixity and malleability of the BME recruitment target. It provides a specific way of seeing contestation and negotiability, and how both categories and numbers are at the same time changing and unchanging in the politics of race, racism and the police.

A representative workforce

The drive to change the look and make-up of the Metropolitan Police that emanated from the Stephen Lawrence Inquiry (Macpherson 1999) was the highest-profile policy development to make the organisation more diverse. However, race and recruitment, and diversifying the police, have been a concern for many years, although earlier efforts were sporadic and diffuse and not founded on any formal target.

In the 1950s and 1960s, historical research shows that the MPS actively opposed the recruitment of any 'coloured' officers, maintaining that it was unnecessary to do so. Whitfield's (2004) history of the post-war period brings out the tensions between the Metropolitan Police and black communities, as well as suspicion from across the ranks of the police to recruiting any black officers in the early and mid-1960s because 'coloured men' [as they were described at the time] were deemed unsuitable. One reason is that the migrants at that stage were not generally born in Britain, but there was also a concern that any black officers would be at a 'serious disadvantage' and unable to fulfil the work of policing in a 'predominantly white' society, which suggested the antipathy they could face (see Whitfield 2004: 118). It was 1967 before the first black constable in the post-war period joined the MPS. For many years afterwards, seeking to increase the numbers of black officers was a vexed issue, because voices in the rank and file treated it as a case of 'lowering standards', meaning that special measures were being adopted to admit black and Asian people who had not qualified by having the required educational qualifications or by passing the initial recruitment test, and criticism of their view was dismissed as 'political correctness'. In addition, there was a minimum height requirement that people of South and East Asian origins were once less likely to be able to reach, and changing that was also treated by some police unions as a matter of making changes for political reasons.

Apart from those barriers, various reasons for the relatively small numbers of black and Asian people who became officers were suggested. These included: the hostility felt towards the police by black communities; the difficulties that people who joined faced, in being regarded as 'traitors' in their communities; a limited pool of eligible candidates (HMIC 2001); and continuing racism in the ranks of the police (Holdaway 1996). Indeed, in the past decade those continued to be the main themes in accounts of why black people may opt not to join the police (Waters et al 2007) and in progress towards the BME target (see Ishaq and Hussain 2006, Johnston 2006).

While Scarman (1981) rejected institutional racism (see Chapters Four and Five), he did propose various measures to improve relations between the (overwhelmingly white) police and black communities, particularly in the inner cities, including speeding up the recruitment of black and Asian officers to make the police more representative. Scarman also saw this as a means to improve communication between the police and local communities, and the number of 'minority' officers did rise slowly over the following decade.

The view that having more BME officers will improve relations with communities continues to be heard, particularly in relation to trust and confidence in the police (Home Office 2008, Home Affairs Committee 2009, 2016), because a representative force would 'look more like London', as it was often phrased informally. This representative claim for race categories and counting is a significant driver (though it has wider consequences[14]), as it formed the foundation of the BME target. It comes also from organisations such as the National Black Police Association and the MetBPA, which illustrates that racial projects

(Omi and Winant 2015) come from 'below' and not just 'above'. The appeal call for 'a representative workforce' became a touchstone phrase in the wake of the Macpherson target, but what 'representativeness' is or means – in terms of numbers and categories – is itself subject to contestation.

The BME target did provide a decisive spur to change the composition of the police. Although the Metropolitan Police had had a difficult relationship with the Macpherson inquiry (see Cathcart 1999, Stone 2013), at the highest levels the Commissioner and the MPS Management Board promised to use the report to institute decisive change in the MPS, including in its composition by recruiting more BME officers (see Metropolitan Police 1999). Following that, a regular theme over the decade that followed was how far the organisation had changed, as well as a common suggestion that the police service has done more than any other organisation in terms of equality and diversity policies and practices (Loftus 2008, Hall et al 2009; see also Chapter Six).

Speaking to a number of very senior people in the MPS and the MPA, I heard that the common (though internal and private) view from the outset was that the 25% BME target was thought to be 'clearly unachievable', as one respondent said to me, and a 'total nonsense', according to another. The reason for this, it was argued, is that police officers have a 30-year career structure and could not be made redundant in the way that employees in most other lines of work can. Because of this, over the course of 10 years there simply would not be enough staff turnover to make it possible to alter a quarter of the workforce to the extent that one in four officers would be of BME origins.[15] The setting of an unrealistic target was seen as demonstrating a simple lack of 'police lore' – an understanding of the structure of the police career and turnover in the organisation – by Macpherson, which had then been perpetuated by central government.

From the very beginning, therefore, some senior figures in the MPA and the MPS who were responsible for developing policies to meet the target and to oversee progress, questioned the goal they had been set. While the comments reported here relate to the period from 1999, it is also evident in public and a few years later. In 2005, the chief officer for equality and diversity for the Association of Chief Police Officers (ACPO) said that the BME target was not feasible and would not be met. He suggested that the only way of making significant progress towards the target would be for successive 'all black' intakes at probationer level. Unsurprisingly, the press and media treated this as an example of political correctness and discrimination against white candidates, while black police associations interpreted ACPO's intervention as mischief making by senior officers, who had already decided the target was unachievable.[16]

A worry that the BME target entailed positive discrimination in favour of people of BME origins was also present from the outset. When the target was announced, both the MPS and the MPA received complaints against it from a number of prospective white entrants, and on occasion their parents as well, because they felt that it meant fewer white people would be admitted. In the late 1990s, the Labour government had pledged to significantly increase police numbers; in the case of the MPS this would take it from around 26,000 officers to over 31,000. In preparing for that step change, the MPS had a 'waiting list' of people who had passed the initial tests and were waiting to join; it consisted overwhelmingly of white people. In order to progress BME recruitment and to start addressing the BME target, the MPS and the MPA sought to find ways in which BME people could be moved higher up, or could 'jump the queue', but without opening themselves to a legal challenge. A concern that something like this would happen was what the potential officers were complaining about. A 'finessed' solution to this emerged via a proposition that because there were so many people waiting to join the organisation, the MPS was justified in prioritising the skills most needed; one of those was to prefer candidates who had a second language, something that tended to bring some BME candidates higher up the list.[17]

Even while pursuing measures to increase BME numbers (Metropolitan Police 1999), the MPS was at the same time 'minding its back'. So while it worked to progress BME recruitment, MPS officials stated to the Home Office that the overall target could not be met, because there would not be enough staff turnover, as mentioned earlier. Over time, the MPS added to that, by arguing that the target had been incorrectly set up, as it was based on the BME population of London – of about 25%. However, given the age structure of the BME population, the MPS instead sought to establish that the correct baseline should be the economically active BME population available for employment, which was a significantly lower figure or proportion.

The exasperation of senior MPS officials was clear when they told me that they believed that Home Office officials agreed on this point, only to find no change in the annual monitoring report, which continued to measure MPS progress against the 25% target. So, far from 'joined up' or expert government, this seems like a complete disconnect about a 'technical' number. Whether the Home Office accepted the argument or not I cannot say, although it is clear that the MPS believed it had established its case. In my view, a reason for the disconnection could be that having issued the target in 1999/2000, for the Home Office to then revise it would have required an explanation to, and approval by, ministers. This likely would have become a public and media battle that would require a somewhat dry explanation of why they had it 'wrong' in the first place. Years later, however, it is notable that the Home Affairs Committee's (2016) numbers are benchmarked in the way the MPS had argued for in the early 2000s. Nationally, the Committee set the 2% of BME officers in 1999 within a 6.5% BME population and 9.5% of the UK workforce; the equivalents in 2015 being 5.5% of BME officers against 14% of the population, and 11.4% of the workforce. Yet in London it reported the headline figures as BME police officer representation at 12.4%, compared to 40.2% of the population in the city.

As well as contesting the numbers and their achievability, the MPS also questioned the extent to which race was still a key issue in London. It suggested to the Home Office that the race base of the BME target was narrow and out of date, because the demographic make-up of London was changing so rapidly. The arrival of newer migrant communities, partly white ones in the wake of new accession countries joining the European Union, led to a significant change in the population. Vertovec (2007) saw this as marking a far-reaching shift beyond the politics of race that had defined debates about ethnicity and difference in Britain and in London for the previous five decades.

The 'bottom up' way this claim emerged within policing is an interesting insight into the practical world of policing. A senior MPS official told me that the demand being heard in New Scotland Yard (the headquarters of the MPS) from the boroughs was for more people with skills in the languages and cultures of people from Poland and Eastern Europe. This pressure reflected, in their view, the reality of the challenges around diversity and difference that operational police officers were actually facing, which were no longer dominated by race, but rather by linguistic as well as cultural diversity of a 'non-racial' kind. While no one in the MPS or the MPA ever used the term 'superdiversity' to me, to all intents and purposes they were employing the idea in the early to middle part of the 2000s.

The shift from race to diversity was perceived as a loss of the hard-won gains made by black organisations and campaigns through – as well as before and after – the Macpherson inquiry. While diversity became an increasingly commonplace term, for some that reflected a policy of detracting or moving away from race (meaning what were sometimes called 'visible minorities'). The MetBPA saw it as part of what they had long feared and warned about: a convenient means for the MPS to back away from race equality. This persistent concern is evident in various reports (Morris 2004, Home Office 2008, Home Affairs Committee 2009, Race and Faith Inquiry 2010), as well as in Hall et al (2009).

For campaigning and pressure groups who took race to be central, the feeling was that of a steady slippage away from that towards an equalities agenda encompassing gender, sexualities, age and religion – as became the case in the Equality Act 2010. This is the underlying reason for accusations of bad faith by government and institutions such as the Metropolitan Police, where diversity talk is seen as a betrayal of race by some campaigners (see also Stone 2013). But, as with so much else around race and the BME target, it is a very uneven process: for many years after Macpherson, both the MPS and the MPA publicly maintained a policy focus on 'race and diversity', which highlighted the distinctive status of race, as well as indicating its primacy by placing it first. As shorthand, race retains a significance that diversity does not, as in the 2009 *Daily Mail* headline discussed earlier. Yet, in retrospect, the Race Relations (Amendment) Act 2000 passed by the Labour government was a high water mark of race politics under Labour. In spite of the significance of that legislation and of Macpherson, it can reasonably be claimed that the MPS's move from race to diversity had started from the very year that Macpherson was published in 1999 (see Chapter Five).

Although most of this chapter points to the declining significance of race, it is important to emphasise the dynamic and recursive nature of race politics, and that race, like institutional racism, continues to matter, albeit in a different register to the past decade. Consequently, this means that the BME target, which flows on and off the political and policy agendas, defies any linear narrative; and race and employment pop up again, as in the Prime Minister's comments in 2016.[18] Some earlier and other public events and reports since Macpherson also make this unevenness evident:

- An MPS internal review occurred in the wake of a 2003 BBC undercover documentary titled 'The secret policeman',[19] which showed stark racism among probationary officers. That review restated the need for anti-racist policies, including the progression of BME officers already in the ranks.
- The fallout from various employment tribunals and cases of racism in the MPS led the MPA to commission an inquiry into employment

practices in the MPS (Morris 2004),[20] which observed that racism in the ranks was a factor that could impact on BME recruitment figures.

While both of these reports were wider than the BME target, the likely failure of the MPS to achieve the target and broader issues – of race, racial discrimination and the retention and progression of BME officers in the organisation – were raised at various points and places throughout the decade (for instance, CRE 2004, Home Affairs Committee 2008, 2009).

Two later reports reinforce the argument about the patchiness of the politics of race and the BME target. In 2008, the UK policing minister published a review of progress made on recruitment and progression nationally (Home Office 2008). To a significant extent, that review was prompted by complaints from the MetBPA about the slow rate of progress, especially in terms of the promotion of BME officers in the senior ranks of the Metropolitan Police. The MetBPA's threatened boycott of MPS recruitment efforts contributed to an inquiry by the MPA into Race and Faith issues (as discussed in Chapter Six), which reported in 2010 (Race and Faith Inquiry 2010). One recommendation from that inquiry was that the government should consider 'direct entry' into the higher ranks of the police (rather than all officers starting at the 'ground floor', as is the current practice), as this would speed up diversity in the higher echelons.

Yet, by 2015–16 the Home Affairs Committee (2016) and the Home Secretary/Prime Minister (as outlined at the start of this chapter) were still calling for more to be done to achieve a representative workforce, with race being a major element in that.

While the policing minister's report and the MetBPA's boycott were clearly about race, the title of the MPA Race and Faith Inquiry (2010) is significant for raising faith to an almost equal status. Like other developments in that decade, around hate crime and hate speech for example, and debates about increasing sanctions against the incitement of religious hatred, this reflects the shifting and dynamic nature of politics around race/ethnicity, racism and anti-discrimination measures. The term 'institutional racialization' as outlined by Rattansi (2005) aims to capture this process of multiple and uneven shifts around race.

In terms of the make-up of the police, issues of faith/religion can also be linked to the fact that, at the time, the three most senior BME officers in the MPS were of Muslim origins. Each of them had been involved in public conflict with the organisation (one of these is covered in Chapter Six), in which accusations of racism were paramount (see Dizaei 2007). While the MPA's final report does not say much on faith per se, and focused mostly on race, the conjoining of race and faith signals a changing climate, in which BME issues became as much about religion as race. After the 2005 London Underground bombings, there was a prolonged debate about whether Muslims were being disproportionately targeted by police stop-and-search practices, as well as calls for the 'faith monitoring' of police stops. Significantly, this parallels the 'race monitoring' of such stops developed in the wake of Macpherson. The connection between race and faith suggests how they could be linked in policy terms, as well as conceptually through racialisation, as seen in Chapter Two (see also Meer 2013). While faith has a different historical context to race in the UK, this call underscored the extent to which both categorisation and enumeration are the dominant means of assessing issues of over-representation and under-representation.

The paradoxes of the BME target

Viewed retrospectively, it seems obvious that the BME target was always going to fail, because the 25% London target could not be achieved, even though the 7% national target may have been possible. Whether this is a failure of governing by targets, or is due to gaming, or is caused by institutional racism and resistance to change is a matter of debate and degree.

For the black police associations and anti-racist campaigners, the target was a matter that required constant reminders to senior managers who wanted to 'move on' from race. For MPS senior managers, the target was a 'non-starter' and a problem created for them by the Home Office acting peremptorily. Those managers questioned both the numerical and categorical basis of the target, although it was not formally removed until 2009. For the MPA, the BME target was not, narrowly, the main concern; rather it sought to diversify the make-up of the MPS in terms of race, gender and other dimensions of equality, while keeping 'race and diversity' as a term to be used in reports to the authority.

Hence the politics of the BME target came into focus in quite different ways. For senior MPS figures, it came to the surface when they were pressed on it in public, but otherwise it was another number among the many targets they faced. But in a large bureaucracy the rising and falling prominence of the target and ongoing processes to address it are variably connected. So while the target could disappear from view from time to time, there were ongoing action plans, policies and regular recruitment efforts aimed at the target. This suggests that it can be seen as being implemented and changed/ignored almost simultaneously.

Yet another paradoxical feature of the BME target is that while the overall target was a key number for the MetBPA, it was also, for them, negotiable in some ways. So at times they argued that the progression and seniority of BME officers was just as important as recruitment, and that the treatment of serving officers mattered as much as those seeking to join (Bowling et al 2005, Home Office 2008, Race and Faith Inquiry 2010).

This account seeks to sketch the shifting politics of the call for a representative workforce as a matter never ever fully 'on' or 'off' the agenda, but, rather, moving in and out of focus due to events and campaigns. The appearance and disappearance of race and the BME target is a tale of myriad political manoeuvrings moving them 'off stage' or keeping them 'on stage'. Race and racism can re-emerge and become public issues for the police, as evidenced by the return of debates that seem 'settled' – around targets, policy, diversity and institutional racism, for instance. The finding that public sector organisations manoeuvre around targets is well known. Here I have sought to demonstrate gaps between what an organisation says it is committed to in public, while it negotiates around both the enumerative and categorical aspects of the BME target. These movements reveal some discordance between levels of government and within a single organisation, making the target simultaneously negotiable/contested and fixed/unchanging.

A wider social science question is the capacity of various frameworks to capture the paradoxical quality identified: of how a target can be simultaneously 'present' and 'absent', implemented and changeable. This is more than 'game playing' (Bevan and Hood 2006), or governing through numbers and at a distance (Miller and Rose 2008). Rather, enumeration and categorisation in the BME target produce some kind of partial, contradictory and spasmodic congruence (Allen and Cochrane 2007, 2010), in which flux and stasis co-exist. The regime of numbers that constituted the BME target and the race categories it rested on are sustained, despite both being built on seemingly shaky sands.

Notes

[1]   This is a revised and updated version of an article that was published as: K. Murji (2014) 'A representative workforce: The BME police recruitment target and the politics of enumeration and categorisation', *International Journal of Sociology and Social Policy*, vol 34, no 9/10, pp 578-92.

[2]   This newspaper story displays some of the data underlying the speech: www. independent.co.uk/news/uk/politics/the-four-charts-that-expose-the-incredible-lack-of-diversity-in-britains-police-force-a6704161.html

[3]   BBC News (2015) 'Theresa May condemns lack of black police officers', www. bbc.co.uk/news/uk-34600290

[4]   See: http://www.policeoracle.com/news/'No-need-for-positive-discrimination'-in-police-recruitment,-government-says_92528.html. Another aspect is that the rate of progress means that the police in London would not be representative in these terms until 2050 at least. See: https://www.theguardian.com/uk-news/2016/jun/14/race-failures-damaging--police-says-top-met-officer

[5]   See: www.independent.co.uk/news/uk/politics/theresa-may-racial-inequality-racism-public-services-difficult-truths-jeremy-corbyn-hate-crime-a7212186.html

[6]   In a response that echoes some of the responses to Macpherson discussed in Chapter Four, *The Times* (29 August 2016) declared that the 'notion that Britain is intrinsically prejudiced and discriminatory is grossly unfounded' and that the Prime Minister had fallen for the 'left's warped view of British society'.

[7]   For an indication, see Cohen (2003) as well as 'Many forces at work in crisis at the Met', www.guardian.co.uk/politics/2008/sep/14/police.race?INTCMP=SRCH

[8]   From 2000 to January 2012, the MPA was the police authority for London, the body responsible for governance of the MPS, when it was replaced by the Mayor's Office for Policing and Crime.

[9]   I am referring here to a period in 2012. In order to keep it manageable, I generally refer to the various organisations as if they are singular or homogenous. Of course, they are actually a coalition of different voices and views.

[10] While it is possible that some of the people I spoke with could be identified through assiduous searching, they were aware of that because they occupied prominent public roles. While all of them have moved on from those positions, I believe that the correct ethical stance is to maintain the terms of the agreement made at the time we spoke.

[11] Kelman (2006), for instance, provides an insider view of policy formulation within the Prime Minister's Delivery Unit.

[12] In addition, there is BAME (Black, Asian and Minority Ethnic), which reflects the emergence of the view that some or many Asians do not regard themselves as Black (Modood 1994). Reflecting recent migrations, BAMER is evident sometimes (where the R stands for Refugees).

[13] This can be seen in arguments around migration numbers in the UK. 'Disproportionality' in the form of over-representation of black people in police stop-and-search practices is the more common political number in race and policing debates. A reversal of this can be seen in the headline and story that most UK police forces have a disproportional number of white officers. See: https://www.theguardian.com/uk-news/2016/jan/01/most-uk-police-forces-have-disproportionate-number-of-white-officers

[14] For an example, see: www.guardian.co.uk/uk/2003/oct/13/race.ukcrime?INTCMP=SRCH

[15] Brown et al (2006) estimated it would take at least 20 years.

[16] For an indication of this debate, see: www.guardian.co.uk/uk/2006/mar/31/race.ukcrime

[17] For another aspect of this debate, see: www.guardian.co.uk/uk/2004/apr/17/race.world?INTCMP=SRCH

[18] See: www.independent.co.uk/news/uk/politics/theresa-may-racial-inequality-racism-public-services-difficult-truths-jeremy-corbyn-hate-crime-a7212186.html

[19] See: http://news.bbc.co.uk/1/hi/magazine/3210614.stm

[20] More than a decade on, this continues to be an issue for the MPS, most recently (in 2016) through an Equalities and Human Rights Commission investigation into discrimination complaints by MPS staff. See: https://www.equalityhumanrights.com/en/publication-download/section-20-investigation-metropolitan-police-service

EIGHT

Framing riots

As this book has examined the links between race, racism, policy and policing – and academic scholarship on those – it has raised issues and questions about change and sameness in them as interconnected fields of study. A degree of 'stop–start' and circularity in academic research and writing is evident concerning what race is, on institutional racism, and in policy. The underlying argument is not that the past is simply being repeated, not least because, as mentioned in the Introduction to this book, contexts change and there is a drastically altered environment for academic work – including engagement and impact. This means that there are some recognisable elements of continuity with the 1980s, as well as some discontinuities.

This final chapter confirms that, by bringing the argument full circle through an examination of a topic that was prominent then and in recent times – riots, protests and violent disorder. It focuses on scholarly commentary and research on riots that occurred in August 2011 in England. As incidents of violent disorder occurring in urban settings, they were commonly linked to recent historical and contemporary concerns about policing operations, in which race occupies a significant place, particularly through the over-policing of black people. This association serves to make the 2011 riots seem familiar and explainable in relation to events in the 1980s. It can be observed in a range of sources, although there are differences of emphasis between them in how strongly (or not) the 1980s is invoked as a comparative frame (Riots Communities and Victims Panel 2012, Home Affairs Committee 2011, Solomos 2011, Smith 2013, Newburn et al 2016). Taking the cause of the 2011 riots as primarily connected to race and policing flowed from tracing them in a particular line back to disorders at the 1976 Notting Hill Carnival, and then in various inner cities, most notably Brixton in 1981 (Scarman 1981) and in Brixton and Broadwater Farm in 1985 (Gifford 1986). The race connection was reinforced through discussions of the 1980s riots as British developments akin to the 1960s US civil rights protests and demonstrations (Benyon and Solomos 1987, Peplow 2015).

As in 2011, the most direct moment that led to the riots in 1985 resulted from police encounters with black people, one of which resulted in a fatality. Referring to these as 'trigger' events (as in the

Home Affairs Committee 2011, for instance) is hardly appropriate in circumstances such as the death in a 'hard stop' of Mark Duggan, a young man of mixed-race origins in Tottenham in August 2011. The Metropolitan Police officers who shot him gave as the reason for the stop that Duggan had a gun. While an illegal firearm was found, it was at some distance from the car he was in. The shooting sparked local community anger, and a protest was held at the local police station. This later tipped over into widespread disorder and some looting in the area. Violence and disorder continued into the next day and spread into riots, including looting, across various parts of north, east, south and west London. Riots of varying scale and intensity also occurred in other cities, such as Birmingham, Bristol, Liverpool and Nottingham, on the following days (Lewis et al 2011, Morell et al 2011, Riots Communities and Victims Panel 2012). As this potted account signals, it is a misnomer to refer to these as 'UK riots', since they occurred only in England. This point about elisions of a part for the whole is also made because it reflects another tendency that can at times be seen in scholarship, such as in the foundation of British policing studies itself (Murji 2009).

In this vein, rioting connected to race can be seen as an episodic but familiar part of the British landscape that made it an archetypal form of protest or mobilisation, associated with racism, exclusion and over-policing (Keith 1993, Rowe 1998). Yet while the 2011 riots seem to speak to this history of race relations (Smith 2013), this is not as self-evident as it appears; moreover, there are other scholarly viewpoints of the 2011 events in which race can be erased altogether.

This chapter provides a heuristic framework of ways in which the riots were read. It is the ways of making sense of riots that are at issue, not a competition about claiming to present what 'really' happened. I do not attempt to 'read the riots', but rather to use them as a way into examining some tendencies and partialities in scholarly work, some of which I discuss in this chapter. (On reading riots generally, see also Benyon and Solomos 1987, Gooding-Williams 1993, Lewis et al 2011). I analyse here some different and critical 'ways of seeing' or framing, interpreting, capturing and explaining riots. The argument is that these frames lend weight to particular ways of thinking about riots, while obscuring others (Keith 1987). They provide a 'preferred narrative' of events that draws attention to some things, yet often this is done in a generalised way that does not hint at the limits of the explanation. This is about more than language and terminology; it suggests processes of 'sense making' that are – or may be – consequential in recognising the formation of social science thinking on events such as riots.

Three broad explanatory frames of the 2011 riots are outlined. These are:

1. seeing the riots as primarily an issue of racism, and policing;
2. seeing them as an expression of nihilistic 'post-politics'; or
3. seeing them as events in response to the politics of neoliberalism.

The first draws on and stresses continuity about race and policing matters across time and space; the second 'deracinates' riots, by treating them as primarily about consumerism; while the third 'politicises' them as inchoate though essentially political action. The frames are not intended as sealed or discrete categories; nor am I claiming that these are the only ways that the 2011 riots have been, or can be, understood.[1] Nor is it my aim to make a case for a typology or an overarching frame to capture other frames.

To underline that the frames are not wholly distinct, I start with an example of one text that could fall into all three of them – Alain Badiou's (2012) commentary on riots and other protests, including 'the Arab spring'. Generally, Badiou, like Harvey (2012), sees these as: 'the first stirrings of a global popular uprising ... [that] resembles the first working-class insurrections of the nineteenth century' (Badiou 2012: 5). In linking all of these events as the 'time of riots' that signifies a rebirth of history, his view could be placed in the third (politicising) frame. But the account can also be located elsewhere, when Badiou goes on to say that the often-forgotten 'real crime [is] the person (often persons) killed by the police ... The spark that "lights a prairie fire" is always a state murder' (Badiou 2012: 17). To the extent that 'real crime' is associated with victims who are impoverished and young, often living in the *banlieues* and ghettoes (see also Jobard 2009, Fassin 2013), this indicates an element of race and racism that would place this analysis closer to the first frame that treats racist policing as a core concern. Yet, further on in the same text, Badiou discusses riots as: 'dominated by negation and destruction [which] does not make it possible clearly to distinguish between ... universalizable intention and what [is] rage with no purpose other than [to] find objects to destroy or consume' (Badiou 2012: 25). So this shares common ground with the second (post-political) frame.

Clover (2016) does something similar in reading events across time periods and continents, as well as in terms of political struggles, thereby straddling the first and third frames. In flagging this overlap between the frames, my point is to reinforce that I am more interested in setting them out in this way to explore how critical accounts are set up, and some consequences of what they overlook or neglect. While my argument is also about and against over-generalised explanations of messy and distributed events such as riots, the focus on scholarly work is further intended to provide a critique of the ways in which race and riots are drawn on, even 'shoehorned' to fit a preferred framework. In making that point, I draw on Paul Rock's (1981) observation of commentaries on the 1980s riots that:

> Interpretative schemes are generally orderly themselves and are designed to impose order on what they describe. In the main, those who analyse riots would claim that they have an authority to do so. They are reluctant to retreat uncomprehendingly, stating that they are baffled or that the riots are fundamentally absurd. Riots may be messy and fluid, but commentaries tend to unearth a simple pattern underlying their surface. The bulk of social scientists and political writers would actually claim that it is their special competence to identify structures which are invisible to the layman. (Rock 1981: 3)

Riots which cover a wildly different range of dispersed events, in which the agency, identity and motives of actors, as well as their causes, are disputed, provide a means to assess the value and limits of critical accounts. The analysis here draws mainly on scholarly accounts of the riots, ranging from conventional academic publications to reports, blog posts and social media. In Hammersley's (2014) terms, these accounts are explanations, and go beyond description, because they infer or claim to know the causes of rioting.[2]

Frames and framing are commonly applied in media studies (Fairhurst and Sarr 1996), and are utilised in an analogous way by Butler (2009), to suggest how a frame is a device to identify what is being brought to attention, or into the centre of the analysis or explanation. It is this sense of framing I am relying on here, but for the purpose of drawing attention to partialities in scholarly analysis. My argument is that instead of challenging 'mainstream' views, such analyses repeat well-established tropes and perspectives that riots provide a pretext or a headline for.

The significance of the choice of words, images and contexts in analysis is not merely incidental, but actively promotes certain kinds of reading, a 'preferred reading' as Hall (1980) called it. Alternatively, what Hall, in the context of media studies, called an 'oppositional reading' might disturb the intended meaning and seek to disrupt conventional or established readings. A simple example of this from the recent history of riots in the UK is when some writers and activists in the 1980s stressed that riots should only be called 'uprisings', because this word is seen as taking the events out of the realm of law-and-order politics and instead lays stress upon them as intrinsically and primarily political events rather than criminal ones. Indeed, one book of the time by left-leaning but mainstream journalists is even called *Uprising!* (Kettle and Hodges 1982). Seeking to re-define rioting in this way also occurred in the 2011 riots when, during an interview on BBC News, the black activist Darcus Howe said, "I don't see them as riots, I see them as insurrections" (cited in Kelley and Tuck, 2015: 1); this is a term that Badiou (2012) also uses.

However, as the role of 'primary definers' (Hall et al 1978) has changed, what is and what is not a preferred/oppositional reading is not clear-cut. There is not one kind of oppositional reading but several kinds. As each of the three frames are forms of that, there can be multiple, incongruent and contradictory oppositional readings; they can also be quite conventional rather than critical. Arguing for events to be called 'uprisings', or even insurrections, is made in opposition to their labelling as riots, but it is also an alternative preferred reading.

My approach, as reflected in Chapter Three, is not against scholarly engagement, commentary and framing as such. Rather, in drawing attention to partialities and problems, I hope for more measured, but also more critical, commentary and analysis on riots, and on issues beyond that. This is in contrast to those such as Hammersley (2014), who think that the role of social science should not primarily be about its immediate relevance to public debate and policy.

The race and policing frame

The most common and easily recognised trope employed in understating the 2011 riots is by reading and comparing them in relation to other times and places. This comparative approach is one way that connecting occurs – and what most of this section focuses on – though I will outline later that the use of contrast rather than comparison is deployed to paint a quite different picture of the riots.

Connecting by comparison is usually done in a critical sense to suggest continuity between past and present, or between different places – usually ones with clear and recent histories of conflict between the police and black communities. The connections made between the events of 2011 across time and space to other events and places are illustrative of how racial connections are imagined and made, by either implying or asserting a connection between them. In that vein, similar kinds of underlying causes are invoked, and most often racism and/or racially discriminatory policing are at the core of this approach. In titles such as 'Policing the riots: From Bristol and Brixton to Tottenham, via Toxteth, Handsworth etc' (Jefferson 2011) and 'From Tottenham to Baltimore …' (Tyler and Lloyd 2015), the core of this approach is observable. These titles display the 'from X to Y' style of connection being made, temporally as well as in spatial terms, between the 2011 riots and other places and other times. In both of these, and whether within Britain or across the Atlantic, the usual and common link is race, or rather racism, and policing and social justice (see also Kelley and Tuck 2015). Jefferson connects 2011 events to a time – the period of the 1980s riots – and to places with significant black or African-Caribbean populations, some of which were designated as 'symbolic locations' for policing in the 1980s, where police–community conflict had become entrenched and routine (Keith 1993). Tyler and Lloyd make a more contemporaneous but transatlantic connection between racially unjust policing in England and in the US, which, for Kelley and Tuck (2015), forms 'the other special relationship' linking the two nations.

The strength of this frame is that it centres an understanding of the 2011 riots as events that are deeply rooted in the antagonistic relationship of race and policing in urban locations, although there are differing criminological understandings of what underlies that (see Chapter Seven). The 'spark' that can light a fire (Badiou 2012) and move rapidly from low-level to violent disorder is embedded in the everyday encounters between the police and black people that, in spite of multiple changes to police procedure and policy in the decades from the 1980s, remain a key source of tension and an aggravating feature of everyday interactions (see Fassin 2013, Camp and Heatherton 2016). Extensive empirical evidence of persistent complaints about police harassment, in tactics such as stop and search (or stop and frisk in the US), underscores that link (Bowling et al 2005, Reiner 2010, Lewis et al 2011). Statistical disproportionality – the greater likelihood that black people, especially young males, will be stopped by the police – plays a key part in this argument about 'endless pressure', where black people, often young ones, are simultaneously over-policed as 'criminals' but under-protected as victims (McGhee 2005) with regard to gun and knife crime, particularly in large cities such as London.

While Jefferson (2011) and Tyler and Lloyd (2015) demonstrate the 'X to Y' style of connecting places and times, a significant factor in 2011 is more the link from 'X to X', 'from Tottenham 1985 to Tottenham 2011', as it were. Looking at this further is revealing for the ways in which claims in this frame are made, as well as for what is obscured or overlooked. The 2011 disturbances began in Tottenham and were commonly linked by commentators and other analysts (see Murji and Neal 2011, Solomos 2011) to, and read in light of, violent disorders in the same general area, at Broadwater Farm in 1985 (Gifford 1986, Keith 1993). The shared location of these two events, even spread over 36 years, speaks powerfully to a sense of ongoing racial subjugation and to unresolved problems between police and black people. Both events, in 2011 and in 1985, are connected to the deaths of black people in contact with the police, itself a matter of concern over more than five decades (Athwal and Bourne 2015). In this light, the riot in Tottenham in 2011 was not 'meaningless' violence, but haunted by the events of 1985. Tottenham was referred to as a place with a history of riot, one made more charged because the 1985 riot involved the death of a police officer, PC Keith Blakelock (Murji and Neal 2011). In discussing with me her verbatim play *The Riots* (Slovo 2011), the writer Gillian Slovo noted the extent to which the police officers she interviewed were still troubled by that event.

However, while no explanation or single frame can cover everything, the partialities, reach and applicability of the race and policing frame ought to be a moment to pause before asserting linkages with any far-reaching confidence. For all its apparent obviousness, the connection between the events is not as plain as it seems. Looking to continuities rather than change means that demographic shifts can be overlooked. The racial and ethnic composition of inner cities areas like Tottenham has altered towards what Vertovec (2007) called superdiversity, with newer and different migrant communities. This made both the rioters and some of the victims, such as local shopkeepers who used self-defence campaigns to protect their property, utterly multicultural and heterogeneous. Moreover, even the 'same' location – Tottenham in north London – is not quite the same in 2011 as it was in 1985, when rioting centred on the Broadwater Farm estate; in 2011 it was more dispersed and included looting at a shopping centre that did not exist in 1985.

Moreover, there are other, and neglected, ways of understanding race and policing connections that are arguably more powerful and far reaching. There is a stronger narrative case for thinking of Tottenham 2011 in relation to the disorders in Brixton in 1985. The protests that followed the Duggan shooting eerily echoed the events surrounding the police shooting of a black woman, Mrs Cherry Groce, in Brixton in 1985, in a raid at her home where the police were targeting her son. That also led to a protest around the local police station and, eventually, to disorder. Linking those events to a common starting point, a shooting by the police, thus provides a base from which to assert that the start of the 2011 riot is, arguably, less about everyday policing and stop and search and more to do with rarer, but highly consequential practices such as police use of firearms.

Furthermore, the two events can be connected further in a manner that is not commonly evident in scholarly work on the 2011 riots.[3] Following the shooting of Mark Duggan, there was an onus on the police to communicate with and support his family. As the Home Affairs Committee (2011: 7) concluded: 'it is essential that the force concerned communicates swiftly with the victim's family. There is no excuse for confusion about whose role this should be: a family liaison officer should be dispatched immediately by the force in question.' The shortcomings or failures of the Metropolitan Police to implement their family liaison procedures in the immediate aftermath of the shooting contributed directly to the mood of the organised protest at Tottenham police station on 6 August 2011. Poor (or zero) communication with the family of Mrs Groce was undoubtedly a factor in Brixton in 1985.

Yet by 2011, this is hardly something the police can claim to be surprised by since, in between those dates, the most high-profile issue of race and policing was their inadequate service to Stephen Lawrence's family after he was stabbed in 1993. After Macpherson (1999), family liaison techniques became a policy focus for improvement. I saw and took part in this myself via the Metropolitan Police Service critical incident management training course that Griffiths (2009) provides an insight into, and in which John Grieve (see Chapter Five) was an active participant. Alongside that, there was sustained training on community relations, stop and search (Foster et al 2005, Rowe 2007, Hall et al 2009), as well as initiatives on race and recruitment (see Chapter Seven). Despite all of that, what appeared to be weak or ineffectual family liaison and poor critical incident management in 2011 speaks to a sense of policy and institutional failure. This perspective still locates the core issue as rooted in race and policing, yet it puts the police centre stage in a notably different way to the connections outlined above. The different analysis it suggests shows that another kind of framing leads to quite different notions of policy and politics after riots.

This discussion of the race and policing frame indicates how comparison or continuity is the most significant aspect, but the comparisons that are *not* made are also significant. The 2011 riots were not, or were only rarely, linked to the 2001 riots in Bradford and Burnley – northern English towns with South Asian descended populations (Cantle 2001) – nor to 'white' riots in places such as the

Blackbird Leys estate in Oxford in 1991. Drawing attention to these absences and different geographies shows how the racial underpinnings of the 2011 riots are imagined in relation to the disorders of the 1980s.

The use of contrast rather than comparison also puts the 2011 riots in a different light. One instance of this is how the 2011 events were regarded as the first riots of the social media age, or as so-called 'Twitter riots' (Morell et al 2011), as the use of instant messaging services and Twitter were presented as instrumental in coordinating and transmitting information about riots. While this is clearly not something that could have been said of events in the 1980s, it is not as distinct as it first seems. Both in the 1980s and in 2011 the spread of rioting was seen as a kind of copycat effect due to the media coverage of events, social media, or just word of mouth. A second kind of contrast is about the perceived legitimacy of violent disorder as an expression of political disaffection. In this light, the 2011 riots are contrasted unfavourably with earlier or other events, such as the 1960s Civil Rights demonstrations in the US or protests against austerity. Treating the latter as legitimate protests enables some writers to dismiss the 2011 events in the UK as lacking any substantial or meaningful cause; this is the nub of the post-political and deracialising frame.

The post-political frame

While the previous frame looks to the antagonisms between racial minorities and the police over decades, the plainest flipside to that has been a 'knee jerk' defence of the police, along with calls for more law and order in the form of public order policing and tough punishment. In this way, any political motivation or underlying social or economic cause is denied or deemed illegitimate. Such refrains around the 2011 riots are easy to find and widely cited in critical commentaries. For instance, 'pure thuggery' is how the Home Secretary, Theresa May, described them; 'It is criminality pure and simple and it has to be confronted and defeated', said the Prime Minister, David Cameron (cited in Badiou 2012: 17), while the Mayor of London, Boris Johnson, added: "It's time we stopped hearing all this (you know) nonsense about how there are deep sociological justifications for wanton criminality and destruction of people's property" (cited in Hammersley 2014: 123, n 10). Indeed, the hostile mainstream media and political reaction to the onset of the 2011 riots did feed through into swift and tough penalties for some of those caught (Lewis et al 2011, Clover 2016).

Although the law and order reflex is a well-worn trope (see, for example, Hall et al 1979, Benyon and Solomos 1987), it is not as simple and narrow as it seems. Despite Mayor Johnson's oft-quoted remark he went on from dismissing 'deep sociological justifications' to later suggest that: 'We need to know what is going on in these people's lives and why they can feel such a sense of exclusion' (cited in Hammersley 2014: 128). While these comments do not excuse rioting they do include a sense that there could be real grievances and social exclusion behind it. In a similar vein, while both the Prime Minister and the Leader of the Opposition condemned violence, they also hinted that there were complex causes behind the riots, reflecting that the law and order reaction can change over time and is not only on one plane (Hammersley 2014). This is also evident in the response of Iain Duncan Smith, at the time the Secretary of State with responsibility for social welfare and a politician commonly regarded as being on the right wing of the Conservative Party, who wrote that:

> While we have to be tough on the perpetrators and on the gangs, we also have to ask ourselves what lies behind this. We cannot simply arrest our way out of these riots ... The riots have provided a moment of clarity for all of us, a reminder that a strong economy requires a strong social settlement, with stable families ready to play a productive role in their own communities. The challenge of our generation is to reforge our commitment to reform society so that we can restore aspiration and hope to communities that have been left behind.[4]

The 'strong and stable families' refrain is far from being a non-punitive approach and has to be viewed within the austerity policies of the 2010–15 UK government (Tyler 2013). Nonetheless it is not the same as 'law and order' demands as seen in previous decades. While the denial of any political intention behind rioting is commonly linked to right-wing, authoritarian and enforcement/police-led perspectives, the supposedly more social democratic or liberal response is usually associated with calls for amelioration and stressing 'repair' rather than punishment, through social rather than criminal justice policy. Yet, as the comments from Duncan Smith, and the change in tone from Johnson, indicate, there is not quite such an easy dividing line between left and right.

Indeed, there was also some crossover between authoritarian and liberal elements in the 1980s. For all the criticism of the Scarman report (see, for example, Barker and Beezer 1983), it did try to combine some social policy with police reform through recommendations for better community facilities and police–community consultation. Yet it also paved the way for a decade of increased public order 'tooling up' by the police in preparation for more violent disorder (Keith 1993). Thus, in Hall's (1982) incisive reading of the Scarman report, it did not conform to a simple liberal/reactionary divide.

In terms of politics, scholarly or academic responses to the 2011 riots take divergent forms, even if they agree on the context. While the politics of the 1980s was dominated by monetarism, by the 21st century the master category is neoliberalism. Combined with the banking and financial crises from 2008, both Harvey (2012) and Badiou (2012) see riots and protests globally in that context. This outlook produces two almost diametrically opposite points of view. On the one hand, riots are a kind of political revolt against the structural inequalities sharpened by neoliberalism (this is covered in the next section). On the other hand, rioting is seen as a futile, politically vacuous response to social and economic inequalities, where it does not signify political consciousness or intent but rather the absence of politics – an apolitical or 'post-political' condition where alterative and progressive political movements are deemed invalid in an era of neo-liberal domination. In this light, the 2011 riots are framed as an expression of impotent rage by failed consumers who have no aim other than acquisition of material goods.

Remarkably, matters of race and racism are accorded little significance in this, and race and policing – crucial to the first frame and a factor in the third frame – almost disappears from the picture. Instead of racially based or racialised explanations, this frame produces a largely deracinated view of 2011. The consumerist 'shopping for free' perspective was typified by Bauman's (2011) widely quoted remarks about the events: 'These are not hunger or bread riots. These are riots of defective and disqualified consumers.' Responding to and building on this, Žižek[5] (2011) commented that more than anything else the riots were:

> A manifestation of a consumerist desire violently enacted when unable to realise itself in the 'proper' way – by shopping. As such, they also contain a moment of genuine protest, in the form of an ironic response to consumerist ideology: 'You call on us to consume while simultaneously depriving us of the means to do it properly – so here we are doing it the only way we can!' … the problem with the riots is not the violence as such, but the fact that the

> violence is not truly self-assertive. It is impotent rage and
> despair masked as a display of force.

The refusal to see any political intent in violent disorder is not just the preserve of social theorists, media commentators or government. The Parliamentary Home Affairs Committee (2011: 31) observed that while there could have 'been an element of disengagement' among some of those involved in the riots, nonetheless, 'unlike some events in the past, including the riots in the 1980s, there does not seem to be any clear narrative, nor a clear element of protest or clear political objectives'. This does rather beg the questions of what 'clear' means in relation to the 2011 events, which is widely understood as stemming from a black death in contact with the police, and so clearly provides some linkage from 1985 to 2011. The spread of disorder to many other places may lack the 'clear narrative' that the Committee refers to[6], but to wilfully fail to recognise race as a starting point seems to be a determined attempt to read the events in a non-political or post-political light.[7]

The most developed exposition of the post-political perspective on the 2011 riots comes from Treadwell et al (2013) and Winlow et al (2015). Taking their cue from the view that the dominance of neoliberal and managerial logics has undermined left-wing political alternatives and displaced the role of the state as a force capable of producing social change, their analysis follows Žižek in seeing rioters as post-political subjects incapable of collective action and driven by individualism and consumerism, or the 'shallow pleasures and distractions of consumer culture'. Significantly, Treadwell et al (2013) do regard previous riots and other forms of protest as political: 'In previous eras, the marginalized subject was able to join and become active in ... political collectives ... [and] able to find collective support ... to articulate [its] rage onto the real socio-economic, ethical and political causes of dissatisfaction'.

However, unlike the impulse behind earlier disorders, which were informed by universalism and class solidarity, the 2011 events are different because: 'in the post-political present, it seems almost impossible for a potential collective of marginalized subjects to construct a universal political narrative that makes causal and contextual sense of their own shared suffering and offers a feasible solution to it' (Treadwell et al 2013: 1–2). This 'pessimistic' view of the potential for political solidarities is founded on a wider rejection of cultural politics and the politics of difference, or 'identity politics', which has undermined working-class cohesion as these authors see it (Winlow et al 2015).

Apart from the glaring neglect of race politics in the riots, this view is symptomatic of a kind of narrative of decline. A sense of nostalgia that things were better in earlier times is one of the forms of cultural pessimism that Bennett (2001) saw as a symptom of postmodern times, in which a nation or culture is regarded as in irreversible decline. By placing this in a historical framework, Bennett makes clear the long histories that such narratives can have. He reads the appeal of, and recourse to, nostalgia as revealing something about a psychic disposition on the part of those proffering them. Appeals to 'political collectivities', 'universalism' and what seems like a time when class politics plain and simple demarcated an 'us' – all chime with that sense of nostalgia, as can also be seen in Harvey (2012).

Moreover, while riots are indeed messy and complex, as Treadwell et al (2013) acknowledge, their refusal to see in them, or at least in parts of them, some elements of solidarity and collective action narrows the domain of politics into a quite traditional sense of the political. New social movements, including surprising and 'globalised' protests such as Occupy[8], generally also fail to pass muster. Indeed, in a further dismissive step, Harvey unfavourably contrasts the 2011 riots as a poor relation to 'real' politics 'elsewhere', as he claims that the London riots bear no relation to 'various glimmers of hope and light around the world' such as the movements in Spain and Greece, and in Latin America. Unlike the 2011 rioters, Harvey maintains that, in other cases, actors can 'see through the vast scam that a predatory and feral global capitalism has unleashed upon the world' (Harvey 2012: 157).

The way in which this frame not only overlooks but also denies the centrality of race – and the relationship of that to policing – is a major problem. This extends across all the views described in this section. The empirical evidence it relies on is also questionable. Newburn et al (2015) challenge the 'shopping for free' viewpoint, in pointing out that looting is a usual – rather than an exceptional – feature of riots. The stress on looting that appears in accounts from Bauman (2011), Žižek (2011), Treadwell et al (2013) and Winlow et al (2015) enables them to identify the events as an instance of a particular kind of disaffected consumer capitalism, where rioters protest merely because they are excluded from objects of consumption and so take what they want for free.

Yet based on their more comprehensive LSE/Guardian study, which interviewed around 270 people in the first phase (Treadwell et al interviewed 30 people involved in the riots by comparison), Newburn et al (2015) show that rioters express a mixture of motives. Reducing that to, or focusing only on, the desire to acquire free goods is to neglect or to miss that range of views, as well as the rioters' sense of dissatisfaction with politics and the police. Drawing on Thompson's (1971) 'moral economy', Newburn et al (2015) also suggest that the targets of looting are not random, and violence can be understood in political terms. This paves the way for the third frame delineated here – resistance to neoliberalism.

The resistance to neoliberalism frame

In direct contrast to the post-politics viewpoint, a third frame or perspective asserts a determinedly political angle to the riots as a revolt against the conditions created by neoliberal austerity policies. As with the previous frames, it includes a range of positions that entail stronger or weaker senses of what politics means but, across the board, there is some measure of consensus that economic conditions, and neoliberalism in particular, have exacerbated inequality as well as racism, and that this is what lies behind the riots. This too has echoes from the 1980s, as when Rock (1981) listed 'unemployment, [and] monetarism' as indicative of the kinds of things that predominantly left-wing or critical commentators attributed the 1981 riots to.

This frame overlaps with the first frame, in making allusions to over-policing and local histories of police–community conflict, but here they are placed in a wider political-economic framework. Indeed, even the 'post-political' argument sees that there are 'real' material and economic factors that underlie rioting. The contrast between the two forms of structuralist approach in the second and third frames (which both reference an economic base or context within which violent disorder occurs) is that in one rioting is seen as misguided or ineffective in recognising or addressing the causes of the rioters' grievances, while in the other rioting is treated as a nascent form of rebellion.

One aspect of this frame can be found in the arts, as for example in Gillian Slovo's (2011) play *The Riots*. This was staged in late 2011 and drew on eyewitness accounts of the events. The author told me she felt it important to include a wide range of views and voices to try and make sense of the events. Nonetheless, the second part of the play, which focuses on lessons to be learnt, does stress the need for political and policy responses to inequality and discrimination, suggesting that these things underlie violent disorder.

Another verbatim play of the 2011 riots, Alecky Blythe's (2013) *Little revolution*, could be cast in the non- or post-political mould because of its satirical approach. Yet at another level, the play is deeply political, because it centres on and, in the main, mocks some of the professional and middle-class people of Hackney, east London, who have added to the gentrification of the area. In *Little revolution* those people rally to support a local shopkeeper, but are unable to respond when faced with concerns about policing and racism when these are raised by campaigners. The play does not present any easy trade-offs between these things, but in putting them side by side, Blythe does highlight the different kinds of 'community' politics – collective/institutional versus individualistic/charitable – that are at stake in one location.

A near-contemporaneous stress on the politics behind the 2011 riots is evident through internet sites such as *Ceasefire* magazine. In September 2011, Adam Elliot-Cooper (2011a) wrote of the riots in terms of 'redefining the political'. Beginning from comments made by rioters about the police as a lawless, 'institutionalised gang' in inner-city areas, Elliot-Cooper regards the police in blunt terms as part of the repressive state apparatus, being 'used by the state to control and repress, not maintain stability and or uphold justice' on behalf of 'a state machine which racialises, impoverishes and dehumanises' black communities. This is not just his own view, as he also draws in the experience of young people:

> affected by the uprising ... [who] offer their own analysis of the political ... Working with large numbers of young people from North London, they have recorded their feelings on unemployment, the cuts to EMA[9] and youth services, police powers, media and political corruption, poverty and racism. (Elliot-Cooper 2011a)

In a following post, he focused on the looting that is so key to the post-political frame. Elliot-Cooper (2011b) shares with that viewpoint, and with Millington (2016), an understanding of looting of particular sport-branded clothes and shoe stores, like JD Sports and Footlocker, as 'hyper-consumerism' in an era of global neoliberalism. However, he differs from it by implicitly drawing on moral economy (Thompson 1971) to treat looting as purposive, as the shops targeted are both purveyors of desirable brands, as well as exemplars of (symbolic) violence towards poor people in deprived areas who find that the goods are well beyond their reach. Similarly, in other social media posts there were suggestions that these shops were targeted because of their exploitative approach in paying minimum wages and refusing to employ local people.

The stress on poverty, inequality and racism, exacerbated by global neoliberalism, therefore draws in local as well as global social and economic contexts. Locally, factors such as the gentrification of poor areas and the lack of resources for young people provide causes for the discontentment that lies behind rioting; locally and nationally, welfare reform or withdrawal, as well as poverty, add to it. Globally, the banking crisis, finance capitalism and neoliberalism frame and inform the other levels that contribute to violent disorder. In Tyler (2013), for instance, there is a clear link to the abjection and stigmatisation of the poor in the UK under neoliberal economic policies, while others emphasise social inequalities underlying rioting in history (Grover 2011) and casino finance capitalism (Monaghan and O'Flynn 2011). In all of these, violent disorder is treated as a symptom requiring a political diagnosis, which in a more global vein centres on critiques of capitalism and the financial crisis. Others focus on measures to improve social policy and to address community conflict, although all of these can intersect analytically, as Elliot-Cooper's posts suggest (2011a, 2011b), with the question of how they are interconnected being developed further in Tyler (2013) and Millington (2016).

However, thinking in terms of levels is subject to a common problem of structuralist analysis: how to link the 'objective' social and economic conditions with the 'subjective' motives, and actions of individuals and groups. This frame shares the same problem as the post-political frame in how to account for the diversity of events and actors. 'Political' motivation, in either narrow or wider senses, may apply to some people and events in some places, but is the explanatory reach intended to encompass all events or just particular ones? Even when applied to particular events and places, such as Tottenham, which can be closely contextualised in terms of local histories of policing and a widening gap between rich and poor, is the explanation pitched at the level of the riot as a whole, or can it include the diversity of actions and actors that took part in that? The messiness of riots do not lend themselves to any neatly bounded explanations (Keith 1987, 1993), and the need for differentiated accounts is difficult when events and actions are scattered and diffuse, and actors are not always able to provide post-hoc rationales.

Akram (2014) partially fills in this gap, in developing a theoretical approach to the politics of riots. Taking politics to refer to the contestation of the uneven distribution of power and resources, Akram identifies the key problem as the gap between the sense of grievance expressed by rioters – and their general demographic profile as people from socially deprived backgrounds – and the lack of an explicit political strategy or even any great sense of engagement with politics. Drawing on the concept of habitus, Akram argues that:

grievances and motivations are stored until they are triggered in the rioter's habitus. This means that, whilst individuals may have concerns about issues, they may not feel able to do anything about them, or there are few channels to do so. However, the riot, or its 'triggering' event, represents an opportunity for stored grievances to be expressed, because the riot represents a rupture in the habitus. (Akram 2014: 383)

The implication of 'latency' within individuals places emphasis on the 'triggering' or disrupting event. One shortcoming of all such 'flashpoints' (Waddington 1992) models is the difficulty of accounting for how many flashpoints – or even daily possible flashpoints – do not lead to riots (compare Newburn 2015). Another shortcoming is the arguably excessive focus on more expressive events of violent disorder, rather than ongoing and everyday low-level social disorder, or 'slow rioting'.

Beyond framing

This chapter has set some of the analyses of the 2011 riots into three frameworks. While the first 'race and policing' frame can persuasively link past and present and 'here' and 'there', the associations made beg questions about why some events are included and others are left out. The second 'post-political' frame shows how the dismissal of riots comes not just from the political right, but also from the left and from critical commentators. For the latter, the 2011 riots were expressions of excluded consumerist rage, which highlight a failure of organised politics to understand and channel that. This perspective underplays the ways in which rioters do express recognisable grievances; it also ignores some of the demographic characteristics of rioters, including race, and local histories of conflict. The third 'resistance' frame aims to understand the riots and rioters as politically grounded in social deprivation and economic conditions. It exceeds the first frame, by going beyond policing and local histories to bring in economic forces such as neoliberalism; and it inverts the second frame's denial of politics. Similarly, Hammersley (2014) also observes how different ways of seeing rioting can be mirror images of one another, in noting that while Bauman (2011) and others portray rioters negatively as gullible consumers, 'other sociological accounts tend to defect responsibility and blame away from the rioters' (Hammersley 2014: 126, n 16) and provide a positive evaluation.

These three frames are not fixed categories or intended as an unassailable typology. I have presented them in this way to highlight particular 'ways of framing' that suggest quite different kinds of causes and where politics and policy can have very different consequences. My argument is not that there is any correct way of seeing or reading the events of 2011. While each of the frames may have some explanatory value, their over-reach is one major problem, particularly when the explanation is applied to riots across time and place.

Riots as essentially disorderly events lend themselves to a case against neat and totalising approaches, my wider aim, though, has been to shed light on and to question styles of scholarly analysis that fit such events into a preferred framework or narrative. In all three frames, riots are summoned in order to develop a preferred reading, even when this is cast as a form of oppositional reading of the events. These types of framings shape understandings, including the wider ones that this book has been concerned with – policy, policing and the politics of race and racism. The usual scholarly style is to critique one frame and replace it with something seemingly better. In stressing overlap between the frames, I have tried not to enter into that style of analysis here; equally, in previous chapters, it has not been my purpose to try to suggest that there are pat and 'off the shelf' answers to the challenges and dilemmas of seeking to be critical and engaged in the politics of race.

Rioting and violent disorder, as seen in 2011, undoubtedly have some link to issues of race, policing and social and economic inequalities. But either over-generalising (as in the first and third frames) or denying (as in the second frame) that link risks falling into the same political and policy dead-ends as the analyses of such events in the 1980s. The circular and sometimes repetitive debates and issues that this book has charted are not external to critical scholarship, but a situation which it has in some ways contributed to. To move beyond that, at least one key lesson of this book is that critique around race and politics requires sustained engagement with – and better understanding of – policy and political domains, while remaining cognisant of the academy itself as a site of knowledge production around race and racism.

Notes

[1]   For instance, Stott et al (2016) provide a social psychology based social identity approach to the 2011 riots in distinction to structural and ideological theories in and from sociology.

[2]   P.A.J. Waddington provides another sceptical account of explanations of riots in social science in this 2013 blog post: http://blog.oup.com/2013/10/riots-collective-meaning-social-phenomena/

3 It is a connection made by the National Black Police Association in its evidence to the Home Affairs Committee (2011) inquiry into the riots.
4 In *The Times*, 15 September 2011.
5 On Žižek's public profile as a celebrity academic, see: https://www.thesociologicalreview.com/blog/slavoj-zizek-between-public-intellectual-and-academic-celebrity.html
6 It said: 'In other locations, the link to the original trigger is even more tenuous and provides no explanation for what went on' (Home Affairs Committee 2011: 31).
7 See also Stott's 'Five years after the English riots, we still don't know why the violence spread' at: http://theconversation.com/five-years-after-the-english-riots-we-still-dont-know-why-the-violence-spread-63618
8 For instance see: http://occupywallst.org/about/
9 EMA refers to an Educational Maintenance Allowance that was withdrawn by the coalition government of 2010–15.

References

Afridi, A (2016) 'Identity, representation and the "acceptable face" of equalities policy making in Britain', *Journal of Poverty and Social Justice*, 24(1), 77–83

Ahmed, S (2012) *On being included: Racism and diversity in institutional life*, Durham, NC: Duke University Press

Akram, S (2014) 'Recognizing the 2011 United Kingdom riots as political protest: a theoretical framework based on agency, habitus and the preconscious', *British Journal of Criminology*, 54, 375–92

Alcoff, L (1999) 'Towards a phenomenology of racial embodiment', *Radical Philosophy*, 95, 15–27

Alexander, C (ed) (2009) *Stuart Hall and 'race'*, Abingdon: Taylor & Francis

Alexander, P and Halpern, R (eds) (2000) *Racializing class, classifying race: Labour and difference in Britain, the USA and Africa*, New York: St Martin's Press

Allen, J and Cochrane, A (2007) 'Beyond the territorial fix: regional assemblages, politics and power', *Regional Studies*, 41, 1161–75

Allen, J and Cochrane, A (2010) 'Assemblages of state power: topological shifts in the organization of government and politics', *Antipode,* 4(5), 1071–89

Alves, J (2014) 'From necropolis to blackpolis: necropolitical governance and black spatial praxis in São Paulo, Brazil', *Antipode*, 46(2), 323-339

Andersen, M and Hill Collins, P (1998) *Race, class and gender: An anthology*, Belmont, CA: Wadsworth/Thomson Learning (6th edn, 2006)

Anderson, E (1999) *Code of the Street: Decency, violence, and the moral life of the inner city*, New York: W W Norton

Anthias, F and Yuval-Davis, N (1992) *Racialized boundaries: Race, nation, gender, colour and class and the anti-racist struggle*, London: Routledge

Appiah, KA and Gutman, A (1996) *Colour conscious: The political morality of race*, Princeton, NJ: Princeton University Press

Ashe, SD and McGeever, BF (2011) 'Marxism, racism and the construction of "race" as a social and political relation: an interview with Professor Robert Miles', *Ethnic and Racial Studies* 34(12), 2009-26

Aspinall, P (2000) 'The challenges of measuring the ethno-cultural diversity of Britain in the new millennium', *Policy & Politics* 28, 109–18

Athwal, H and Bourne, J (eds) (2015) *Dying for Justice*, London: Institute of Race Relations

Back, L (2007) *The Art of Listening*, Oxford: Berg

Back, L (2011) 'Intellectual Life and the University of Commerce' *Academe*, 97(6), 19-23

Back, L (2015) 'On the side of the powerful: the 'impact agenda' and sociology in public', *Sociological Review*, www.thesociologicalreview. com/ information/blog/on-the-side-of-the-powerful-the-impact-agenda-sociology-in-public

Back, L and Solomos, J (eds) (2009) *Theories of Race and Racism*, 2nd edn, London: Routledge

Back, L, Keith, M, Khan, A, Shukra, K and Solomos, J (2002) 'The return of assimilationism: race, multiculturalism and New Labour', *Sociological Research Online*, 7, 2

Back, L and Solomos, J (1993) 'Doing research, writing politics: the dilemmas of political intervention in research on racism', *Economy and Society*, 22, 178-99

Back, L and Tate, M (2014) 'Telling about racism. W.E.B. Du Bois, Stuart Hall and sociology's reconstruction,' in W. Hund and A. Lentin (eds) *Racism and sociology*, Berlin: Lit Verlag

Badgett, MV (2016) *The Public Professor: How to Use Your Research to Change the World*, New York: New York University Press

Badiou, A (2012) *The rebirth of history: Times of riots and uprisings*, London: Verso

Baert, P (2012) 'Positioning theory and intellectual interventions', *Journal for the Theory of Social Behaviour*, 42(3), 304-24

Bailey, M and Freedman, D (2011) *The assault on universities: A manifesto for resistance*, London: Pluto Press

Banton, M (1967) *Race relations*, New York: Basic Books

Banton, M (1977) *The idea of race*, London: Tavistock

Banton, M (1991) 'The race relations problematic', *British Journal of Sociology*, 42, 115-30

Banton, M (2002) *The international politics of race*, Cambridge: Polity

Banton, M (2005) 'Historical and contemporary modes of racialization', in K Murji and J Solomos (eds) (2005) *Racialization: Studies in theory and practice*, Oxford: Oxford University Press

Banton, M (2015) 'Superseding race in sociology: the perspective of critical rationalism', in K Murji and J Solomos (eds) *Theories of race and ethnicity: Contemporary debates and perspectives*, Cambridge: Cambridge University Press

Barkan, E (1992) *The Retreat of Scientific Racism: Changing Concepts of Race in Britain and the United States Between the World Wars*, Cambridge: Cambridge University Press

Barker, M (1981) *The New Racism*, London: Junction Books

Barker, M and Beezer, A (1983) 'The language of racism: An examination of Lord Scarman's Report on the Brixton riots', *International Socialism Journal*, 2(18), 108–25

Barot, R and Bird, J (2001) 'Racialization: the genealogy and critique of a concept', *Ethnic and Racial Studies*, 21(4), 601-18

Bassel, L (2016) 'The Casey review on opportunity and integration: Re-inventing the wheel', http://discoversociety.org/2016/12/09/the-casey-review-on-opportunity-and-integration-re-inventing-the-wheel/

Bauman, Z (1987) *Legislators and interpreters*, Cambridge: Polity

Bauman, Z (1989) *Modernity and the Holocaust*, New York: Random House

Bauman, Z (2011) 'The London riots – on consumerism coming home to roost', *Social Europe Journal*, 9 August

Bauman, Z (2014) *What use is sociology?*, Cambridge: Polity

Baxi, U (2007) *Human Rights in a Posthuman World*, New Delhi: Oxford University Press

Bell, M (2008) *Racism and Equality in the European Union*. Oxford: Oxford University Press

Bennett, O (2001) *Cultural Pessimism: Narratives of Decline in the Postmodern World*, Edinburgh: Edinburgh University Press

Bennetto, J (2009) *Police and racism: What has been achieved 10 years after the Stephen Lawrence Inquiry report?*, London: EHRC

Benyon, J and Solomos, J (eds) (1987) *The Roots of Urban Unrest*, Leicester: Scarman Centre

Better, S (2008) *Institutional Racism: A Primer on Theory and Strategies for Social Change*, 2nd edn, Maryland: Rowman and Littlefield

Bevan, G and Hood, C (2006) 'What's measured is what matters: targets and gaming in the English public health care system', *Public Administration*, 84(3), 517–38

Bevir, M and Rhodes, R (2003) *Interpreting British Governance*, London: Routledge

Bhambra, G (2014) *Connected sociologies*, London: Bloomsbury

Bhatt, C (2004) 'Contemporary geopolitics and alterity research,' in M Bulmer and J Solomos (eds) *Researching race and racism*, London: Routledge

Bhatt, C (2010) 'The spirit lives on: races and disciplines', in PH Collins and J. Solomos (eds) *The Sage handbook of race and ethnic studies*, London: Sage, 90–128

Bhatt, C (2012) 'The new xenologies of Europe: civil tensions and mythic pasts', *Journal of Civil Society*, 8(3), 307–26

Bhatt, C (2016) 'White sociology', *Ethnic and Racial Studies*, 39(3), 397–404

Bhattacharyya, G, Gabriel, J and Small, S (2002) *Race and power*, London: Routledge

Biko, S (1986) *I write what I like*, San Francisco, Harper and Row

Billingsley, A (1973) 'Black families and White social science', in J Ladner (ed) *The death of White sociology*, New York: Vintage, 431–50

Blackburn, D (2000) 'Why race is not a biological concept', in B Lang (ed) *Race and racism in theory and practice*, Maryland: Rowman and Littlefield, 3–26

Blair, I (2009) *Policing controversy*, London: Profile

Bliss, C (2012) *Race decoded: The genomic fight for social justice*, Stanford: Stanford University Press

Blum, L (2002) *"I'm not a racist, but...": The moral quandary of race*, Ithaca: Cornell University Press

Blythe, A (2014) *Little revolution*, London: Nick Hern Books

Boatca, M (2007) 'No race to the swift: negotiating racial identity in past and present Eastern Europe', *Human Architecture: Journal of the Sociology of Self-Knowledge*, 5(1), 91-104

Bobo, L.D. (2014) 'The stickiness of race', *Du Bois Review: Social Science Research on Race*, 11(02), 189–93

Bobo, L.D. (2015) 'A troublesome recurrence', *Du Bois Review: Social Science Research on Race*, 12(01), 1-4

Bonilla-Silva, E (2001) *White supremacy and racism in the post-civil rights era*, Boulder, CO: Lynne Rienner Publishers

Bonilla-Silva, E (2006) *Racism without racists: Color-blind racism and the persistence of racial inequality in the United States*, 2nd edn, Maryland: Rowman and Littlefield

Bonilla-Silva, E with Ray, E (2015) 'Getting over the Obama hope hangover: the new racism in "post-racial" America', in K. Murji and J. Solomos (eds) *Theories of Race and Ethnicity: Contemporary Debates and Perspectives*, Cambridge: Cambridge University Press

Bonnett, A (2000) *White identities: Historical and international perspectives*, Hemel Hempstead: Prentice Hall

Bourdieu, P and Wacquant, L (1999) 'On the cunning of imperialist reason', *Theory, Culture and Society*, 16(1), 41–58

Bourne, J and Sivanandan, A (1980) 'Cheerleaders and ombudsmen: the sociology of race relations in Britain', *Race & Class*, 21(4), 331–52

Bowling, B (1998) *Violent Racism*, Oxford: Oxford University Press (revised edn, 1999)

Bowling, B (2013) 'The borders of punishment: towards a criminology of mobility,' in KF Aas and M Bosworth (eds) *Migration and punishment: Citizenship, crime control, and social exclusion*, Oxford: Oxford University Press

Bowling, B with Grieve, J (2009) 'Violent racism, policing, safety and justice 10 years after Lawrence', in N Hall et al (eds) *Policing and legacy of Lawrence*, Cullompton: Willan

Bowling, B, Philips, C, Campbell, A and Docking, M (2005) 'Policing and human rights', in Y Bangura and R Stavenhagen (eds) *Racism and public policy*, Basingstoke: Palgrave Macmillan, 117–45

Brah, A (1996) *Cartographies of Diaspora: Contesting Identities*, London: Routledge

Braham, P, Rattansi, A and Skellington, R (eds) (1992) *Racism and Antiracism: Inequalities, Opportunities and Policies*, London: SAGE

British Academy (2008) *Punching our weight: the humanities and social sciences public policy making*, London: British Academy

British Academy (2010) *Past, present and future: the public value of the humanities and social sciences*, London: British Academy

British Journal of Sociology (2005) 'Continuing the public sociology debate', articles in vol 56(2) and vol 56(3)

Brooks, D (2003) *Steve and me: My friendship with Stephen Lawrence and the search for justice*, London: Abacus

Brown, J (ed) (2013) *The future of policing*, London: Routledge

Brown, J, Hegarty, P and O'Neill, D (2006) *Playing with numbers: A discussion paper on positive discrimination as a means for achieving gender equality in the police service in England and Wales*, Guildford: University of Surrey

Brown, M (2016) *Back to academia, in struggle*, www.socialjusticejournal. org/back-to-academia-in-struggle

Bulmer, M and Solomos, J (eds) (1999a) *Ethnic and Racial Studies Today*, London: Routledge

Bulmer, M and Solomos, J (eds) (1999b) *Racism*, Oxford: Oxford University Press

Burawoy, M (2005) 'For public sociology', *British Journal of Sociology*, 56(2), 259-94

Burawoy, M (ed) (2014) 'Precarious engagements: combat in the realm of public sociology', special issue, *Current Sociology*, 62(2)

Butler, J (2009) *Frames of war: When is life grievable?*, London: Verso

Cairney, P (2016) *The politics of evidence-based policy making*, London: Palgrave Macmillan

Camp, J and Heatherton, C (eds) (2016) *Policing the planet: Why the policing crisis led to Black Lives Matter*, London: Verso

Cantle, T (2001) *Community Cohesion: Report of the Independent Review Team*, London: Home Office

Carmichael, S (later known as Kwame Ture) and Hamilton, C (1992, originally 1967) *Black Power: The politics of liberation*, New York: Vintage

Carter, B (2000) *Realism and racism: Concepts of race in sociological research*, London: Routledge

Carter, B (2007) 'Genes, genomes and genealogies: the return of scientific racism?', *Ethnic and Racial Studies*, 30(4), 546–56

Carter, B, Harris, C and Joshi, S (1987) *The 1951–55 Conservative Government and the racialization of black immigration*, Warwick: Centre for Research in Ethnic Relations

Casey, L (2016) *A review into opportunity and integration*, available at: https://www.gov.uk/government/uploads/system/uploads/attachment_data/file/575973/The_Casey_Review_Report.pdf

Cashmore, E (2002) 'Behind the window dressing: ethnic minority police perspectives on cultural diversity', *Journal of Ethnic and Migration Studies* 28(2), 327–41

Cathcart, B (1999) *The Case of Stephen Lawrence*, London: Viking

Chatterton, M, Hodkinson, S and Pickerill J (2010) 'Beyond scholar activism: making strategic interventions inside and outside the neoliberal university', *ACME*, 9, 245–75

Chouhan, K and Sian, K (2010) *The Equanomics UK Index*, available at: https://issuu.com/equanomics/docs/equanomics_index_jan2010

Clarke, S (2015) 'Racism: psychoanalytic and psychosocial perspectives', in K Murji and J.Solomos (eds) *Theories of race and ethnicity: Contemporary debates and perspectives*, Cambridge: Cambridge University Press, 198–213

Clawson, D, Zussman, R, Misra, J, Gerstel, N, Stokes, R and Anderton, D (eds) (2007) *Public sociology: Fifteen eminent sociologists debate politics and their profession in the twenty-first century*, Berkeley, University of California Press

Clover, J (2016) *Riot. Strike. Riot: The new era of uprisings*, London: Verso

Coates, T (2015) *Between the world and me*, New York: Spiegel & Grau

Cohen, N (2003) 'Why the Met faces a crisis over race', *New Statesman*, 1 December

Cohen, P (1992) 'Its racism what dunnit', in J Donald and A Rattansi (eds) *Race, culture and difference*. London: Sage

Cohen, R (1994) *Frontiers of identity: The British and the others*, Harlow: Longman

Cole, M (2009) *Critical race theory and education: A Marxist response*, New York: Palgrave Macmillan

Collins, J, Noble, G, Poynting, S and Tabar, P (2000) *Kebabs, kids, cops and crime*, Annandale, NSW: Pluto

Commission on Social Justice (1994) *Social justice*. London: Vintage

Connell, R.W. (1997) 'Why is classical theory classical?', *American Journal of Sociology*, 102(6): 1511–57

Cottle, S (2004) *The racist murder of Stephen Lawrence: Media performance and public transformation*, London: Praeger

CRE (Commission for Racial Equality) (2004) *A Formal Investigation of the Police Service in England and Wales: An interim report*, London: CRE

Critical Social Policy (2008) Special Issue: Social Science and Public Policy: Reflections on the Link, 28(3)

Curnoe, D (2016) *The biggest mistake in the history of science*, https://theconversation.com/the-biggest-mistake-in-the-history-of-science-70575

Dalal, F (2002) *Race, colour and the process of racialization: New perspectives from analysis, psychoanalysis, and sociology*, Hove: Brunner-Routledge

Daley, J (1999) 'Coming soon: A new offence – institutional thought crime', *Daily Telegraph*, 23 February

Das Gupta, T, James, C, Maaka, R, Galabuzi, G and Andersen, C (2007) (eds) *Race and racialization: essential readings*, Toronto: Canadian Scholars Press

Davis A (1974) *Angela Davis: An autobiography*, New York, Random House

Davis, A (1981) *Women, race and class*, London: Women's Press

Davis, A (2005) *Abolition democracy: Beyond prisons, torture and empire*, Berkeley: Seven Stories Press

Daynes, S and Lee, O (2008) *Desire for race*, Cambridge: Cambridge University Press.

Delgado, R and Stefancic, J (2012) *Critical race theory: an introduction*, 2nd edn, New York: New York University Press

Demeritt, D (2002) 'What is the 'social construction of nature'? A typology and sympathetic critique', *Progress in Human Geography*, 26(6): 767-90

Dennis, N, Erdos, G and Al-Shahi, A (2000) *Racist murder and pressure group politics*. London: Institute for the Study of Civil Society

Dikötter, F (1992) *The discourse of race in Modern China*, London: Hurst

Dizaei, A (2007) *Not one of us*, London: Serpent's Tail

DoJ (Department of Justice) (2015) 'Investigation of the Ferguson Police Department, by United States Department of Justice', https://www.justice.gov/sites/default/files/opa/press-releases/attachments/2015/03/04/ferguson_police_department_report.pdf

DoJ (2016) 'Investigation of the Baltimore City Police Department, by United States Department of Justice', https://www.justice.gov/opa/file/883366/download

DoJ (2017) Investigation of the Chicago Police Department, by United States Department of Justice, https://www.justice.gov/opa/file/925846/download

D'Souza, D (1995) *The end of racism*, New York: Free Press

Dyson, M (2003) *Open Mike, Reflections on Philosophy, Race, Sex, Culture and Religion*, New York, Civitas

Edwards, A and Sheptykci, J (2009) 'Third wave criminology', *Criminology and Criminal Justice*, 9(3), 379–97

EHRC (2015) *Is Britain fairer?*, https://www.equalityhumanrights.com/en/britain-fairer

EHRC (2016) *Healing a divided Britain*, https://www.equalityhumanrights.com/en/race-report-healing-divided-britain

Eisenstein, ZR (1996) *Hatreds: Racialized and sexualized conflicts in the twenty first century*, New York: Routledge

Elias, S and Feagin, J (2016) *Racial theories in social science: A systemic racism critique*, New York: Routledge

Elliot-Cooper, A (2011a) 'Redefining the political', https://ceasefiremagazine.co.uk/the-anti-imperialist-12-1/ 11 Sept 2011 The UK riots: redefining the political

Elliot-Cooper, A (2011b) 'Advertising as a form of violence', https://ceasefiremagazine.co.uk/anti-imperialist-12-2/

Emirbayer, M and Desmond, M (2015) *The racial order*, Chicago: University of Chicago Press

Entine, J (2000) *Taboo: Why Black athletes dominate sport and why we are frightened to talk about it*, Boston, MA: Public Affairs

Epstein, S (2007) *Inclusion: The politics of difference in medical research*, Chicago: University of Chicago Press

Erel, U, Murji, K and Nahaboo Z (2016) 'Understanding the contemporary race–migration nexus', *Ethnic and Racial Studies*, 39(8): 1339–60

Ericson, R. (2005) 'Publicizing sociology', *British Journal of Sociology* 56: 36–72

Erikksen, T (2006) *Engaging anthropology*, Oxford: Berg

Essed, P (1991) *Understanding everyday racism*, London: Sage

Essed, P (2013) 'Women social justice scholars: risks and rewards of committing to anti-racism', *Ethnic & Racial Studies*, 36 (9), 1393–411

Essed, P and Goldberg, D (eds) (2002) *Race critical theories*, Malden, MA: Blackwell

Eyerman, R and Jamison, A (1991) *Social movements, A cognitive approach*, Pennsylvania: Pennsylvania State University Press

Fairhurst, G and Sarr, R (1996) *The art of framing*. San Francisco: Jossey-Bass

Faist, T (2009) 'Diversity: a new mode of incorporation?', *Ethnic and Racial Studies*, 32(1): 171–90

Fanon, F (1967) *The wretched of the earth*, Harmondsworth: Penguin

Farrar, M (2013) 'How can we meet "the demands of the day"? Producing an affective, reflexive, interpretive, public sociology of "race"', *Ethnic and Racial Studies*, 36(9), 1446–64

Fassin, D (2011) 'Racialization: how to do races with bodies' in F Mascia-Lees (ed), *A companion to the anthropology of the body and embodiment*, Oxford: Blackwell

Fassin, D (2013) *Enforcing order: An ethnography of urban policing*, Cambridge: Polity

Feagin, J (2006) *Systemic racism: a theory of oppression*, New York: Routledge

Finney, N and Simpson L (2009) *'Sleepwalking to segregation'?: challenging myths about race and migration,* Bristol: Policy Press

Ford, R (2008) 'Is racial prejudice declining in Britain?', *British Journal of Sociology,* 59 (4): 609–36

Fortier, AM (2005) 'Diaspora', in D Atkinson, P Jackson, D Sibley and N Washbourne (eds) *Cultural geography: A critical dictionary of key concepts*, London: IB Tauris, 182–87

Foster, J (2008) 'It might have been incompetent but it wasn't racist', *Policing and Society*, 18(2): 89–112

Foster, J, Souhami, A and Newburn, T (2005) *Assessing the impact of the Stephen Lawrence Inquiry, Research study 294*, London: Home Office

Foucault, M (1977) 'The political function of the intellectual', *Radical Philosophy*, 17: 12-14

Fuss, D (1989) *Essentially speaking: feminism, nature and difference*, London: Routledge

Gallagher, C (2015) 'Color-blind egalitarianism as the new racial norm', in K Murji and J Solomos (eds) *Theories of Race and Ethnicity: Contemporary Debates and Perspectives*, Cambridge: Cambridge University Press

Gans, H (2017) 'Racialization and racialization research', *Ethnic and Racial Studies,* 40(3): 341–52

Garner, S (2004) *Racism in the Irish experience*, London: Pluto

Garner, S (2009) *Racisms*, London: SAGE

Garner, S and Fassin, E (2013) '"Race", sexualities and the French public intellectual: an interview with Eric Fassin', *Ethnic and Racial Studies*, 36(9), 1465–84

Gifford, T (1986) *The Broadwater Farm inquiry:Report of the independent inquiry into disturbances of October 1985 at the Broadwater Farm Estate, Tottenham*, London: Karia Press

Gillborn, D (2008) *Racism and education: Coincidence or conspiracy?* Abingdon: Routledge

Gilroy, P (1987) *There ain't no black in the Union Jack: The cultural politics of race and nation*, London: Routledge

Gilroy, P (1993) *The black Atlantic: Modernity and double consciousness*, Cambridge, MA.: Harvard University Press

Gilroy, P (2000) *Between camps: Race, identity and nationalism at the end of the colour line*, London: Allen Lane

Glasgow, J (2009) *A theory of race*, New York: Routledge

Golash-Boza, T (2016) 'A critical and comprehensive sociological theory of race and racism', *Sociology of Race and Ethnicity*, 2(2): 129-141

Goldberg, D [originally 1992] (1999) 'The semantics of race' edited extract in M. Bulmer and J. Solomos (eds) *Racism*, Oxford: Oxford University Press

Goldberg, D (1993) *Racist Culture: Philosophy and the Politics of Meaning*, Oxford: Blackwell

Goldberg, D (1997) *Racial subjects: Writing on race in America*, New York: Routledge

Goldberg, D (2002) *The racial state*, Oxford: Blackwell

Goldberg, D (2005) 'Racial Americanization' in K Murji and J Solomos (eds) (2005) *Racialization: Studies in theory and practice*, Oxford: Oxford University Press

Goldberg, D (2015) 'Racial comparisons, relational racisms: some thoughts on method', in K. Murji and J. Solomos (eds) *Theories of Race and Ethnicity: Contemporary Debates and Perspectives*, Cambridge: Cambridge University Press

Gooding-Williams, R (1993) *Reading Rodney King/reading urban uprising*, New York: Routledge

Goulbourne, H (1998) *Race relations in Britain since 1945*, Basingstoke: Macmillan

Gramsci, A (1971) *Selections from the prison notebooks*, edited and translated by Q. Hoare and G. Nowell Smith, London: Lawrence & Wishart

Griffiths, B (2009) 'Doing the right thing', in N Hall et al (eds) *Policing and legacy of Lawrence*, Devon: Willan

Grover, C (2011)' Social protest in 2011: material and cultural aspects of economic inequalities', *Sociological Research Online*, 16(4)

Gržinić, M and Tatlić, S (2014) *Necropolitics, racialization, and global capitalism*, Maryland: Rowman & Littlefield

Guillaumin, C (1995) *Racism, sexism, power and ideology*, London: Routledge

Gunaratnam, Y (2003) *Researching 'race' and ethnicity*, London: Sage

Hacking, I (1999) *The social construction of what?*, Cambridge, MA: Harvard University Press

Halady, S (2011) *The reality of race: Against racial eliminativism*, Ann Arbor MI: Proquest

Hale, C (2008) *Engaging contradictions: Theory, politics, and methods of activist scholarship*, Berkeley: University of California Press

Hall, N (2005) *Hate crime*, Devon: Willan

Hall, N, Grieve, J and Savage, S (eds) (2009) *Policing and legacy of Lawrence*, Devon: Willan

Hall, S (1980): 'Encoding/decoding', in Centre for Contemporary Cultural Studies (ed): *Culture, Media, Language.* London: Hutchinson

Hall, S (1982) 'The lessons of Lord Scarman', *Critical Social Policy*, 2(2), 66–72

Hall, S (1988) *The hard road to renewal*, London: Verso

Hall, S (1990) 'Cultural identity and diaspora', in J Rutherford (ed) *Identity: Community, culture, difference*, London: Lawrence & Wishart

Hall, S (1999) 'From Scarman to Stephen Lawrence', *History Workshop Journal*, 48(1), 187–197

Hall, S (2000) 'Conclusion: The multicultural question', in B Hesse (ed) *Un/settled multiculturalisms: Diasporas, entanglements, 'transruptions'*, London: Zed Books

Hall, S, Critcher, C, Jefferson, T, Clarke, J and Roberts, B (1978) *Policing the crisis: Mugging, the state and law and order*, London: Macmillan

Halliday, J (2015) 'Met chief admits institutional racism claims have "some justification"'. www.theguardian.com/uk-news/2015/jun/05/met-chief-admits-institutional-racism-claims-have-some-justification#img-1

Hammersley, M (2013) *The myth of research-based policy and practice*, London: SAGE

Hammersley, M (2014) *The limits of social science: Causal explanation and value relevance*, London: SAGE

Hanchard, M (ed) (1999) *Racial politics in contemporary Brazil*. Durham: Duke University Press

Haraway, D (1991) *Simians, cyborgs and women: The reinvention of nature*, London: Free Association Books

Harvey, D (2012) *Rebel Cities: From the Right to the City to the Urban Revolution*. London: Verso

Herrnstein, RJ and Murray, C (1994) *The Bell Curve: Intelligence and Class Structure in American Life*. New York: Free Press

Hesse, B (ed) (2000) *Un/settled multiculturalisms: Diasporas, entanglements, "transruptions"*, London: Zed Books

Hesse, B (2004) 'Discourse on institutional racism: genealogy of a concept', in I Law et al (eds) *Institutional racism in higher education*, Trent: Trentham

Hesse, B (2007) 'Racialized modernity: An analytics of white mythologies', *Ethnic and Racial Studies*, 30, 4: 643-663

Hesse, B (2014) 'Racism's alterity: the after-life of black sociology', in W. Hund and A. Lentin (eds) *Racism and sociology*. Berlin: Lit Verlag: 141-74

Hesse, B, Rai, D, Bennett, C and McGilchrist, P (1992) *Beneath the surface*, Aldershot: Avebury

Hill Collins, P (2000) *Black feminist thought: Knowledge, consciousness and the politics of empowerment*, 2nd edn, New York: Routledge

Hill Collins, P (2013) *On intellectual activism*, Philadelphia. PA: Temple University Press

Hill Collins, P and Bilge, S (2016) *Intersectionality*, Cambridge: Polity

Hirschfield, L (1996) *Race in the making*, Boston: MIT Press

HMIC (2001) *Winning the race – embracing diversity*, London: Home Office

Holdaway, S (1996) *The racialization of British policing*, London: Macmillan

Holdaway, S (1999) 'A sociologist's involvement with the Lawrence Inquiry', *Network*, no 7

Holdaway, S and O'Neill, M (2006) 'Institutional racism after Macpherson', *Policing and Society*, 16: 349–69

Holohan, S (2005) *The search for justice in a media age: Reading Stephen Lawrence and Louise Woodward*, Aldershot: Ashgate

Home Affairs Committee (2008) Seventh report, London: House of Commons

Home Affairs Committee (2009) *The Macpherson Report – Ten Years On*, London: The Stationery Office

Home Affairs Committee (2011) *Policing Large Scale Disorder: Lessons from the disturbances of August 2011*, London: The Stationery Office

Home Affairs Committee (2016) *Police diversity*, www.publications. parliament.uk/pa/cm201617/cmselect/cmhaff/27/27.pdf

Home Office (2008) *Policing Minister's review of recruitment, retention and progression of Black and Minority Ethnic Officers*, London: Home Office

Hood, C (2006) 'Gaming in Targetworld: the targets approach to managing British public services', *Public Administration Review*, July–August: 515–21

Hood, C (2007) 'Public service management by numbers: why does it vary? Where has it come from? What are the gaps and the puzzles?', *Public Money & Management*, April: 95–102

hooks, b (1990) *Yearning: Race, Gender, and Cultural Politics*, South End Press

Hughey, M (2015) 'The sociology of whiteness', in K Murji and J Solomos (eds) *Theories of Race and Ethnicity: Contemporary Debates and Perspectives*, Cambridge: Cambridge University Press: 214–32

Hund, W and Lentin, A (eds) (2014) *Racism and sociology*, Berlin: Lit Verlag

Iganski, P (2008) *'Hate crime' and the city*, Bristol: Policy Press

Independent Committee of Inquiry (1989) *Policing in Hackney 1945–1984*. London: Karia Press

Institute of Employment Studies (2003) *A Review of Community Race Relations Training in the Metropolitan Police Service*, Sussex: IES

Isaacman, A (2003) 'Legacies of engagement: scholarship informed by political commitment', *African Studies Review* 46(1): 1–41

Ishaq, M and Hussain, A (2001) 'Race and recruitment from a uniformed services' perspective: the Scottish dimension', *Policy Studies*, 22(3); 217–32

Jacobson, M (1998) *Whiteness of a different color: European immigrants and the alchemy of race,* Cambridge, MA: Harvard University Press

Jefferson, T (2011) 'Policing the riots: from Bristol and Brixton to Tottenham, via Toxteth, Handsworth, etc', *Criminal Justice Matters*, no 87: 8–9

Jenkins, R (1997) *Rethinking ethnicity: Arguments and explorations.* London: Sage

Jennings, J and Kemp-Welch, A (eds) (1997) *Intellectuals in politics: From the Dreyfus Affair to Salman Rushdie*, London: Routledge

Jhally, S and Hall, S (1996) *Race: The floating signifier*, Northampton, MA: Media Education Foundation

Jobard, F (2009) 'Rioting as a political tool: the 2005 riots in France', *Howard Journal of Criminal Justice*, 48(3): 235–44

Johnson, D, Warren, P and Farrell, A (2015) *Deadly injustice: Trayvon Martin, race, and the criminal justice system*, New York: New York University Press

Johnston, L (2006) 'Diversifying police recruitment? The deployment of Police Community Support Officers in London', *Howard Journal of Criminal Justice*, 45(4): 388–402

Kahn, J (2013) *Race in a bottle: The story of BiDil and racialized medicine in a post-genomic age*, New York: Columbia University Press

Kay, D and Miles, R (1992) *Refugees or migrant workers? European volunteer workers in Britain, 1946–1951*, London: Routledge

Keith, M (1993) *Race, riots and policing*, London: UCL Press

Keith, M (1987) '"Something happened": the problems of explaining the 1980 and 1981 riots in British cities', in P. Jackson (ed) *Race and Racism: Essays in social geography*, London: Allan and Unwin, pp 275-303

Keith, M (2008) 'Public sociology?', *Critical Social Policy*, 28(3): 320–34

Kelley, R and Tuck, S (eds) (2015) *The other special relationship: Race, rights, and riots in Britain and the United States*, New York: Palgrave

Kelman, S (2006) 'Improving service delivery performance in the United Kingdom: organization theory perspectives on central intervention strategies', *Journal of Comparative Policy Analysis, Research and Practice*, 8(4); 393–419

Kesten, J, Murji, K, Neal, S and Ruppert, E, (2013) 'Knowing riots', CRESC working paper no 120, http://www.cresc.ac.uk/publications/working-papers/

Kettle, M and Hodges, L (1982) *Uprising! The police, the people and the riots in Britain's cities*, London: Macmillan

Kibria, N, Bowman, C and O'Leary, M (2013) *Race and immigration*, Cambridge: Polity

Knowles, C (2010) 'Theorizing race and ethnicity: contemporary paradigms and perspectives', in PH Collins, P and J Solomos (eds) *The SAGE Handbook of Race and Ethnic Studies*, London: Sage

Krieger, N (2010) 'The science and epidemiology of racism and health: racial/ethnic categories, biological expressions of racism, and the embodiment of inequality – an ecosocial perspective', in I Whitmarsh and DS Jones (eds) *What's the use of race? Modern governance and the biology of difference*, Cambridge, MA: MIT Press: 225–58

Kuklick, H (1991) *The savage within: The social history of British anthropology, 1885–1945*, Cambridge: Cambridge University Press

Kushner, T (2005) 'Racialization and 'White European' immigration to Britain', in K Murji and J Solomos (eds) (2005) *Racialization: Studies in theory and practice*, Oxford: Oxford University Press, 207–26

Kuzawa, C and Sweet, E (2009) 'Epigenetics and the embodiment of race: developmental origins of US racial disparities in cardiovascular health', *American Journal of Human Biology* 21(1): 2–15

Kyriakides, C (2008) 'Third way anti-racism: a contextual constructionist approach', *Ethnic and Racial Studies* 31(3): 592–610

Ladner, J (ed) (1973) *The death of white sociology*, New York: Vintage

Lal, J (2008) 'On the domestication of American public sociology: a postcolonial feminist perspective', *Critical Sociology*, 34 (2): 169–91

Latour, B (1993) *We have never been modern*, London: Harvester Wheatsheaf (trans. from French by Catherine Porter)

Law, I (2010) *Racism and ethnicity: Global debates, dilemmas, directions*, London: Pearson

Law, I, Phillips, D and Turney, L (eds) (2004) *Institutional racism in higher education,* Trent: Trentham Books

Lawrence, E (1982) 'In the abundance of water a fool is thirsty', in Centre for Contemporary Cultural Studies, *The Empire Strikes Back*, London: Hutchinson

Lawrence, R (2000) *The politics of force: Media and the construction of police brutality*, Berkeley: University of California Press

Layton-Henry, Z (1984) *The politics of race in Britain*, London: Harper Collins

Lea, J and Young, J (1984) *What is to be done about law and order?*, Harmondsworth: Penguin

Lee, S (2015) 'Race and the science of difference in the age of genomics', in K Murji and J Solomos (eds) *Theories of race and ethnicity: Contemporary debates and perspectives*, Cambridge: Cambridge University Press: 26–39

Le Grand, J (2007) *The other invisible hand*, Oxfordshire: Princeton University Press

Lentin, A (2014) 'Migration and racism research', in W Hund and A. Lentin (eds) *Racism and sociology*, Berlin: Lit VerlagLentin, A (2015) 'What does race do?, *Ethnic & Racial Studies*, 38(8): 1401–06

Lentin, A (2017) 'Race', in W Outhwaite and S Turner (eds) *Sage handbook of political sociology*, London: Sage

Lewis, A and Embrick, D (2016) 'Working at the intersection of race and public policy', *Sociology of Race and Ethnicity*, 2(3): 253–62

Lewis, P, Newburn, T, Taylor, M, McGillivray, C, Greenhill, A, Frayman, H and Proctor, R (2011) *Reading the riots: Investigating England's summer of disorder.* London: LSE and The Guardian

Loader, I and Sparks, R (2011) *Public criminology?*, Abingdon: Routledge

Lockwood, D (1970) 'Race, conflict and plural society', in S Zubaida (ed) *Race and racialism*, London: Tavistock: 57-72

Loftus, B (2008) 'Dominant culture interrupted recognition, resentment and the politics of change in an English police force', *British Journal of Criminology*, 48(6) 756–77

Lorde, A (1984) *Sister outsider*, Berkeley: Crossing Press

Loveman, M (2014) *National colors: Racial classification and the state in Latin America*, New York: Oxford University Press

Mac an Ghaill, M (1999) *Contemporary racisms and ethnicities*, Buckingham: Open University Press

McGhee, D (2005) *Intolerant Britain? Hate, citizenship and difference*, Maidenhead: Open University Press

McGowan, J (2008) '"Dispute", "Battle", "Siege", "Farce"? Grunwick 30 years on', *Contemporary British History*, 22: 383–406

MacKinnon, D (2000) 'Managerialism, governmentality and the state: a neo-Foucauldian approach to local economic governance', *Political Geography* 19: 293–314

McKinstry, L (1999) '"Macpherson was just a useful idiot"', *Sunday Telegraph*, 28 February

McLaughlin, E (2005) 'Recovering blackness/repudiating whiteness', in K Murji and J Solomos (eds) *Racialization*, Oxford: Oxford University Press

McLaughlin, E and Murji, K (1998) 'Resistance through representation: "storylines", advertising and Police Federation campaigns', *Policing and Society*, 8: 367–99

McLaughlin, E and Murji, K (1999) 'After the Stephen Lawrence report', *Critical Social Policy*, 19(3), 371–85

Macpherson, W (1999) *The Stephen Lawrence Inquiry*, London: The Stationery Office

Mahony, N and Clarke, J (2013) 'Public crises, public futures', *Cultural Studies*, 27(6), 933–54

Malik, K (1996) *The meaning of race*, Basingstoke: Macmillan

Malik, K (2008) *Strange fruit: Why both sides are wrong in the race debate*, London: Oneworld

Marable, M (1998) *Speaking truth to power: Essays on race, resistance, and radicalism*, Boulder: Westview Press

Marrin, M (1999) 'How racism fever gripped the nation', *Sunday Telegraph*, 14 March

Martínez, D (2013) 'Intellectual biography, empirical sociology and normative political theory: an interview with Tariq Modood', *Journal of Intercultural Studies*, 34(6); 729–41

Martinot, S (2003) *The rule of racialization: Class, identity, governance*, Philadelphia: Temple University Press

Martinot, S (2011) *The machinery of whiteness: Studies in the structure of racialization*, Philadelphia: Temple University Press

Mason, D (1982) `After Scarman: A note on the concept of institutional racism', *New Community* X(1): 38-45

Mayberry, D (2008) *Black deaths in police custody and human rights: the failure of the Stephen Lawrence inquiry*, London: Hansib

Meer, N (2013) 'Racialization and religion: Race, culture and difference in the study of antisemitism and Islamophobia', *Ethnic and Racial Studies*, 36 (3), 385-98

Meer, N (2014) *Key concepts in race and ethnicity*, London: Sage

Meer, N and Modood, T (2012) 'How does interculturalism contrast with multiculturalism?', *Journal of Intercultural Studies* 33(2): 175-96

Meer, N and Nayak, A (2015) 'Race ends where? Race, racism and contemporary sociology', *Sociology*, 49(6): NP3–NP20

Meloni, M (2014) 'Biology without biologism: social theory in a postgenomic age', *Sociology*, 48(4): 731–46

Meloni, M. (2017) 'Race in an epigenetic time: thinking biology in the plural', *The British Journal of Sociology*. doi:10.1111/1468-4446.12248

Metropolitan Police (1999) *Protect and respect – The Met's diversity strategy*, London: Metropolitan Police

Mignolo, W (2009) '"Dispensable and bare lives": coloniality and the hidden political/economic agenda of modernity', *Human Architecture: Journal of the Sociology of Self-Knowledge*, 7: 2

Miles, R (1982) *Racism and Migrant Labour*, London: Routledge

Miles, R (1989) *Racism*, London: Routledge

Miles, R (1993) *Racism after 'race relations'*, London: Routledge

Miles, R and Brown, M (2003) *Racism*, 2nd edn, London: Routledge

Miles, R and Torres, R (1999) 'Does "race" matter?', in R Torres, L Miron and J Inda (eds) *Race, identity and citizenship*, Malden, MA: Blackwell

Miller, P and Rose, N (2008) *Governing the present*, Cambridge: Polity

Millington, G (2016) '"I found the truth in Foot Locker": London 2011, urban culture, and the post-political city', *Antipode*, 48 (3), 705–23

Mills, C (1998) *The Racial contract*, Ithaca: Cornell University Press

Mitchell, WJT (2012) *Seeing through race*, Cambridge, MA: Harvard University Press

Mirza, H (2009) *Race, gender and educational desire: Why black women succeed and fail.* London: Routledge

Modood, T (1994) 'Political blackness and British Asians', *Sociology*, 28(4): 859–76

Monaghan, L and O'Flynn, M (2011) 'More than anarchy in the UK: "social unrest" and its resurgence in the Madoffized society', *Sociological Research Online*, 17(1): 9

Monahan, MJ (2011) *The creolizing subject: Race, reason, and the politics of purity*. New York: Fordham University Press

Montagu, A (1942/1997) *Man's most dangerous myth: The fallacy of race*, Walnut Creek, CA: Alta Mira

Moore, D, Kosek, J and Pandian, A (eds) (2003) *Race, nature, and the politics of difference*, Durham, NC: Duke University Press

Morgan, R and Newburn, T (1997) *The future of policing*, Oxford: Oxford University Press

Morrell, G, Scott, D, McNeish, D and Webster, S (2011) *The August riots in England Understanding the involvement of young people*, London: NatCen

Morris, A (2015) *The scholar denied: WEB Du Bois and the birth of modern sociology*. Berkeley: University of California Press

Morris, W (2004) *The case for change*, London: MPA

Morton, M, Dolgon, C, Maher, T and Pennell, J (2012) 'Civic engagement and public sociology: two "movements" in search of a mission', *Journal of Applied Social Science*, 6(1): 5–30

Mosse, GL (1978) *Toward the final solution: A history of European racism*, London: JM Dent

Murji, K (2002) 'It's not a black thing', *Criminal Justice Matters*, 47: 32-3

Murji, K (2009) 'Enacting the sacred: nation and difference in the comparative sociology of the police', *Journal of Transatlantic Studies*, 7(1): 23–37

Murji, K (2011) 'Working together: governing and advising the police', *Police Journal*, 84(3): 256-71

Murji, K and Bhattcharyya, G (eds) (2014) *Race critical public scholarship*, London: Routledge

Murji, K and Neal, S (2011) 'Riot: race and politics in the 2011 disorders', *Sociological Research Online* 16, 4

Murji, K and Solomos, J (eds) (2005) *Racialization: Studies in theory and practice*, Oxford: Oxford University Press

Murji, K and Solomos, J (2015) *Theories of race and ethnicity: Contemporary debates and perspectives*, Cambridge: Cambridge University Press

Murji, K and Solomos, J (2016) 'Rejoinder: race scholarship and the future', *Ethnic and Racial Studies*, 39(3): 405–13

Nayak A (2006) 'After race: Ethnography, race and post-race theory', *Ethnic and Racial Studies* 29(3): 411–30

Neal, S (2003) 'The Scarman report, the Macpherson report and the media', *Journal of Social Policy*, 32: 55–74

Neal, S, Bloch, A and Solomos, J (2013) *Race, multiculture and social policy in Britain*. London: Palgrave

Neal S and McLaughlin E (2007) 'The public sphere and public interventions on race and nation', *Cultural Studies*, 21(6): 911–31

Newburn, T (2015) 'Reflections on why riots don't happen', *Theoretical Criminology*, 20(2): 125–44

Newburn, T, Cooper, K, Deacon, R and Diski, R (2015) 'Shopping for free? Looting, consumerism and the 2011 riots', *British Journal of Criminology* 55: 987–1004

Newburn, T, Diski, R, Cooper, K, Deacon, R, Burch, A and Grant, M (2016) '"The biggest gang"? Police and people in the 2011 England riots', *Policing and Society*, 1–18

Nijjar, J (2015) '"Menacing youth" and "broken families": a critical discourse analysis of the reporting of the 2011 English riots in the *Daily Express* using moral panic theory', *Sociological Research Online*, 20(4)

Omi, M and Winant, H (2015, originally 1986) *Racial formation in the United States*, 3rd edn, New York: Routledge

Ossorio, P and Duster, T (2005) 'Race and genetics: controversies in biomedical, behavioral, and forensic sciences', *American Psychologist* 60(1): 115–28

Outlaw, LJ (1996) *On race and philosophy*. New York: Routledge

Outram, S and Ellison, G (2010) 'Arguments against the use of racialized categories as genetic variables in biomedical research: what are they, and why are they being ignored?', in I Whitmarsh and DS Jones (eds) *What's the use of race? Modern governance and the biology of difference*, Cambridge, MA: MIT Press: 91–124

Parekh, B (2000) *The future of multi-ethnic Britain*, London: Profile Books

Peplow, S (2015) *Race, policing, and public inquiries during the 1980–81 collective violence in England*, unpublished PhD thesis, University of Exeter

Phillips, A (1995) *The politics of presence*, Oxford: Clarendon Press

Phillips, A (2010) 'What's wrong with essentialism?', *Distinktion: Scandinavian Journal of Social Theory*, 11(1): 47-60

Phillips, C (2005) 'Facing inwards and outwards? Institutional racism, race equality and the role of Black and Asian professional associations', *Criminology & Criminal Justice*, 5 (4): 357–77

Phillips, C (2011) 'Institutional racism and ethnic inequalities: an expanded multilevel framework'. *Journal of Social Policy*, 40(1): 173–92

Phillips, M (2000) 'Now we know the truth: the police are not racist ', *Sunday Times*, 24 September

Phillips, T (2009) 'Institutions must catch up with public on race issues', 19 January, http://www.equalityhumanrights.com/en/newsandcomment/speeches/Pages/Macphersonspeech190109.aspx #

Phoenix, A (2005) 'Remembered racialiastion', in K Murji and J Solomos (eds) *Racialization: Studies in Theory and Practice*, Oxford: Oxford University Press

Pidd, M (2012) *Managing the performance of public services*, Cambridge: Cambridge University Press

Pilkington, A (2003) *Racial disadvantage and ethnic diversity in Britain*. Basingstoke: Palgrave

Pitcher, B (2014) *Consuming Race*, London: Routledge

Pittman, CT (2012) 'Racial microaggressions: the narratives of African American faculty at a predominantly white university', *Journal of Negro Education*, 81(1): 82–92

Platt, J (2003) *The British Sociological Association*. Durham: Sociology Press

Pollitt, C (2006) 'Academic advice to practitioners', *Public money and management*, 26 (4), 257

Pollitt, C and Bouckaert, G (2011) *Public Management Reform: A Comparative Analysis – New Public Management, Governance, and the Neo-Weberian State*, 3rd edition, New York: Oxford University Press

Posnock, R (1997) 'How it feels to be a problem: Du Bois, Fanon, and the "impossible life" of the black intellectual', *Critical Inquiry*, 23(2): 323–49

Public Money and Management (2007) Special issue on Academic advice to practitioners, 27(4)

Puwar, N (2004) *Space Invaders: Race, Gender and Bodies Out of Place*. Oxford: Berg

Race and Faith Inquiry Report (2010) London: MPA

Ratcliffe, P (2004) *'Race', Ethnicity, and Difference: Imagining the Inclusive Society*. Maidenhead: Open University Press

Rattansi, A (2005) 'The time/spaces of racialization', in K Murji and J Solomos (eds) *Racialization: Studies in Theory and Practice*, Oxford: Oxford University Press

Rattansi, A (2007) *Racism: A very short introduction*, Oxford: Oxford University Press

Rattansi, A (2011) *Multiculturalism: A very short introduction*, Oxford: Oxford University Press

Rattansi, A and Westwood, S (eds) (1994) *Racism, Modernity and Identity*, Cambridge: Polity

Ray, V (2017) 'A theory of racialized organizations', Retrieved from http://osf.io/yhrne

Razack, S, Smith, M and Thobani, M (eds) (2010) *States of Race*, Toronto: Between the Lines

Reed, A (2000) '"What are the drums saying, Booker?': the curious role of the Black public intellectual', in *Class notes: Posing as politics and other thoughts on the American scene*, New York: New Press

Reeves, F (1983) *British racial discourse: A study of British political discourse about race and race-related matters*, Cambridge: Cambridge University Press

Reiner, R (2010) *The politics of the police*, 4th edn, Oxford: Oxford University Press

Rex, J (1970) *Race relations in sociological theory*. London: Weidenfeld and Nicolson.

Rex, J (1979) 'Race relations research in an academic setting', *Home Office Research Bulletin* 8: 29–30.

Rex, J (1986) 'The role of class analysis in the study of race relations – a Weberian perspective', in J Rex and D Mason (eds) *Theories of race and ethnic relations*, Cambridge: Cambridge University Press

Rex, J and Mason, D (eds) (1986) *Theories of race and ethnic relations*. Cambridge: Cambridge University Press

Riots Communities and Victims Panel (2012) *After the riots*, http://webarchive.nationalarchives.gov.uk/20121003195935/http://riotspanel.independent.gov.uk/wp-content/uploads/2012/03/Riots-Panel-Final-Report1.pdf

Ritzer, G (2006) 'Who's a public intellectual?', *British Journal of Sociology*, 57(2): 209–13

Rock, P (1981) 'Rioting', *London Review of Books*, 17 September

Rock, P (2004) *Constructing victims' rights*, Oxford: Clarendon

Rose, N (1991) 'Governing by numbers: figuring out democracy', *Accounting, Organizations and Society*, 16: 673–92

Roth, W (2016) 'The multiple dimensions of race', *Ethnic and Racial Studies*, 39: 1310–38

Rowe, M (1998) *The racialization of disorder in twentieth century Britain*, Aldershot: Ashgate

Rowe, M (ed) (2007) *Policing beyond Macpherson*, Devon: Willan

Rowe, M and Garland, J (2007) 'Police diversity training: a sliver bullet tarnished', in M Rowe (ed) *Policing Beyond Macpherson*, 43–65

Runnymede Trust (2009) *The Stephen Lawrence Inquiry 10 Years On: An Analysis of the Literature*, London: Runnymede Trust

Runnymede Trust (2015) *Local ethnic inequalities*, London: Runnymede Trust

Rushton, J.P. (1995) *Race, evolution, and behavior*, 2nd edn, Port Huron, MI: Charles Darwin Institute

St Louis, B (2005) 'Racialization in the zone of ambiguity', in K Murji and J Solomos (eds) *Racialization*, Oxford: Oxford University Press

St Louis, B (2015) 'Can race be eradicated? The post-racial problematic', in K Murji and J Solomos (eds) *Theories of race and ethnicity: Contemporary debates and perspectives*, Cambridge: Cambridge University Press, 114–39

Said, E (1978) *Orientalism*, New York: Pantheon Books

Saldanha, A (2006) 'Reontologising race: the machinic geography of phenotype', *Environment and Planning D: Society and Space* 24(1): 9–24

Sandel, M (2012) *What money can't buy: The moral limits of markets*, London: Allen Lane

Sandoval-García, C (2013) 'To whom and to what is research on migration a contribution?', *Ethnic and Racial Studies*, 36 (9): 1429–45

Sayer, A (1997) 'Essentialism, social constructionism, and beyond', *Sociological Review* 45(3): 453–87

Sayer, D (2014) *Rank hypocrisies: The insult of the REF*. London: Sage

Scarman, L (1981) *The Brixton disorders 10–12 April 1981*. London: HMSO

Scott, J (2005) `Who will speak, and who will listen?', *British Journal of Sociology* 56: 405–9

Scott, J and Marshall, G (eds) (2005) *Oxford dictionary of sociology*, 3rd edn, Oxford: Oxford University Press

Sexton, J (2011) 'The social life of social death: on Afro-pessimism and black optimism', *InTensions*, 5(1)

Shattock, M (2008) 'The change from private to public governance of British higher education'. *Higher Education Quarterly*, 62(3): 181–203

Shiner, M (2010) 'Post-Lawrence policing in England and Wales: Guilt, innocence and the defence of organizational ego', *British Journal of Criminology*, 50: 935–53

Sian, K, Sayyid, S and Law, I (2014) *Racism, governance and public policy: Beyond human rights,* London: Routledge

Sim, J (1982) 'Scarman: the police counter-attack', *The Socialist Register 1982*, London: Merlin

Singh, N (2004) *Black is a country*, Cambridge, MA: Harvard University Press

Skellington, R (1996) *'Race' in Britain today*. London: Sage (2nd edn)

Slovo, G (2011) *The riots*, London: Oberon Books

Smaje, C (2000) *Natural hierarchies: The historical sociology of race and caste*, Malden: Blackwell

Small, S (1994) *Racialised barriers: The Black experience in the United States and England in the 1980s*, London: Routledge

Small, S and Solomos, J (2006) 'Race, immigration and politics in Britain: changing policy agendas and conceptual paradigms 1940s–2000s', *International Journal of Comparative Sociology* 47(3–4): 235–57

Smith, AM (1994) *New Right discourse on race and sexuality: Britain, 1968–1990,* Cambridge: Cambridge University Press

Smith, E (2013) 'Once as history, twice as farce? The spectre of the summer of '81 in discourses on the august 2011 riots', *Journal for Cultural Research*, 17(2): 124–43

Smith, S (ed) (2007) *Applying theory to practice,* Aldershot: Ashgate

Sociology (2007) Special issue on 'Sociology and its Public Face(s)', 41(5)

Solomos, J (1988) *Black youth, racism and the state: The politics of ideology and policy,* Cambridge: Cambridge University Press

Solomos, J (1999) 'Social Research and the Stephen Lawrence Inquiry', *Sociological Research Online,* 4, 1.

Solomos, J (2003) *Race and Racism in Britain,* 3rd edn, Basingstoke: Macmillan

Solomos, J (2011) 'Race, rumours and riots: past, present and future', *Sociological Research Online,* 16(4)

Song, M (2014) 'Challenging a culture of racial equivalence', *British Journal of Sociology,* 65, 1, 107–29

Souhami, A (2014) 'Institutional racism and police reform: an empirical critique', *Policing and Society* 24(1): 1–21

Sowell, T (2006) *Black Rednecks and White Liberals,* New York: Encounter

Stanfield, J (2011) *Historical Foundations of Black Reflective Sociology.* California: Left Coast Press

Stanko, B (2007) 'From academia to policy making', *Theoretical criminology,* 11(2), 209–19

Staples, R (1973) 'What is black sociology?', in J Ladner (ed) *The death of white sociology,* New York: Vintage: 161–70

Staples, R (1976) *Introduction to black sociology,* New York: McGraw-Hill

Stepan, N (1982) *The idea of race in science: Great Britain 1800–1960.* Basingstoke: Macmillan

Stevens, A (2007) 'Survival of the ideas that fit', *Social Policy and Society,* 6(1), 25–35

Stone, R (2009) *Stephen Lawrence review: An independent commentary,* London: Uniting Britain Trust

Stott, C, Drury, J and Reicher, S (2017) 'On the Role of a Social Identity Analysis in Articulating Structure and Collective Action: The 2011 Riots in Tottenham and Hackney', *British Journal of Criminology* 57(4): 964–81

Stout, B, Yates, J and Williams, B (eds) (2008) *Applied criminology*, London: Sage

Stumpf, J (2006). 'The crimmigration crisis: immigrants, crime, and sovereign power', *American University Law Review* 56(2): 367–419

Sudbury, J and Ozakawa-Rey, J (2009) *Activist scholarship: Antiracism, feminism, and social change*, Boulder, CO: Paradigm

Swartz, DL (2003) 'From critical sociology to public intellectual: Pierre Bourdieu and politics', *Theory and Society*, 32(5-6): 791–823

Theoretical Criminology (2007) Special issue on 'Public Criminologies', 11(2)

Thompson, EP (1971) 'The moral economy of the English crowd in the eighteenth century', *Past and Present*, 50: 76–136

Tonry, M (2004) *Punishment and politics*, Devon: Willan

Torgerson, D (1986) 'Between knowledge and politics', *Policy Sciences*, 19: 33–59

Touraine, A (1981) *The voice and the eye*, New York: Cambridge University Press

Treadwell, J, Briggs, D, Winlow, S and Hall, S (2013) 'Shopocalypse now: Consumer culture and the English riots of 2011', *British Journal of Criminology*, 53(1): 1–17

Turda, M (2007) 'The nation as object: race, blood, and biopolitics in interwar Romania', *Slavic Review* 66(3): 413–41

Turda, M and Quine, S (2018, in press) *Historicizing race*, London: Bllomsbury.

Tyler, I (2013) 'The riots of the underclass? Stigmatisation, mediation and the government of poverty and disadvantage in neoliberal Britain', *Sociological Research Online*, 18(4)

Tyler, I and Lloyd, J (2015) 'From Tottenham to Baltimore, policing crisis starts race to the bottom for justice', *The Conversation*. http://theconversation.com/from-tottenham-to-baltimore-policing-crisis-starts-race-to-the-bottom-for-justice-40914

Tyler, TR (2001) 'Public trust and confidence in legal authorities: What do majority and minority group members want from the law and legal institutions?', *Behavioral Sciences & the Law*, 19(2): 215–35

Urry, J (2000) *Sociology beyond societies*, London: Routledge

Vázquez, R (2010), 'Modernity, the greatest show on earth: thoughts on visibility', *borderlands e-journal*, 9: 2

Vertovec, S (2007) 'Super-diversity and its implications', *Ethnic and Racial Studies* 30(6): 1024–54

Virdee, S (2010) 'Racism, class and the dialectics of social transformation', in PH Collins and J Solomos, J (eds) *The Sage handbook of race and ethnic studies*, London: Sage, 135–66

Waddington, D (1992) *Contemporary issues in public disorder*, Routledge, London

Wade, N. (2014) *A troublesome inheritance: Genes, race and human history*, London: Penguin.

Wade, P (1997) *Race and ethnicity in Latin America*. London: Pluto Press

Wade, P (2002) *Race, nature and culture: An anthropological perspective*. London: Pluto Press

Wade, P (2010) 'The presence and absence of race', *Patterns of Prejudice* 44(1): 43–60

Wade, P (2014) 'Race, ethnicity, and technologies of belonging', *Science, Technology & Human Values*. 39(4): 587–96

Ware, V and Back, L (2002) *Out of whiteness: Color, politics, and culture*, Chicago: University of Chicago Press

Warren, JW and Twine, FW (1997) 'White Americans, the new minority?', *Journal of Black Studies* 28: 200–18

Waters, I, Hardy, N, Delgado, D, and Dahlmann, S (2007) 'Ethnic minorities and the challenge of police recruitment', *The Police Journal* 80: 191–216

Webster, C (2007) *Understanding race and crime*, Berkshire: Open University Press

Webster, YO (1992) *Racialization of America*, New York: St Martin's Press

Whitfield, J (2004) *Unhappy dialogue: The Metropolitan Police and black Londoners in post-war Britain*, Cullompton: Willan

Whitmarsh, I and Jones, DS (eds) (2010) *What's the use of race? Modern governance and the biology of difference*, Cambridge, MA: MIT Press

Wight, C (2003) 'The agency-structure problem and institutional racism', *Political Studies*, 51: 706–21

Williams, J (1985) 'Redefining institutional racism', *Ethnic and Racial Studies* 8(3): 323-348

Williams, JE (2016) *Decoding racial ideology in genomics*. Maryland: Lexington

Winant, H (1994) *Racial conditions*, Minneapolis: University of Minnesota Press

Winant, H (2004) *The new politics of race: Globalism, difference, justice*. Minneapolis: University of Minnesota Press

Wing, A (2015) 'Critical race feminism', in K Murji and J Solomos (eds) *Theories of race and ethnicity: Contemporary debates and perspectives*, Cambridge: Cambridge University Press: 162–79

Winlow, S, Hall, S, Treadwell, J and Briggs, D (2015) *Riots and political protest: Notes from the post-political present*, Abingdon: Routledge

Wise, T (2010) *Colorblind: The rise of post-racial politics and the retreat from racial equity*, San Francisco: City Lights Books

Wolpe, H (1970) 'Industrialism and race in South Africa', in S Zubaida (ed) *Race and racialism*, London: Tavistock: 151–70

Young, J and Evans-Braziel, J (eds) (2006) *Race and the foundations of knowledge: Cultural amnesia in the academy*, Urbana: University of Illinois Press

Zack, N (2002) *Philosophy of Science and Race*. New York: Routledge

Žižek, S (2011) "Shoplifters of the World Unite", *London Review of Books*, 19 August

Zubaida, S (ed) (1970) *Race and racialism*, London: Tavistock

Index

U

UK context, sociology and
  institutional racism in 81–8
undercover policing 4
universities
  changing context 59, 74–5
  critical perspective on 58, 59
University of Michigan 88
Urry, J. 65, 66
US Department of Justice (DoJ)
  reports 2, 3
US police race relations 2–3
US social science 24, 40, 81–5

V

veil of race 43
victim-centred approach 111, 112
violent disorder *see* riots

W

Wade, N. 28
Wade, P. 26–7
war on terror 119
Webster, Y.O. 45
West, C. 67–8
white racial frame viewpoint 37–8
whiteness, and racialisation 53–4
Whitfield, J. 149
Williams, J. 91
Williams, J.E. 29
Winant, H. 40–1, 43, 148, 149
Winlow, S. 172

Y

Yuval-Davis, N. 50–1

Z

Žižek, S. 171–2